The Dutch
Resistance Revealed

Silence in the face of evil is itself evil . . . not to speak is to speak.
Not to act is to act.

Dietrich Bonhoeffer,
German pastor who fought Nazism and was executed

The Dutch Resistance Revealed

The Inside Story of Courage and Betrayal

Jos Scharrer

Pen & Sword
MILITARY

First published in Great Britain in 2018 by
Pen & Sword Military
an imprint of
Pen & Sword Books Ltd
47 Church Street
Barnsley
South Yorkshire
S70 2AS

ISBN 978 1 52672 813 5

Printed and bound in England by TJ International Ltd, Padstow, Cornwall

Pen & Sword Books Limited incorporates the imprints of Atlas, Archaeology,
Aviation, Discovery, Family History, Fiction, History, Maritime, Military,
Military Classics, Politics, Select, Transport, True Crime, Air World,
Frontline Publishing, Leo Cooper, Remember When, Seaforth Publishing,
The Praetorian Press, Wharncliffe Local History, Wharncliffe Transport,
Wharncliffe True Crime and White Owl.

For a complete list of Pen & Sword titles please contact
PEN & SWORD BOOKS LIMITED
47 Church Street, Barnsley, South Yorkshire, S70 2AS, England
E-mail: enquiries@pen-and-sword.co.uk
Website: www.pen-and-sword.co.uk

Contents

Acknowledgements   vii
Prologue   ix

Stories of Hope and Heroes   1

Chapter 1   Henri's Fatal Day   2

Chapter 2   American Airmen Down   13

Chapter 3   The Escape of Rudy Zeeman – an *Engelandvaarder*   28

Chapter 4   The Initial Fiasco   46

Chapter 5   Restructuring the Dutch Resistance   52

Chapter 6   The Escape Lines   56

Chapter 7   Henri Scharrer, his Operation   61

Chapter 8   *Engelandvaarder* Jack Charles Bottenheim's Lucky Escape   73

Chapter 9   British Airmen Down   86

Chapter 10 Other Amazing Escapes   92

Stories of Enemies and Traitors   97

Chapter 11 The Gestapo, SiPo, SD and Waffen-SS   98

Chapter 12 Christiaan Lindemans ('King Kong'),
                His Early Resistance Work   103

Chapter 13 Christiaan Lindemans the Double Agent,
                and Other Pro-German Sympathizers   106

Chapter 14 The KLM False Line and Other Collaborators   119

Stories of Plots and Betrayals   125

Chapter 15 The Ransom and the Plot   126

Chapter 16 Revenge, Hunger and the Holocaust   140

Victory and Survival   151

Chapter 17   New Beginnings   152

Chapter 18   Extraordinary People We Cannot Forget   159

Chapter 19   Richard Scharrer Writes about his Father   163

Epilogue   167
Concise Bibliography   170
Index   173

Acknowledgements

I am extremely grateful to a number of people who helped me with this book on the story of my late father-in-law, Henri Scharrer.

First and foremost is Professor Doeko Bosscher of the University of Groningen, who gave me a couple of copies of his book on his uncle Fritz Conijn entitled *Haast om te Sterven* (Hurry to Die), published in 2015. This book contains far more about Henri Scharrer than the family ever knew. It is only published in Dutch, and so I had to overcome language difficulties in trying to follow the story. If I misunderstood anything or read the information incorrectly, he has kindly sent me corrections.

Linda Libourel Morison, the daughter of Caroline (Carry) Libourel, also gave me important insights into her mother's character and relationship with Henri Scharrer.

I am grateful, too, to Robert Courtois of Brussels, who contacted me out of the blue as a result of his research into the death of Emmanuel Scharrer; he sent me what information he had about Emmanuel's murder and the involvement of a group which included his own great-uncle, Georges Dumont, who was found guilty of this murder and who died in the Buchenwald camp shortly before the end of the war. His emails spurred me to start searching in earnest for material in order to capture the true story of Henri Scharrer.

Bruce Bolinger of California has an important website on which he has posted information on the Dutch Resistance obtained from British National Archives and helper files (people who helped the Resistance) from the National Archives II (NAII) in College Park, Maryland, outside Washington DC. Bruce sent me scans of some of the information he found on Henri and people associated with him, including the Stichting files with correspondence on the education of Henri's sons, Richard and Raymond.

Through Bruce I was able to contact Michael Moores-LeBlanc of New Brunswick, Canada, who has been studying the KLM line (a false escape line) for over 25 years and has developed a file on 235 airmen, their Dutch-Belgian helpers and the members of the Abwehr III/f who ultimately entrapped them. He also sent me scans from his files, and photographs, with advice to follow the story of the relationship between Henri Scharrer and Christiaan Lindemans ('King Kong'), who turned traitor and whose counter-espionage activities resulted in the

Allied defeat at the Battle of Arnhem. He is also believed to have betrayed Henri, although the information on this is sketchy.

It was also a real stroke of luck that Bruce Bolinger gave me the email address of one of the few surviving *Engelandvaarders* (people who successfully escaped Holland and reached England) – by the name of Rudy Zeeman, of Tasmania, Australia. The day after I emailed him, he replied saying that Henri Scharrer was one of the men who had helped him escape and they had met on a number of occasions; also that he had written a memoir, *Luck through Adversity*, in which he tells the story of his escape. He arranged for me to get a copy of the memoir from his nephew, Don Conner, who lives in Durban, South Africa.

Megan Koreman (who researched the Dutch-Paris escape route, and launched her book *Children of Dutch-Paris* with publisher Boom in Amsterdam in November 2016), sent me some files on her articles to check details, as well as a few names. Her assistance was much appreciated.

My brother, Eyre Shaw, read the first draft of the manuscript and gave me many comments which I have implemented. He also proofread one of the final drafts, picking up typos and errors which had escaped me. The book could not have been finalized without him.

Many thanks also go to Tim Cooke, Vernae Vermaak, Alistair and Yvette Barclay and Keith Partridge who also read the manuscript, seeking out typos and giving me useful comments and suggestions. Thanks are also due to my other friends and family who have been both helpful and understanding of the limited time I have had to socialize over the past year, while I put this story together.

Extensive research has been done to source copyright and royalties on images used in order to ensure that no infringement has incurred.

Prologue

Henri Scharrer is my late father-in-law, and when I started this project I had little information about him. I knew he was a French-speaking member of the Dutch Resistance. There were also recollections of Henri as told by my husband, Richard Scharrer, Henri's eldest son, most of which at the time I thought somewhat exaggerated.

Initially, what the family knew was that he had been arrested on a train and a few days later had been executed by firing squad on 6 September 1944 for helping Allied airmen. And that was more or less it. As my search went along I uncovered stories of bravery, treachery, murder, assassinations, deceit and an astonishing devotion to the Resistance cause by large numbers of people.

Once I decided I could write the true story, no matter how brief, I found several researchers in other parts of the world who are also investigating the Dutch Resistance movement. The most important of these is Professor Doeko Bosscher of the University of Groningen, whose book *Haast om te Sterven* (Hurry to Die) about his uncle, Fritz Conijn, contained much missing information on Henri Scharrer, as Fritz and Henri had not only worked together but were executed together. Many people have assisted me, suggesting numerous websites to visit, emailing me scans of documents from war archives in the United States and the United Kingdom and passing along personal letters from characters involved in these activities.

Gradually the character and achievements of Henri Scharrer emerged. More importantly, what was also revealed was the story of an extraordinary group of Resistance people. These were the brave men and women who put their lives on the line to help their fellow citizens, their Jewish friends and shot-down Allied airmen. Their deeds are well documented in war archives and letters, as are numerous accounts of the betrayals and treachery they faced. From these sources I have gathered what facts appear to be true and are substantiated by more than one report. However, I am only too well aware that in some instances information sent to me may have been incorrect.

I have found it necessary to keep close to Henri Scharrer's story and to the people directly or indirectly involved in the background to his life. Therefore, the stories of all the Resistance people revealed here have a link or association to Henri's underground cell and his helpers. The limitations of space have meant that I have had to leave out many other stories of brave Dutch and Belgian Resistance men and women whose heroic actions await to be told. The stories of the traitors and villains, too, I have of necessity limited to the important few. The shocking truth is that there were far too many of these unpleasant people to be incorporated in one book. War and greed bring out the evil in many people, just as they bring out the good.

To assist the reader and maintain the flow of the story, I have omitted many technical details and facts and figures, such as ranks, aircraft numbers, service numbers, names and addresses of organizations. These are available in my background files.

This book is a tribute not only to Henri Scharrer, but also to the brave people of the Dutch Resistance who fought the horrifying Nazi danger with their sheer endurance, sacrifice, bravery and perseverance.

STORIES OF HOPE AND HEROES

Chapter 1

Henri's Fatal Day

In the beginning, the family had little information on Henri Scharrer. There was a picture of him, and another of his wife Geertruida (Truus). We also had two framed certificates in acknowledgement of his work saving Allied airmen: one signed by President Eisenhower and another by Air Marshal Sir Arthur Tedder.

The most interesting item, however, was a framed identification letter with a photograph; these were his press credentials, which allowed him to travel in the Netherlands, France and Belgium during the war seeking material for his articles, but also facilitated his underground work in setting up safe houses and escape routes.

Despite the war, it appears that life had been going well for the Scharrer family in Amsterdam. Henri was often away on trips, and the German occupation of the Netherlands had not been a hardship for them. Every now and then, in the dark of night, people would arrive at the house. There would be whispers and steps going up the stairs to the attic. All the windows were blacked out according to the new laws. Nobody spoke about what was going on and nobody really knew – 'Never say a word'.

On the fatal day when the lives of the Scharrer family were turned upside down, the Netherlands had been under German occupation for over four years. The Battle of the Netherlands was part of *Fall Gelb* (Case Yellow), the German invasion of the Low Countries (Belgium, Luxembourg and the Netherlands). The German army, 700,000 strong, had swept into the Netherlands and Belgium in a sudden blitzkrieg early on 10 May 1940. The battle saw one of the first mass paratroop drops, occupying tactical points to assist the advance of ground troops. Several important airfields and bridges were captured within hours.

The entire centre of Rotterdam was carpet-bombed, razed to the ground, and the Dutch army and airforce was crushed in four days. Around 3,000 Dutch military personnel died, as did 2,500 civilians – many in the Rotterdam bombing. Germany then threatened to bomb Amsterdam and other cities unless the Dutch surrendered immediately.

Barely in the nick of time, the Dutch royal family and other leaders, together with their treasury, diamond stocks and gold bullion, fled to Britain on a British destroyer. The previous evening, Princess Juliana and Prince Bernhard had sailed to Harwich. After some hesitation and heated discussions, the cabinet also decided it was wise to flee. They knew they would be among the first to be arrested when the Germans arrived.

The Dutch were ill-prepared to resist invasion. Although Britain and France had declared war on Germany in 1939 following the German invasion of Poland, no major operations occurred in Western Europe during the period known as the Phoney War. The Netherlands had hoped to remain neutral, as they had done in the First World War. They limited their reaction to the growing crisis as much as they could, the most important measure being a partial mobilization of 100,000 men in April 1939.

The main Dutch defensive strategy was a system called the Holland Water Line. Built two centuries before, this protected all major cities in the west by flooding part of the countryside. Easterly defences were hastily constructed in 1939, including the northern Grebbe line. These lines were protected by pill boxes. Most civilians, however, cherished the illusion that their country might be spared, and the Netherlands adhered to a policy of strict neutrality so as not to upset their powerful neighbour.

In a radio broadcast of January 1940 Winston Churchill tried to convince the Low Countries not to wait for the inevitable German attack but to join the Anglo-French Entente. Both the Belgians and the Dutch refused his pleas. A couple of months later, however, as the situation grew more alarming, the Dutch government did declare a state of emergency. Border troops were placed under greater alert and counter-measures were taken at ports and airfields against a possible assault. These were only token gestures, as the reality was that the Netherlands had not been involved in military action for many years. The Dutch army was hopelessly inadequate, poorly equipped and poorly trained. The most conspicuous deficiency lay in its shortage of armour. It possessed only one tank that was operational – a Renault FT. Another area of neglect was radio. The Netherlands was the seat of the large Phillips organization, Europe's largest producers of radio equipment, but the Dutch army mostly used telephone connections. Only the artillery had radio sets – 225, to be exact.

It is true to say that the German population and troops generally disliked the idea of violating Dutch neutrality. So the Nazi propaganda machine started to spread the idea that an invasion was justified because France and Britain might attempt to occupy the Low Countries in advance of an attack on Germany.

Hitler in his war room meetings hammered home the vital importance of the Low Countries to his expansion plans. From their large western ports it would be a short trip to the Thames estuary. His tacticians estimated that with the poor quality of Dutch military the core region of Holland could be conquered in about three to five days maximum. Various strategies were discussed. In the end it was decided to use the Eighteenth Army under General Georg von Küchler to defeat the main Dutch force.

Hitler summoned his commanders and ordered the shock attack for the early morning 10 May. The suddenness of this blitzkrieg left the people of the Netherlands stunned. They were awakened from their beds by the sound of aircraft roaring overhead and the noise of their own anti-aircraft batteries. These batteries put up a fierce fight, shooting down nearly 250 Ju transport planes. One of the Luftwaffe wings, the KG4, which attacked Dutch airfields, lost eleven Heinkels and three Junkers.

The first German attack on the Hague was an operational failure, as they were not able to secure the main airfield at Ypenburg in time for the airborne infantry to land safely in their Junkers. But they soon overwhelmed Dutch troops at other airfields and bombed the city centre of Rotterdam.

For the Dutch it was a brave but hopeless fight.

Before the Dutch people knew it, German vehicles were rolling down the streets of Amsterdam and other cities. All it had taken had been a series of heavy bombardments, the landing of airborne infantry and a huge, powerful army with heavy armour moving at lightning speed.

Dutch commander General Winkelman concluded that it had apparently become German policy to devastate any city offering resistance; so in view of his mandate to avoid unnecessary suffering, and fully realizing the hopelessness of the Dutch military position, he decided to surrender.

Four days after the invasion he sent telex messages of his decision to all higher-level army units, ordering them to first destroy their weapons and then offer their surrender to the nearest German units. He then made an early evening radio broadcast to the Dutch nation informing them of the capitulation; this is how the German command became aware the Dutch had surrendered. This implied that in principle a ceasefire should be observed by both parties. Large parts of the Dutch army were reluctant to accept this surrender, as many had not seen any fighting. The commander of the Dutch naval base at Den Helder wanted to resist, and it was with difficulty that Winkelman convinced him to obey the surrender order.

Early the next morning, a German messenger reached the Hague, inviting Winkelman to Rijsoord for a meeting with von Küchler to negotiate the articles of a written capitulation document. They quickly agreed on most conditions. Interestingly, Winkelman only agreed to surrender the armed forces in the Netherlands (with the exception of Zeeland) and not the country itself. The document was signed, and the occupation started officially on 17 May.

Soon thereafter, Winkelman left Holland secretly to head up the Dutch Government-in-Exile in London.

The occupation started fairly peacefully, and the Scharrer family carried on as usual. Henri wrote his articles and travelled to the press offices, the children went to school and Truus managed the house.

The reason for this calm, non-threatening start was that the Germans behaved well, stood in queues for their food and were polite to the population. Hitler and the Nazi leaders regarded the Dutch as a 'brother' nation. Another reason for this friendship was that a surprising number of Dutch citizens were National Socialists and pro-German. The Dutch National Socialist movement, under the leadership of its founder, Anton Mussert, had grown substantially since the early 1930s. The NSP held huge rallies in the main cities and people joined them in droves. The party had gained 8 per cent of the vote and two seats in the Senate.

Trouble was soon brewing, however. Gradually more regulations, laws, curfews, blackouts, confiscations, forced labour, food rations and censorship were put in place. Thousands of able-bodied Dutchmen were recruited into the Waffen SS. Posters persuading young men to join up were plastered all over the country. Freedom was restricted. Jews were rounded up and first placed in a ghetto in Amsterdam, then shipped to a transit camp at Westerbork.

In protest against these developments, trade unions ordered strikes, against which the Nazis retaliated, and the Dutch underground movement started gaining strength.

By this time Henri had proved himself a successful journalist, but one of the laws passed required that all foreigners and Jews be fired from companies, and Henri, being a French national, did not escape. He was fired from his job on the ANP (*Algemeen Nederlands Persbureau*), rounded up and sent to the Schoorl prison camp, where he was held for five months.

It was here that he spent his time producing many sketches, including self-portraits. More importantly, he became involved in the Dutch Resistance movement and by the time of his release, which followed the French capitulation, he was ready to play an active role. He joined the Swiss publication STP (*Schweizer Press-Telegraph*) which had offices on the Voorburgwaal near the Dam in Amsterdam. Soon he became one of their most respected correspondents, writing in French on his specialized areas of politics and economics.

By August 1944 he had been working not only for the STP, but also for the Resistance, for nearly two and a half years, without his cover ever being blown. Considering how many pro-German collaborators were about, only too keen to pass on suspicions to their conquerors, this in itself was an achievement.

He personally set up an escape route which was one of the most successful and was used by other cell leaders in the Resistance. He was responsible for assisting a number of Allied airmen (some say twenty-eight) and Dutch citizens; he was an important supplier of intelligence information to the French and British in London; and in Resistance circles he was regarded as one of the leading suppliers of excellent false identity and travel documents.

'You could not tell Henri's documents from the originals', several reports have stated.

Then suddenly, without warning, the blow fell.

On 18 August 1944 Henri was arrested by the Gestapo on a train travelling to the Hague. The questions we have asked were: what had led up to this? How had it all happened? How did it all end? Was it worth the suffering and anxiety? It has taken a couple of years of research, a visit to Amsterdam and about 14kg of documents, besides the much appreciated scans and emails sent to me from all over the world, to slowly fill in the details of the remarkable story.

We still do not know much about Henri's activities during July and August 1944. We do know that he had started to find that his work for the Dutch Resistance was becoming too dangerous. He made the escape arrangements for an American airman, Frank Hart, whose Liberator bomber had been shot down. He had been working with his mistress, Carry Libourel, and their friends Arnold and Xenia Verster, to have Frank hidden in the attic of the Scharrer house in Amstelveen, before being sent on his way on one of the escape routes.

There had been some recent betrayals along this escape line, which went through Belgium and France and finally reached Spain. Henri was also reported to have travelled to Belgium and France in those two months, most likely to check on his helpers, investigate reports of traitors and set up new safe houses and points of contact to replace those that appeared to have been infiltrated by collaborators. He spent time at home with his family, as they had recently moved to an apartment in Amsterdam in a building near the Amstel River.

Behind the scenes, the Netherlands-based Gestapo and Waffen-SS were desperate to detain a real thorn in their flesh – a Resistance man with the code name 'Sandberg'. Particularly obsessed by this was Sicherheitsdienst (SD) Officer Herbert Oelschlägel, the cunning hunter of Resistance people and based in the SD-Assenstelle in the Euterpestraat. They did not know Sandberg's identity and he always remained frustratingly out of German reach, protected by the smallness of the Resistance cells and, because lives were at stake, their high levels of control and confidentiality. Until this time captured Resistance men, although heavily interrogated and tortured, did not know who Sandberg was or where he lived.

Sandberg, as we now know, was the main code name for Henri Scharrer, although he also used a few others from time to time.

There are two different opinions about the fateful day when Henri was arrested. Some maintain it was pure accident that the Germans came across Henri on that train. Others, though, believe that somebody knew he was on it. If so, who tipped them off? It could easily have been the notorious double agent, Christiaan Lindemans, as there is no evidence to suggest that Henri or any members of the Resistance suspected that only five months earlier Lindemans, highly regarded as a brave and respected colleague, had turned traitor and was supplying information to the Germans. They all believed Lindemans to be a ruthless and deadly anti-Nazi, responsible for some twenty-eight assassinations of German supporters and officials. So it is likely that Henri, or most probably one of his associates, might have taken Lindemans into their confidence about the plans and schedules Henri and his cell were working on. There were airmen that had to be moved to safe houses, and this is what Henri was busy arranging.

There is one report that states that Lindemans was suspected of betraying Henri. It is worthwhile noting, however, that after his arrest Lindemans was asked by Allied Intelligence to draw up a list of the Resistance members he had betrayed; and although it is not unexpectedly a shockingly long list, Henri's name does not appear. But then he also denied knowing anything about betraying Allied plans to land paratroopers and equipment near Arnhem. We know from the book *London Calling North Pole*, written by the leading German counter-intelligence officer in Amsterdam, Abwehr Major (later Colonel) Hermann Giskes, that Lindemans had in fact made this Arnhem report directly to him. So it is hard to know when Lindemans was telling the truth and when he was not.

In Henri's life at this time was a woman with whom he had fallen deeply in love. We now know this because only a few days before, on 15 August, Henri had written a letter to Carry Libourel, a lawyer and press colleague. The letter is in French, and what follows is a summary of extracts from the Dutch in Doeko Bosscher's book, *Haast om te Sterven.*

Henri writes to tell Carry of his great love for her and promises that after the war they will be married. Because of difficult circumstances recently, the two lovers had seldom seen each other, and have to love each other as if they were strangers. But the war is coming to an end, and the time will come when they will see the results and fruits of their hard work. He writes of the stress of war and the anxieties he feels because of its danger. The slightest negligence or mishap can have fatal consequences. He writes that he is weighed down by his material and moral responsibilities and what will be demanded of him in the future.

He goes on to say that the stress and tensions of the war have also brought something good. He swears with his 'purified soul' that he will come out of this adventure grateful for the lessons he has learned from so many people, as a result of his relationship with her. In addition to his personal messages and thoughts, the letter tells of his future movements and his plans to meet up with Jan Lowey-Ball, for whom he has an urgent task. So he will only be able to embrace her between trains. He promises that on 22 August he will be able to spend the whole night with her 'without fail'. The last two words he underlined.

This letter is in the possession of Carry Libourel's daughter, born some seven years after the war. Linda Morison Libourel today lives in the Hague, where she works for an investment bank.

The Jan Lowey-Ball referred to in the letter was Henri's closest working associate in the Resistance. The meeting with Jan concerned information and contacts with 'Rolls Royce', which was the Resistance information service set up by a friend of theirs.

So here we are on that fatal day, 18 August, with Henri travelling on a train from Haarlem to the Hague with another friend and work colleague, Tom Yardin Millord. From there they were planning to go on to Delft, where both Jan and Carry lived. Henri was to meet a person referred to as Eena, and squeeze in a visit to Carry as mentioned in his letter to her.

In the neighbourhood of Aerdenhout the Germans had set up a document-checking operation on the train. It would appear that both Tom and Henri were taken by surprise and had no time to check or hide any documents, let alone the gun Henri had in a suitcase on the rack above his head. Being in possession of a gun was an offence punishable by death. The Germans searched them and demanded that Henri and Tom hand over their documents. They found Henri's documents, in the name of 'Debordes', suspicious. One of them was false, and was marked in pencil: '*Eena, Maandag, Amsterdam, Roelofs Hartplein*'.

Then a fatal problem! The suspicious Germans noticed the suitcase. According to one report by Tom Millord, when they asked Henri whose suitcase it was, he replied that it belonged 'to the other man'. The Germans, however, believed the suitcase belonged to Henri, opened it and found the gun.

This statement by Tom was made some time after the event and is questionable. It does not make sense, because in the suitcase were also other items that identified Henri as the owner.

Henri was immediately handcuffed. That a man like Henri – the leading specialist in Holland on false documentation – should have been caught in this fashion is ironic. There is no reference in Tom Yardin Millord's statement after the war on Henri's arrest to the effect that Henri had stated the suitcase was his. In her report to the Allies, Carry Libourel also confirms that Henri was in possession of a gun. Why would Tom want to cast aspersions on Henri after the war? There were rumours that Tom believed that Henri was in love with his wife Betty and that there was bad feeling between them at the time. If that is true then Tom would have known nothing of Henri's deep relationship with Carry. This is highly likely as Henri and Carry went to great lengths to keep their love affair a secret.

Whatever took place, it transpired that the Germans did not realize that Tom and Henri were travelling together. Tom was in luck and allowed to go free. At the next station Tom disembarked and saw Henri being taken off the train under arrest. Tom was in a state of shock and also suffering a nosebleed. Holding a handkerchief to his nose, he immediately caught the Blauwe Tram to get home as fast as he could and give his wife Betty the bad news about Henri. When Tom arrived he was as white as a sheet, Betty later reported. Tom led her up upstairs, put his arm around her and said, '*Henri is gepakt*' (Henri is caught).

Henri was first taken to the prison in Scheveningen for questioning. After a few days he was taken to the *Huis van Bewaring* (detention centre) Weteringschans on Amstelveenseweg in Amsterdam. Here he was initially interrogated by Sachbearbeiter (clerk) Emil Rühl. The details of the interrogation are not known. Henri's excellent German would have been of some assistance in warding off the first onslaught of questions. Exactly what information Henri gave the SD (German Secret Police) is difficult to gauge. He was in the hands of one of the most cunning hunters of Resistance people, Herbert Oelschlägel, who led this interrogation and who wanted to bring in more arrests of Henri's cell members and of the larger RVV (*Raad van Verzet*) organization, of which Henri was a member. This was one of the four leading Resistance organizations that had been set up from London. Oelschlägel hoped he could achieve a breakthrough by using Henri as bait.

We also know that in the course of the interrogation Henri was quite severely injured. Exactly what they did to him we do not know, except that Truus was later told he was in need of medical treatment. Oelschlägel was not Henri's only interrogator. Other senior SS officers involved were Wouter Mollis, Maarten Kuiper and Friedich Viebahn. All were leading Nazis and later sentenced for crimes against humanity. The most notorious was Maarten Kuiper, a member of the SS and SD who was present at the arrest of Anne Frank and who took part in the Sibertanne Killings, part of a horrific operation in which many Resistance members were captured, raped, tortured and killed, in retaliation for attacks on pro-German Dutch people.

It appears that Oelschlägel did not get the information he wanted out of Henri, and so he came up with a plan to place a stool pigeon in Henri's cell who might be able to draw out information that he could use profitably. The devious details of this plot and its tragic consequences are revealed later.

There was one arrest the SD were able to make. In studying the false document found on Henri they noted the few words written on it. The German police understood this to mean that Henri had an appointment with Ima van Asbeck, known as 'Eena', as he had written down her address. They wasted no time and arrested her on Monday 21 August on the Roelof Hartplein. It had been Henri's plan to deliver a few Allied pilots to her at this address.

News of Henri's arrest flew around like wildfire. People were shocked. How could such a cunning operator get caught? Truus heard the bad news from Tom and Betty. His close associate, Jan Lowey-Ball, heard the news from Carry's brother, Hans Libourel, who told Jan that Carry was devastated. Jan rushed across to Carry's house to get more information. That he did this was something the SD (German Secret Service) later found suspicious. But Jan's easy explanation was that he had gone there in all innocence to visit his friend Carry, and this satisfied them. It was in this manner that Henri's relationship with Carry became more commonly known. Until that time they had always been discreet, keeping their relationship strictly private and as confidential as they could.

There was an important reason for this: Henri was married to Geertruida (Truus) and had two sons Richard, then fourteen and Raymond, twelve. While his love affair with Carry Libourel was a serious one, they had an understanding that nothing would have a negative impact on Henri's relationship with his wife and family while the war lasted. That was how many wartime love affairs were conducted.

The Scharrer home in Amsterdam, to which they had recently moved, was a first floor apartment at number 16 Rivierenlaan (recently renamed in honour of President Kennedy) overlooking the Amstel river. As news of Henri's arrest spread, Resistance colleagues rushed round and started 'cleaning' the apartment of all incriminating evidence. There was no time to lose. How long would Henri last under interrogation at the hands of Sachbearbeiter Emil Rühl, Maarten Kuiper and Wouter Mollis, all torture experts, before he gave them his address? It was also common knowledge that families of those arrested were also brought in for interrogation. There was concern, too, that Henri's wife and children could be threatened. A fairly common Gestapo tactic would be to promise to leave his family alone if Henri co-operated and gave them the information they wanted.

In those frantic couple of days much had to be done. The false documents stored in their new apartment had to be packed and carted away. The many German uniforms, boots and other paraphernalia hidden for Resistance use were hurriedly put into containers and removed. Every scrap of evidence that linked the home to the Resistance had to be eradicated. Truus, Richard and Raymond were briefed on what to say and how to act when the Germans arrived. There was a grave danger that houses would be searched, everyone arrested and the whole cell would collapse. The tension at this time was acute. Richard always remembered the frantic panic to get everything done in time, and the fear about what would happen to his father.

It took exactly two days for plain clothes police to arrive at Rivierenlaan. Raymond and Richard were at home with Truus. The entire apartment was searched, drawers and cupboards were emptied. Raymond remembers that the search and questioning was calm and conducted in a business-like manner. There were no threats or violence. But it remained one of the most terrifying day of their lives.

Truus was arrested and taken away to Weteringschans for questioning. The children were abandoned, and friends sent for relatives to come and assist them. Fortunately, discretion paid off. Truus knew nothing about Henri's operations and movements and so she had nothing to tell. Richard told the story that when his mother was in custody he visited a senior German official to ask for her release and brought her toiletries and food. She was soon released; knowing nothing, she was of no value.

The main charge Henri faced was of conducting espionage on behalf of the BCRA (*Bureau Central de Renseignements et d'Action*) of DB (Deuxième Bureau) of the French Government-in-Exile. It is interesting to observe that the honours he received after the war did not relate to his espionage work but to his help to Allied airmen and his getting them to safety along his RVV (*Raad van Verzet*) escape route. This was most probably due to his espionage work being so confidential and strictly classified.

From this time Truus did everything she could in her power to get Henri released and acted with bravery and determination. A couple of days later, Truus discussed Henri's situation and the options available to them with friends and Resistance colleagues, Fritz Conijn and Jan Lowey-Ball. During this conversation in the Noord-Zuid Hollandsch Koffiehuis, opposite the Central Station in Amsterdam, there was a discussion on whether a message could be sent to Netherlands SOE-N group in London to seek help. This was the group that organized and financed the Resistance operation in the Netherlands on behalf of the Government-in-Exile. Whether this was done is not known.

Carry Libourel also acted immediately. Unafraid as usual, she went right to the top of German officialdom to visit the Kriminal Kommissar Johannes Heinrich Munt to plead Henri's case. In an unexpected turn of events, this important senior official agreed to see her.

Tough career woman, lawyer, assistant to Henri Scharrer in his journalistic commitments and his reports to MI5, the Free French and others, and helper in the Resistance movement, Carry was no shrinking violet. Despite all the information on Henri that she possessed, including his escape routes, safe houses and helpers, she was not one to be bullied.

Her photographs do not show a beauty, but rather a striking woman of arresting character. She was tall, slim, with a strong face, long dark hair and an athletic appearance.

She walked confidently into Johannes Munt's offices with her head held high and a determination to use her legal training to argue Henri's case clearly and logically. She probably also pleaded on the grounds that she was Henri's fiancée, that they planned to marry and that she was worried sick about the fate of the love of her life. They were a couple in love and soul mates.

Munt listened politely and decided to hold her for a couple of days for further questioning. At one stage she and Henri were questioned together. This meeting was the last time Carry would see Henri. As expected, no further information was forthcoming from Carry, and she was released. Munt was in one of his benevolent moods. In fact, Munt was known in SD circles as a 'white crow'. His colleagues called him 'Munt der Weiche' (the soft). There are several reports that Munt handled his job efficiently but without cruelty or malice. Many are the Resistance men who, because of Munt, found themselves sent to prison rather than executed.

On this occasion, Munt told Carry that he would see what he could do, but that the matter was out of his hands. The case of Henri Scharrer was being looked at by more senior officials in the German hierarchy. Berlin was involved, as was the Austrian National Socialist Arthur Seyss-Inquart, who was in charge of the German occupation government in the Netherlands. An unwavering anti-semite, he was also responsible for ordering the execution of nearly 1,000 political prisoners before the liberation of the Netherlands. On the face of it, Henri was doomed.

Carry left with a beating heart, and went straight to Henri's wife.

'We can only hope and pray for his safe return,' she told her.

The two women embraced. Their love for one man would from now on unite them in their mission to save his life and bring him home.

Chapter 2

American Airmen Down

Now let us step back some two months. How did this all work? How did airmen land up in the Scharrer house, and what exactly did Henri and his Resistance colleagues do in their attempts to get them home safely? We had a stroke of luck here which makes it easy to tell the particular story of Frank Hart. One of the crewmen on his ill-fated US Liberator bomber flight actually wrote a book about their experiences. After the war, Eugene Halmos – a former journalist on the *New York Times*, wrote *The Wrong Side of the Fence*, in which he tells the terrifying yet thrilling tale of the crew's experiences, with several references to Frank.

It was a cold, dank morning. How could Gunner Frank Hart and the Navigator Eugene Halmos ever have imagined that their lives were about to take such unexpected and dangerous twists and turns? Events were about to unfold that would eventually lead to Frank hiding injured in the attic of the Scharrers' Amstelveen house with his life and well-being dependent on the care and kindness of a number of courageous Dutch people, while Eugene and the rest of the crew ended up in the hands of the Nazis.

It was 29 June 1944. Frank and his fellow crew members had been woken at 0400 hrs when the sergeant came banging on their Nissen-hut door. The accommodation was basic. The huts were built of steel, uninsulated, and the walls covered with tarpaper. Inside were the rows of thin-mattressed cots, and the huts reeked of coal-fired stoves and damp clothing.

This was 'Double British War Time', so it was actually 0200 hrs local time. The men fumbled in the darkness of the blackout for their shoes and clothes and stumbled outside to the latrine and showers. Then with their .45s buckled on, they made their way down a dark road to the mess hall.

Bob Cole, lean and tough looking, was the pilot and he strode into the hall first, followed by quiet Bob Post, the co-pilot. Then came Eugene Halmos and Dave Smart, the bombardier. The rest followed, sleepy-eyed, with hardly a word spoken. They were Jack Sorensen, Joseph Santora, John Currie, James Moos, Walter Leonard and Frank Hart, a gunner from Chicago.

Like most Second World War aircrew, they were nearly all in their early twenties. The two eldest were Bob Cole and Eugene Halmos, who were each twenty-seven; one of the others is described as being only nineteen.

Breakfast, which consisted of powdered eggs and greenish coffee, was eaten in haste. They chatted, making feeble jokes about condemned men and their last supper. They were then hurried along into a waiting open truck that took them a mile down the road to the briefing room, past Jeeps that weaved across the airfield. One was driven by an attractive young woman in uniform. Frank and the rest waved and whistled, and she responded with a bright smile.

Once they were all seated in the mess hall, the colonel strode in and greeted them in a curt, business-like manner. The chaplain then opened his prayer book and read in a monotone. He had prayed over many crews that had not made it safely back to base, and he was painfully aware of the dangers that lay ahead for these men. This was their pre-mission briefing. A large map on the wall was unveiled, showing a bold red line running at least 600 miles into Germany. When the men saw this, there was a gasp. It was not good news. They solemnly took their notes and then broke up for individual briefings with a new sense of urgency. There was a rush to the quartermaster to pick up their flying suits, jackets and boots.

With only a few minutes to spare, they were standing in front of their B-24 and had a photograph taken. It still exists, showing smiling young men who had no idea what the next few hours would bring. Some hurriedly lit cigarettes, while last minute pre-flight checks were carried out by the flight engineer and pilots. The big motors, which could be heard miles away, started to growl, and the men climbed into their take-off positions.

Were they scared? They all were, but discipline held their nerves and kept them at the jobs which would take them into danger. Halmos reports that together with his navigational work, which was periodically feverish, he kept on trying to sort out the jumbled thoughts in his mind about the possibility of not getting back.

They were part of the US 489th Bombardment Group (Heavy) stationed near Halesworth, Suffolk, north-east of London near the coast. There were a number of airfields in this area, which is only a short flight from the Dutch coastline. The bombardment group, flying Liberator B-24 bombers, had arrived from the United States in May 1944 and would be operating here for only another few months of that year. Later, in November, the group would return to the USA. They had played an important role in the build-up to D-Day and on D-Day itself, just three weeks earlier on 6 June, when the Allies landed on the beaches of Normandy in Operation Overlord, the largest amphibious assault in history.

Their Liberator had been christened 'Heaven Can Wait', although it was reportedly not the only Liberator to have that most appropriate name. The plane was covered in war paint, and at least one of the Heaven Can Wait bombers had a nose cone decorated with a painting of a seated naked girl. They carried eleven machine guns, and these large bomber formations had fighter plane support.

The crew had already successfully flown many raids, starting shortly before the Allied landings in Normandy. These previous raids were described as 'coal runs'. They had consisted of flying maybe 20 minutes to France, dropping their bomb-loads in support of troops on the ground and going back home to pick up more.

Today's mission was different and more dangerous. They were to head for the factories and railways of eastern Germany, some distance from the Dutch-Belgian border.

In his introduction to *The Wrong Side of the Fence* the navigator, Eugene Halmos, wrote:

> It's a strange thing when you go to war: You somehow never expect to be taken prisoner.
> You figure (academically, of course) that you might be killed – that's always something to be considered with something of a thrill (even though you really don't believe it). You might be wounded. Or you could come out a hero.
> But taken prisoner?
> That's a role few men picture for themselves.
> Of course, we had lectures on the subject of how to conduct ourselves if we fell into enemy hands. So we listened respectfully.
> But we listened with the same feeling we'd had when our parents told us what would happen if we weren't good. Of course, we were going to be good, so there wasn't any reality in the dire punishment promised.
> And, of course, we weren't going to be taken prisoner.

Pilot Bob Cole was confident, although he would have preferred to have flown the B-17 Flying Fortress, because it could reach a higher altitude. The B-24 was more susceptible to flak and machine gun fire; the German fighter planes would fly to the bombers' altitude and inform the anti-aircraft men on the ground so they could more accurately set their sights. Then the German fighters would wheel round and open fire.

The US Air Force and the RAF were organized to fly at different times. The RAF operated mainly at night, while the USAAF worked the day-time operations. They had to be up and gone shortly after dawn. So it was still early by the time all the crew were in their positions in the plane. Some were strapped in, while the gunners had to sit on the floor, and all were wearing their parachutes. They had been instructed how to operate the parachutes, but not a single member of this crew had ever jumped from a plane. There had been rain earlier, but now the sun was coming over the horizon, helping to take away any gloom and foreboding some of them might have felt every time they took off on their deadly missions. After growling noises from the engines, the big, clumsy-looking plane taxied down the runway, before becoming airborne and joining the other bombers in a formation heading for Germany.

This morning it would be a 1,000-bomber raid. These enormous formations were a terrifying sight and sound for anyone on the ground. Like the gathering of the legions, from every point of the compass, tens, twenties and hundreds of aeroplanes arrived and rose above the white billowing clouds, arranging themselves in mathematical formations, rank on rank, each individual engine's noise drowned in the roar of millions of horsepower.

A full air division in the sky could be truly described as awesome. One thousand planes and ten thousand men, and all were headed to Germany to destroy three factory towns. Looking through a window at the rows of planes beside them, Frank Hart found his excitement rise with the sense of the enormous power this sky-filling armada presented. His nerves steadied at the sight. Protecting them were hundreds of Thunderbolt and Mustang fighter planes. This morning the Allies were unleashing an awesome daylight strike at the heart of Nazi Germany.

Within minutes the Liberators were flying over the English Channel on their way to the Netherlands. Richard Scharrer recalled lying in the grass looking up at the sky as these vast formations flew overhead on their way to Germany. He remembered his sense of excitement knowing they were going to attack Germany and his conviction that soon there would be victory and the Germans in the Netherlands would be gone.

Once they passed over the Dutch beaches, the formation started to take flak from the German anti-aircraft cannons, which could hurl fifteen to twenty shells per minute up to 30,000 feet in the air. German fighters swept nearby, and the machine gunners on Heaven Can Wait fired at them. One was hit, and gunners cheered. As they flew on, the flak became heavier, and the noise from the flak concussions, the machine guns and the roaring of the bomber's four Pratt & Whitney engines was deafening. The bomber next to Heaven Can Wait took a couple of hits and went down first, its wings swept upward like a fiery butterfly. Other bombers that had been hit were streaming flames and leaving the formation. One bomber took a direct hit and disintegrated before anyone could shout, 'Hit the silk!', which was the call to parachute out.

The pilots up front were praying they could get back to base in one piece and live to fight another day. Around them enemy fighters swooped and the flak became heavier, exploding in blinding bursts.

The massive formation seemed to have reached their target in Germany in no time at all. They swung into their bombing run, sailing through black puffballs of flak. Advancing rank on rank, they dropped their bomb-loads in curtains, each a little ahead of the other, until the entire town, airfield and factories beneath them had turned into an ever-growing, fiery red blanket, pierced with bright flashes.

As they started to wheel away from the target and toward home, Dave Smart spoke the traditional words, 'Bombs away, let's get the hell out of here.'

The plane was still wheeling round when it took a hit and staggered. The men cursed loudly. Debris flew everywhere and the huge bomber started to drop. Their outboard engine was windmilling crazily, splashing gas and oil on to the fuselage. They were at 28,000ft and had 600 miles to go to get home. At any second they could take another hit and burst into an explosion of flaming gasoline.

Bob Cole struggled to keep the aircraft flying. The crew started to throw equipment out of the plane and pump gas out of the damaged tank. Everybody worked in a frenzy. Across Germany they flew, over the Dutch border and the Zuiderzee. Every man on board was sweating heavily and praying. One was holding his rosary tightly. Now for the first time in their lives they might have to jump from over five miles up, into a rarefied atmosphere. It was a heart-stopping thought!

As they passed over the North Sea coast, Cole called Halmos to tell him they had maybe 150 gallons of gas left (the gauges were not always reliable), they were losing altitude at 200ft per minute, would lose another engine soon (they did, almost immediately), and how about a radius-of-action problem? Could they make it home, Cole wanted to know in his usual calm manner?

There was a 40mph headwind, and Eugene wrote that he would never want to do a navigational calculation like that again. He reported to Bob that it could not be done. They couldn't get home, despite the fact that there were now only 100 miles to go. They would crash into the sea. The great bomber was literally bleeding to death.

Cole did not hesitate. He turned the plane in a wide arc back to the Dutch coast and his voice came over the intercom: 'We'll have to get rid of this kid. Get ready to walk . . . Luck . . .'

Dave Smart climbed out of the nose-turret where he had been riding, freeing himself from a web of wires and hoses. Nobody said a word. He helped Halmos with his 'chute straps. They exchanged a look and a handshake, and then Dave disappeared down the knee-high tunnel that led to the bomb bays. Halmos had another minute during which he gave instructions as to roughly where they were and what direction to take to reach Normandy, where the nearest help would be found, before the intercom went dead. He wrote that he then crouched under his navigation table and pulled the red 'emergency handle'. The nose-wheel doors flopped suddenly open and he was looking down – 17,500ft down, to be exact. Then the crewmen started jumping, flashing past the nose-wheel hole, twisting and turning grotesquely like rag dolls and falling away and out of sight.

There was no time to think. Frank simply leapt into space and experienced a tremendous, breath-taking rush and buffeting in the slipstream. His nerves seemed as tight as cold steel. The air felt solid and it didn't seem as if he was falling to the ground below. At about 8,000ft he pulled his rip-cord, experienced a painful tug from the straps, and suddenly it was all eerily quiet. Down below the Netherlands looked calm and peaceful, with its canals, fields and houses dotted about the farmlands. There was no sign of its harsh occupation by the Germans. Suddenly everything seemed to grow larger and larger; cattle, fields and canals were rushing at him. The ground came up with a shock. Bang! And a sharp pain shot through his legs. Frank was on the ground and surprised to be still alive.

The last man to jump from the crippled bomber was the pilot, leaving the plane to continue on its downward cruise to a fiery explosion in the countryside, fortunately away from any built-up area.

Miraculously, the whole crew made it to the ground alive, with only a couple of men, David Smart and Frank Hart, suffering serious injuries in the jump. They had hit the ground near Ursem on a fine, bright, fresh June morning.

With parachutists from crippled bombers coming down from the skies over a large area, the Germans immediately went on the hunt. Heavily armed military vehicles went flying down the narrow farm roads seeking the crews and arresting all they were able to find.

Eugene Halmos wrote that after landing he looked around and saw friendly looking Dutch people in wooden clogs. They came and helped him up, all smiling and making V-for-victory signs. He asked if there were any Germans around, and a young Dutch lad pointed. There, standing about 30ft away, was a grim-faced German soldier with a machine-pistol pointed right at him. Young Dutch boys were jumping around in glee making rude gestures at the German; he shouted at them, and they skipped and pranced away mockingly.

One by one all were captured, except Frank, whose drop was also spotted by nearby friendly Dutch farmers. While he lay on the ground in agony, the farmers rushed over and, in great haste, hid his parachute. Two men helped carry him to the nearby farmhouse, where he was hidden. A man left urgently on a bicycle to get word to the local Resistance, slowing down when a German military vehicle approached in the hope that they had not noticed his haste. They barked questions at him about parachutists, but he simply shook his head as if he was a simpleton. At a nearby safe house a plan was hurriedly made to remove Frank from the area, which was now under heavy surveillance.

This was the danger period for helpers in the Resistance. If they were caught assisting or hiding an airman it would mean immediate arrest, then deportation or often the death penalty. The German authorities considered helping Allied aviators to be a much more serious offence than helping civilians, tantamount to aiding an enemy combatant. Also the constant Allied bombardment of Germany had meant great suffering amongst the civilian population, and the Germans considered Allied bomber crew to be '*Luftterroristen*' (air terrorists).

The crew had been briefed that they could expect harsh treatment if taken prisoner. Did they think about the huge destruction they had caused in their target areas, or the fire storms that usually followed these massive bombing raids? Most likely they had no idea, and if they thought about it at all they would have considered the terror to be the comeuppance the Germans deserved. The airmen knew that Hitler and the Nazis had a great deal to answer for in what they had done to England, but they had no idea what was happening to the Jewish population of Germany and occupied Europe.

What they did know about were some of the atrocities the Germans had inflicted on Britain and the occupied territories. From 7 September 1940 London was attacked no fewer than seventy-one times on fifty-seven consecutive nights, destroying one million homes and killing more than 40,000 civilians, most in London itself. Other cities had experienced frequent raids: Birmingham, Liverpool and Plymouth suffered eight massive ones, Bristol had six, Glasgow had five, and another twelve other cities, including Coventry, suffered heavy raids.

Air-raid shelters were built, London Underground entrances were protected with sandbags, and here the population fled as the sirens went off, wailing through the night air as the bombers droned over. Thousands of gas masks were issued to civilians. From 1 September to the end of the war, Operation Pied Piper evacuated over 3.5 million people, mostly children, to safe areas in the country and to distant parts of the British Empire.

The destruction of German towns, railways and factories by these bombing raids continued into the final months of the war, until every large city and even many small towns were reduced to rubble. It was this effort, together with the advance of Russian and Allied forces into Europe, that was mainly responsible for the German surrender and the end to the biggest war in history.

Now, in the midsummer fields of the Netherlands, for the crew of Heaven Can Wait the worst of their nightmares had become real. With the exception of Frank, all the other members of the crew were picked up by the Germans and taken by truck to a large farmhouse. How were they going to be treated? It appeared that while their treatment was somewhat on the rough side, and they all looked rather 'banged-up' as Eugene put it, it was not as bad as expected. Everything was efficiently dealt with, their belongings were noted carefully and signed for. Then they were sent on to the town of Hoorn, near the Zuiderzee. There they were imprisoned and interrogated, before being sent first to Venlo in Holland, then to Oberursel in Germany and finally to Sagan, Germany, or to the notorious Stalag Luft IV Gross Tychow.

They speculated about what might have happened to their missing crew member. Had he been killed? Had he escaped? Meanwhile, Frank was lying low, nursing his injuries. Within days, in the dark of an early morning, he was hidden under hay on the back of a farmer's cart and passed to the next person in the line of Resistance helpers.

It took a couple of days, a ride in a motorcycle with sidecar, and several safe houses, before Frank Hart landed up at Henri Scharrer's house on 21 Emmakade, Amstelveen, outside Amsterdam. It was early evening and growing dark. Fuel was unattainable, except for wood- or coal-burner conversions, so there were few vehicles on the road that were not official or had been requisitioned. Getting a wounded man around was not easy, and special arrangements had to be made to transport him. A motor vehicle painted the German field-grey pulled up quietly, and after the driver had first checked that the coast was clear, two men in German uniforms hurried Frank into the house. Here he was greeted by Henri's wife Truus and Henri himself, who had been waiting for this new 'delivery'. Their two sons Richard and Raymond rushed down the stairs in excitement: 'An American! A Yankee! Hello Yankee!'

Henri was well dressed as usual. He greeted Frank warmly and assured him in French-accented English that he was now in safe hands and that plans would soon be made to get him back to his base. But first Frank needed medical treatment, food and rest. Frank was surprised to be told that Henri was a French national and not Dutch.

Henri sent the excited boys back upstairs, scolding them in French with words of warning that this was a serious matter and they had to keep out of the way. The men all sat down and Henri brought out glasses and beer for everybody. Knowing in advance that the crewman had been injured, Henri had arranged through his cell contacts for Frank to be treated by a local doctor. The news travelled fast through the network and the doctor arrived just as the ravenous Frank had finished eating a large plate of stew and potatoes with a welcome glass of beer. The atmosphere in the room was jolly, and indeed they had every reason to feel exhilarated – 'We've foxed the Hun again!' There was much laughter, and Henri especially was in high spirits. It was times like these that made the dangers he faced on a regular basis seem worthwhile.

Once safely housed in the attic, waiting for the worst of his injuries to heal, Frank, who was a friendly young man, regaled Richard and Raymond with stories of life in the United States and gave the boys lessons in English. In his adult years Richard remembered that Frank had given him a small American flag, which he treasured. Richard always spoke English with a slight American accent, which he had originally picked up from his lessons with Frank.

The day after Frank's arrival, Henri left to meet up with other members of his Resistance cell. There was much to be done. Frank had to be given documents, the route had to be planned and messages had to be sent to other cell leaders. Also there were other airmen in the area who needed help. It was a few days before Henri returned and went upstairs to the attic to sit down with Frank and explain how the rest of the escape plan would work. He would organize identity papers and alert his escape line that would take Frank through Belgium to Paris, and then to the perilous trek over the Pyrenees to Spain and the safety of Gibraltar.

This was a similar route to the one he had used for Allied airmen on about twenty previous occasions, and the same route taken by Resistance men who had helped him with the young Dutch student Rudy Zeeman. These escape routes were tricky, and he had to proceed with caution. Sometimes, depending on circumstances and intelligence received, he would change the plan. Men might be sent on their own or in groups, and on at least two occasions they were sent to the coast to be helped by the Resistance man with the boats, twenty-six-year-old Anton (Tonny) Schrader.

Every detail had to be considered, because this was a life or death undertaking. Henri gave detailed instructions on how Frank was to be dressed, how he should behave, what information he had to remember, even how he had to eat. This had to be the European way with knife and fork together and not the American style of cutting up the food first and then eating it with a fork. It was important that Frank should be able to survive initial questioning by the Germans, who continually stopped people and checked them out. The Americans were more conspicuous than other nationalities because of slightly different mannerisms. The biggest problem would be language, as Frank could only speak English. So some key phrases were taught: '*Bitte*' and '*Danke*', '*Jawohl*', '*Ja, natürlich*' and others. Despite his injured legs, Frank was marched up and down the lounge, practising striding purposely and looking confident. Nervous looking men were always regarded as suspicious.

Henri spent a few precious hours with his boys, laughing and joking about the stupid Germans he had tricked. He would go over their homework and warn them never to say a word about their 'visitors'. He did not stay long at the house. Truus was used to his absences. There was much work to do, not only for his Resistance cell but also in arranging false identification for other hidden airmen and Resistance members. This was time-consuming, as one mistake could expose the escapees to grave danger; at worst, the whole fraudulent identification document operation could be compromised.

In spite of the pressures he faced, Henri somehow also managed successfully to handle his journalist duties as this provided him with his *Regeeringspersdienst* (government press card) – an important document that allowed him to travel in the Netherlands and Belgium.

Also behind the scenes, assisting Frank Hart, was Carry Libourel. It was she who organized the supplies and medicine for Frank. These she would give to her close friend Xenia Verster, who also on occasion helped Henri and Carry with their Resistance work. Xenia was one of the few people allowed into the house during Frank's stay, and she brought him the food and medication. After the war both Frank and his mother in Chicago wrote letters to Xenia, thanking her for her kindness during those dark days. These letters have been preserved.

Finally, the day came when Frank had to move. He was shocked when suddenly, without warning, two men dressed in German military uniform opened his attic door and strode into the room. He immediately thought he had been betrayed. But no! These were two Resistance men in disguise who were to take him to the south of the Netherlands.

The Scharrer household had a carefully hidden stock of a large variety of German military and SS uniforms of various ranks, even boots. Henri Scharrer himself used these from time to time, and Richard Scharrer recalled in his memoir how Henri had on one occasion taken him by train to see an aunt while dressed as a German officer and carrying a German newspaper. Richard did not know what the reason was for Henri to dress in this manner, or what his mission was.

As Richard remembered it, Henri cautioned him, 'Do not say a word. Not a word to anyone.' Henri left Richard at his aunt's house and then went back to the station. Why did Henri on occasion impersonate German officers? It would seem that he did so because it was easy. His German was excellent, he was a good actor and, most importantly, he enjoyed it. He also dressed several of his escapees as senior German officers for their own protection, because lower ranking Germans were reluctant to question a higher ranking officer. This reluctance is also reported by Rudy Zeeman in his memoir, and he experienced it when Henri sent Rudy and his friend Robert van Exter on their way to Spain as non-Germans working for the SD. In their travels on these papers through Belgium and France Rudy and Robert only had one near mishap, despite going through several control checks.

Now Frank was being sent on what was still believed to be a safe escape route, as so far it had experienced no betrayals or arrests. All had been working smoothly. According to the debrief report Frank gave to the Allied military after the war, he was then handed over to another Resistance man who moved him south along the escape line. Next he was introduced to a girl who took him to Dordrecht. Here he was handed over to two young fellows who took him to an electrical shop at Waalwijk in North Brabant. At this shop he met a number of people in the Resistance organization. His report listed those who assisted him and their addresses, including a farmhouse at Kaatsheuvel Zundet-Chaam belonging to well-known Resistance leader, Piet Felix, where he stayed for a few days.

Piet operated his own cell and worked with Henri Scharrer from time to time, mainly to obtain the false documentation his escapees needed for travel purposes. Born in the Hague, Piet worked closely with an important Resistance man,

Toon Wagemakers. At the time of Frank's visit he had a group of seven airmen on the farm. These were Eugene Glysynski from Chicago, Clement Leone of Baltimore, Alan Hayden from Brighton, George Packham from Sheffield, William Owens from West Virginia, Horace White from Memphis, and Derrick Coleman from Enfield.

After the war and his release from PoW camp, Frank Hart sent Piet Felix pictures of himself back home in Chicago and on occasion wrote him letters. Piet received the same awards as Henri Scharrer: a signed certificate from President Eisenhower and another signed by the British Air Chief Marshal Sir Arthur Tedder, in recognition of the work he did in assisting Allied airmen.

The other helpers Frank met at the farm and listed in his debrief to the Allies after the war included A. van der Hoof of Breda and Andre Wijlen of Sprang-Capelle.

After his stay on Piet's farm, Frank was taken back to the electrical shop, where he was given his Belgian papers. This time he and a couple of other escapees, William Coedy and Alan Denton Heyden, who was the sole survivor of a Lancaster that crashed near Oosterhaut on 21 July, left on bicycles and rode to the border near Turnhout, Belgium. Here they met two Dutch policemen in blue uniforms. They were the *Marechaussees* (Dutch Mounted Police) Ernst Lems and Wilhelmus Monnier, both underground Resistance members.

The three men waited with Ernst and Wilhelmus for about twenty minutes. Then a man came to the border from the Belgian side and they were instructed to follow him. This they did and they were hidden in bushes for about an hour – a wait that seemed endless to Frank. Finally, much to their relief, the man returned with a pretty young woman, and they walked a short distance to Turnhout, where they boarded a tram.

They had only been travelling on the tram for about five minutes when German soldiers suddenly and dramatically boarded it, with their guns drawn, aimed at Frank, Alan and William. They were arrested and immediately handcuffed. As for the girl, the Germans greeted her in a friendly and familiar manner. All were joking and laughing about their success. Frank realized with shock and anger that she had betrayed them. He cursed her in good backstreet Chicago fashion, but she simply laughed mockingly at him before turning around and leaving the tram. It was 28 July 1944.

Two days later Frank saw her again with a couple of German soldiers as he was being brought in for questioning in Antwerp. She was laughing and talking with her German friends over cups of coffee. Her name was Anna Maria Verhulst-Oomes and she worked directly for a *V-Mann* (informant) with the Abwehr – René van Muylem. Anna Maria was under van Muylem's orders, and so successful was he at finding and arresting Allied airmen that he received an award from his German masters for having trapped a total of 178 of them, with the help of a number of pro-German sympathizers like Anna.

Frank also discovered during his time in detention at Antwerp that at least ten other Americans had been arrested, all of whom had visited the electrical shop in Waalwijk, where an unknown collaborator had been secretly positioned. So in only a few days Henri's escape line had been compromised, and the weak spot was clearly the shop.

Frank reports that he was subjected to a heavy-handed interrogation. At one stage he was knocked down so hard that he injured his back. After Antwerp he was taken to Brussels, then to Aachen, Frankfurt and Oberursel. The interrogators were not interested in his squadron or his flying experiences; all they wanted to know was the identity of the people who had helped him. Somehow, with great bravery and resilience, Frank remained firm, and after his interrogation, which he described as 'not too gentle', he was sent to his first internment camp. An Allied military report on Frank's experiences referred to this camp as Stalag Luft IV Gross Tychow – formerly Heyd. Frank described it in a letter to Xenia Verster as being near Saarbrücken, writing that it was a camp with little food, little clothing and much hard work.

This was the camp from which nearly 6,000 airmen were sent on an infamous forced march as the American forces under Patton were approaching. Known as the Death March, for some men it lasted up to 86 days. Not everyone from the camp was sent in the same direction, but all the marchers experienced great hardship, slept in barns or open fields, suffered trench foot, malnutrition, exposure, dysentery and tuberculosis. There are many reports of heroism, describing how the stronger prisoners helped the weaker and how some made their escape, ducking and diving into ditches, hiding in forests, until rescued by Allied forces.

When Frank's march came to an end, he and his group were then shipped to Xolberg, where he spent a few months. Then in their weakened state they were force-marched a second time to another camp near Rostock.

Here at Rostock, finally, Frank's trials and tribulations came to an end. On one of the great days in history, 1 May 1945, they were liberated by the Russians under Marshal Zhukov. The Russians provided food, clothes and good vodka – which Frank describes as being 'powerful stuff' and much appreciated by everybody. After spending time in a hospital in France, Frank was shipped back to the United States to the Regional Hospital in San Antonio, Texas, where he spent several months having further treatment to his injured back and left leg. One can't help wondering how Frank ever survived two grim forced marches with his injuries. It is a testament to his courage and determination.

In a letter dated Saturday, 6 October 1945, Frank wrote to Xenia Verster, Carry Libourel's friend, who had brought food and medication to Henri's house to help treat his injuries:

Dear Mrs Verster,

I am happy to say that I received your most welcome letter of 11th July, just two days ago. I guess it was due to my moving around so much. I am very happy to hear that you are all alright. And again I am sorry to hear about your brother in law losing all his possessions in the battle of Arnhem.

Of course, the death of the gentleman who was responsible for my spending several enjoyable days with you came as a great disappointment to me as he was a brave fellow. It must be quite hard on his wife and two children whom I met in Amsterdam. I surely hope they will be taken care of by the Allied government. As for myself I had the misfortune of being turned in to the German Military police on the 28th of last July 1944, by a woman who was posing as a member of the organization in Belgium. I had been with her just about an hour and while on a tram in Turnhout she signalled the German Police. I was very disappointed as you can imagine. In attempting to escape I was knocked down and injured my back which as you know had been giving me trouble as a result of the parachute jump I made. I was taken to Antwerpen, Brussels, Aachen, Frankfurt and Oberursel for questioning. They knew by my identification tags that I was an American Airman, but they didn't seem interested in that fact. They wanted to know where and who helped me. This treatment wasn't too gentle but you can rest assured that I conveniently forgot all names and places of anything or anyone I saw in the Netherlands. I was finally sent to a prison camp near Saarbrücken in the latter part of September. As you can imagine it was most unpleasant. Little Food and Little Clothing and hard work.

We were in that camp only forty six days when we were forced to march out as the American forces under Patton were coming near us. We were then shipped to a camp near Xolberg where we spent four months. In the latter part of January of this year we were forced to travel once more to another camp near Rostock where I stayed till May first of this year, when I was liberated by the Russian forces under Marshall Zhukov. I enjoyed meeting the Russians as they fed us and made it possible to remain alive as the German people had a great hate for all Allied Airmen. I also had a taste of your countrymen's national drink (Vodka). It sure was a powerful drink. I was sent to hospital in Le Harve, France from where I was sent back to the United States. At the present time I am in a hospital as my back and left leg are practically useless. They seem to think that my nerves in those parts of my body are shattered. If you would do me the honour of writing again please address it to my home address in Chicago.

I will also mail you some of our American cigarettes as soon as I can get enough of them together as we still have rationing here. I will close for now. Thanking you once again for your fine treatment of myself while in your fine country. I remain,

Your Everlasting Friend
S/Sgt Francis A. Hart (Junior)

Frank's mother, Mrs Genevieve Hart, also wrote to Xenia thanking her for her kindness in looking after her son and told her a little about Frank's experiences, mentioning that he did not like talking about them. She also wrote to his fellow crew members, and one of her letters reached Eugene Halmos. It was only then that Eugene and the other captured crew members of Heaven Can Wait discovered that Frank was alive and had nearly escaped the Germans, before landing in a PoW camp.

The unfortunate consequence of the Frank Hart escape was that the Scharrer Amsterdam-to-Spain line was now known to have been compromised, and at the time nobody knew for sure who the collaborators were. Much time and effort went into trying to identity these traitors. When they were identified, no mercy was shown. Known traitors were swiftly executed by the Resistance. Henri, Carry and their trusted helpers now had to set up a new route, an arduous task that Resistance fighters frequently faced when their safe routes and houses were betrayed. We know that in those two months after Frank's capture Henri was often away from home, travelling to Belgium and France, most likely to do just that.

At the close of the war many collaborators were able to escape the anger and wrath of the occupied populations by fleeing to Germany. They were only identified after the war as a result of debriefings and interviews given by survivors to the Allies. It was partly on the basis of Frank's report and others that the Belgian girl, Anna Maria Verhulst-Oomes, was arrested and charged with serious war crimes. She was known to have fraternized with the Germans, so it is possible she had also been recruited because of this association.

Women who fraternized with Germans were harshly treated. The Dutch called them 'krauts'. The French had a slightly more colourful expression, 'collaborateurs horizontales'. They were paraded as loose women, humiliated, painted orange and often had their hair shorn off in a degrading punishment for all to see.

Anna Maria committed suicide by taking poison a couple of days before her trial in 1945. Her immediate boss, V-Mann René van Muylem, was arrested after the war, tried and executed.

Although Frank's attempt failed in the Belgian part of the escape route, after his return to the United States he spent time over the next few years writing to many of the people who had helped him. Letters went not only to Xenia Verster, but also to Piet Felix of Kaatsheuvel Zundet-Chaam in the southern Netherlands. Frank also sent a happy photograph showing him with his Dalmatian dog. At the same time that Piet assisted Frank he had also been helping a group of his own airmen, and they too were caught in the same trap that ensnared Frank. So it had been a bad day for the underground movement, but a successful day for German counter-intelligence.

Tough as those long months in PoW camps were, on the positive side Frank forged many lasting friendships with a wide range of people. He enjoyed several hearty reunions with a number of his fellow crewmen, swopping stories of their great adventures, escapes and arrests, and their rescues by the liberating Russian and Allied forces.

We do not know how Frank's life progressed and whether he later married and had a family. All searches to track him down after he settled back in Chicago have so far failed. With his bravery and determination it is more than likely that he will have gone on to live a successful and productive life.

One of the positive memories Richard and Raymond Scharrer had of war was of Frank Hart, the American gunner who stayed in their attic. To them he always remained a hero.

Chapter 3

The Escape of Rudy Zeeman – an *Engelandvaarder*

Not all the escapees Henri Scharrer helped were Allied airmen. As we have discovered, Henri also helped young Dutch people escape to safety. During the occupation, while there were many failed escapes, there were also some 1,600 to 1,700 Dutch evaders who successfully made it to England. They were called *Engelandvaarders*, or 'England paddlers', so called because the first groups who made it to England safely went by boat. Henri assisted a number of *Engelandvaarders*, and we have their stories. One in particular needs to be recorded here since he wrote a memoir about his experiences which provides fascinating detail on a successful escape. He is also one of the few people alive at the time of writing who knew Henri Scharrer personally.

This is the story of Rudy Zeeman, a leading *Engelandvaarder*. He vividly describes meeting Henri and then his remarkable escape on one of the dangerous and challenging routes: from Amsterdam, through Belgium and France, over the Pyrenees in the grim cold of winter, and down to Spain.

Today in his late nineties, he lives in Tasmania. In his excellent memoir, *Luck through Adversity*, he describes in detail his escape from the Netherlands as a young student and the wartime adventures that took him to England. It was while in London during the war that Rudy was invited, with several others, to have tea with Queen Wilhelmina at 77 Chester Square. The memoir also deals with his travels to the United States and eventually his experiences as an officer fighting the Japanese in the Far East.

Like many Hollanders he was desperate to get to England to link up with the Government-in-Exile in the fight against the Nazis. In the spring of 1943, at the Amsterdam Golf Club, he met Robert van Exter, an economics student at the University of Amsterdam. Robert had excitedly run into the club house shouting that he had made a hole-in-one at the eighth. Rudy had to explain to him with great sympathy that it would not stand as a hole-in-one, since he did not have a completed scorecard signed by a partner who had witnessed the feat. Following this meeting Robert joined Rudy's small group of *onderduikers* (people who had gone underground to evade the Germans for various reasons).

In October they were having lunch at the flat of Robert's mother on Beethovenstraat. During lunch Robert outlined a plan to reach England by Spain. He explained to Rudy that his father lived in Paris and had important Resistance connections. One of his father's friends was a member of the Dutch Resistance in Paris, a young engineer by the name of Albert Starink, who was involved in the Dutch-Paris escape line. Albert would be their contact and would organize falsified French identity cards. Somehow at that time the two young men believed that escaping to England would be as easy as a walk in the park. Little could they know the dangers they would be getting themselves into or the numbers who had perished attempting the same undertaking.

So the plans were laid. Early in December, while they were in Breda, they received the first bit of bad news regarding their plans. The safe house where they would stay in Brussels had been raided by the Gestapo, and everyone 'was now in hospital', the euphemism for being in jail. This unexpected setback came as a shock, and Rudy and Robert beat a hasty retreat back to Amsterdam to reorganize and start over again.

It took a few weeks before Rudy and Robert could meet up with Albert, which they did at the café of the well-known Hotel Americain on the Leidseplein in Amsterdam. The conversation was brief. Albert told them that Robert would receive a letter from a man called 'Monsieur Henri' – one of Henri Scharrer's pseudonyms. He would need their photographs and other information. Monsieur Henri would then be able to provide them with the SD (German Security Police) identity cards and travel documents and advise them how and when they were to travel to Paris. After this meeting, the group broke up.

A few days after Christmas, Monsieur Henri, also known as 'Sandberg', arrived at the Beethovenstraat apartment and came straight to the point with his instructions. Smartly dressed as usual, in his efficient manner he told them they were to travel on the documents he would be giving them which were only issued to SD employees.

The instructions were not simple. In fact, they were quite intricate and at first glance appeared cumbersome. But there was a reason for everything. The travel documents were to cover them for a journey from Pau, a city in the south of France, to Amsterdam and for the return, again via Paris, to Pau. So the starting point for these documents was Pau.

Genuine SD identity cards with a vertical crossed green stripe had been stolen from an SD office, and would be filled in with the escapees' photos, information and signatures as these appeared on their Dutch identity cards. The SD cards were 'signed' by the commanding *Grüne Polizei* (regular police) officer, an *Untersturmführer*, whose signature had been copied, as had the falsified/copied stamps and signatures of the key German officials stationed along the route from Pau to Amsterdam and on the return trip. This was a highly researched route. Every important address and every key German official's name was known, as were their signatures. Rudy and Robert were astonished.

According to their SD identity cards they were *Vertragsangestellten* (contract employees) attached to the SD in the Pau regional branch office and employed in interrogating Dutch and Flemish prisoners. That would be their cover. Monsieur Henri noted the details of their Dutch identity cards and was given their passport photographs.

Henri must have worked very fast, because the next day he returned with two sets of documents and the SD identity cards with the photos on them. He then briefed them on the cover story for their travel to Pau from Amsterdam. This they had to rehearse.

The story was both clever and creative, and they would have to know it thoroughly and be able to tell it to anyone who questioned them. It was simply that they had been on a short home leave after delivering documents to the SD Headquarters in Holland. This was attested by the stamps and signatures of a host of German authorities on their *Sonderausweis* (official travel order). They had the signature of the officer-in-charge in Pau, and the important *Bescheinigung* (official certificate) issued on behalf of the police. Every detail and possible eventuality had been covered.

Monsieur Henri handed them each the two complete sets of documents. The first *Sonderausweis* showed that on 3 January 1944 they had travelled from Pau to Amsterdam and had reported their arrival at the *Hauptkommandantur* (headquarters) in Amsterdam. It was also provided with another stamp confirming that they had reported their arrival in Paris, on their return journey to Pau, at the bureau of the Kommandant von Gross, on 12 January. Monsieur Henri instructed them to hide the second set of documents, which they did inside a talcum powder tin.

Monsieur Henri carefully explained that the first set, with different and earlier dates, were to be destroyed on the morning of 12 January. (Robert's second set of these documents is now stored in the archives of the Verzetsmuseum in Amsterdam).

It is this detailed account by Rudy Zeeman of the plans Henri made that illustrates not only how thorough Henri was but also how audacious his plans and ideas were. He seemed to have no fear of failure, and his many successes had made him ever more confident.

Rudy enjoyed the irony that they would actually travel as SD employees. The plan was brazen, but Henri was confident of its success. It also explains why Henri preferred setting up escapees as phoney characters and often as senior German officers. This ploy was made all the easier because many Dutchmen who were collaborators had actually joined the German military and Waffen-SS. It meant that speaking German with a Dutch accent did not raise much suspicion when someone was questioned.

Henri did not leave it there. Rudy writes that a few days after New Year Henri visited them again and gave them a 'final interrogation' to make sure they knew the street name and other houses standing in the street where the SD regional branch office was situated. They would need to know this should they ever land up being questioned. Also they would need to act like proper SD employees and adopt an arrogant, stern demeanour to keep suspicious individuals and junior officers at bay. There were plenty of pro-German sympathizers around who would be only too happy to turn them in.

After their final practice run they had lunch with Henri and Mrs van Exter. After an excellent meal, a taxi was arranged to take them to the Central Station in Amsterdam. And so they were on their way to Paris.

On the train from Amsterdam the German Railway Police entered their compartment, examined their 'first' set of documents and handed them back with a '*danke schön*'. They then went through a second German control at Utrecht Station which also went well. They stayed at a hotel at Maastricht and the next morning caught the 9.00 German Army *Fronturlaubzug* (home leave train) for Paris. In their compartment were three German army officers, so they simply sat down and started reading *Das Reich*, a Nazi newspaper, and then pretended to fall asleep. Finally they reached the Gare du Nord in Paris. As they left, Rudy with a stern look on his face, said to the ticket inspector, '*Polizei*', showing the SD Identity documents. The inspector made no comment and let them pass. After that successful brush with German officialdom they adopted this stern approach with more confidence every time they were challenged.

Rudy goes on to describe the progress of his escape route and the dangers they experienced. Short of French francs for the Paris Metro ride to the Trocadero station, Robert and Rudy brazenly showed their SD identity cards to the ticket collector, saying curtly, as Henri had instructed, '*Polizei*'. Once again the man let them pass without comment and they enjoyed a free ride.

The plan was working brilliantly!

Now, following instructions, Rudy and Robert had to meet up again with Albert Starink, who plays an important role in a number of these adventures. Albert was a graduate of the University of Delft and operated mainly in Paris and Brussels; his name is frequently mentioned in Rudy's memoir. His prime bases were the Hôtel de Noailles on the Rue de la Michodiére and the Hôtel Monsieur-le-Prince on the street of the same name. These were two Parisian hotels favoured by Henri.

After meeting Albert, they moved to the Paris apartment of Robert's father. Mr van Exter had been kept informed about their escape plans and also provided the money to pay Henri for their SD documents. He now brought Mr Lahnemann, a Dutch businessman, into the picture and introduced him to the two young men. Lahnemann lent Rudy 20,000 French francs, on the basis of an IOU, trusting time and honour for repayment at the end of the war. Of this sum, 500 guilders was needed to pay for the SD documents.

Many of the guides in the Pyrenees were professional smugglers, herders, local farmers, woodcutters and Maquis members born in the Pyrenees. They knew the tracks inside out. It had been agreed with the escape line negotiators that the fee for the co-operation of the local Maquis groups could be as much as 12,000 francs to get escapees from the foothill towns up the mountains and over to the Spanish border. Henri's part of the fee was for the fraudulent documents he supplied. Theo Koersen also needed to be paid for his expert and essential printing services.

Rudy reports a narrow escape with their 'second' set of documents. At a hotel restaurant it seems that a waiter, clearly a collaborator, overheard Rudy talking quietly in English to Robert's lady friend because his French was not that good. Then at the garderobe Rudy was asked to show his papers to a German official. Robert was still inside the restaurant when Rudy was stopped.

The German commented curtly on the documents, 'They might be all right but I want them inspected at the *Hauptkommandantur.*'

This was a dangerous situation. They both knew that if these documents were checked at the *Hauptkommandantur* it would be clear that the office did not have an entry to correspond with the documents. Luckily, Rudy without hesitation walked out of the restaurant, forcing the officer to follow him and thus leaving the second officer to collect their overcoats at the garderobe. This allowed Robert time to slip out of the front door and make his getaway.

Rudy, however, was put in the back seat of the Quarte Avant behind the Oberleutnant, with the Hauptmann taking the seat to the left of him; both had their pistols in open holsters on their laps. The driver was ordered to proceed to the *Hauptkommandantur*, where all travellers had to report on arrival in Paris. After a few hundred metres the officer changed his mind and ordered the driver to take them to the '*Gestapo auf Avenue Foch*'.

This is where Rudy's luck came into play. In the Citroen Rudy was seated in the right rear seat, one officer seated next to him with his Luger on his lap and the second on the front right seat next to the driver, also with his pistol ready for use. The front doors, as was usual in those days, opened backwards, and the rear doors forward. He also noted that the handle of his door was hidden behind his leg and he immediately gripped it in his right hand.

In blacked-out Paris, with car headlights covered except for a narrow slit, the street signs were hard to read, and the driver was scolded when he missed the left turn he should have taken. The vehicle now slowed down to enable the Germans to read the next street sign. All this caused confusion about the route, and when all three Germans were looking at the street signs on the left, Rudy jumped out of the car on the right side, and escaped in the pitch darkness.

His flight was accompanied by shouts of '*Halt! Da geht der Schwein!*' and '*Ach, wir haben sie doch!*'. But Rudy had a 10-metre head start. He avoided the next side street as that would have been too obvious, but afterwards ran through many small streets before becoming hopelessly lost.

He then approached an unknown elderly lady with a shawl over her head and asked her to direct him to the nearest Metro station. She looked at him for a moment and said, '*Monsieur, prenez mon bras, s'il vous plait*' (Please take my arm, sir'). So he walked, on her arm, as if they were mother and son, to the St Augustin Metro Station, where he thanked her profusely.

Robert, too, had fortunately got away, but Rudy had now lost Henri's documents, which the German officer had taken. Albert Starink came to the rescue immediately. He and the other Resistance members decided that Robert and Rudy could no longer stay at the apartment and had to move to another safe address. Because there might be searches for them, they avoided the Metro and walked to the Hôtel de Medicis on the Rue Monsieur-le-Prince. This was one of the safe addresses in Paris identified by Henri and Jan Lowey-Ball when they first started working together and set up the escape route. During his three-night stay in a narrow, unheated bedroom, with barred window and a broken window pane, Rudy was bitterly cold. Albert also warned him to disguise his appearance it, so Rudy changed his hairstyle and obtained a pair of spectacles.

Although Albert brought him bread and cheese for breakfast and lunch, Rudy felt the need to get out of his chilly confinement. Most evenings he slipped out of the hotel after dark, confident in his disguise, and had a good hot meal in a side street at the Chinese restaurant of Mr Wong, enjoying both the food and the excellent heating.

Through his contact with Albert, the Dutch artist John Ruys offered Rudy a place to stay in Montparnasse. Rudy described John as a tall slim aristocrat and a most charming and considerate host, but someone who totally ignored the dangers faced by escapers like Rudy. John had not changed his lifestyle after the German occupation and had grown complacent about its ever-present dangers. He had foreign resident's papers, allowing him to remain in France but not, of course, to be in the company of illegals. However, this did not bother him that much. In the evenings despite the danger, he would take the now bespectacled Rudy to dine at brasseries like Le Dôme and the still famous La Coupole on the Boulevard de Montparnasse, where he would point out interesting guests, including Picasso. And so Rudy enjoyed the best that occupied Paris could offer in good dining and night life.

Rudy's memoir also tells us what happened to John Ruys, who often helped Dutch escapees with a safe house. He was arrested a couple of months later helping another escapee and transported to the Oranienburg concentration camp.

Years later, John's grandson, US Navy Commander R. E. Ruys, told Rudy that John had been sent on to Natsweiler concentration camp and then to Dachau, where he died.

Robert and Rudy were reunited a couple of weeks later. Because Rudy's falsified SD identity, travel papers and photo were now in the hands of the Gestapo, Albert Starink made arrangements for new French identity cards for both of them. It was also decided to bring forward their departure and include them in the next 'convoy' for Toulouse. After a few days at John Ruys' apartment, Albert picked them up and gave them their new French identity documents.

Robert's alias was Robert Pierre Vancastel, an *employé de bureau* (office worker) born on 2 September 1911. Rudy's alias was Jean Paul Pascal, professional *dessinateur* (designer), born on 5 December 1910 in Saigon, Indo-China, address 4 Rue le Goff, Montaigu-de-Quercy. Jean Paul was the Christian name of his friend J. P. Perez, 5 December was his father's birthday and 1910 was the year of his brother Tom's birth, so these particulars were all easy to remember if Rudy and Robert were ever questioned. Every detail of their aliases was therefore carefully thought out, researched and professionally executed. Nothing was left to chance.

Rudy handed Albert the overcoat and hat he wore at the time of his arrest which he felt had brought him good luck. They then put on their raincoats and an extra pullover to help protect themselves against the bitter January cold.

Albert took 'Jean Paul Pascal' and 'Robert Pierre Vancastel' to the Gare d'Austerlitz. No information about the escape route or the names of helpers was supplied. This precaution was an unwritten rule in the Resistance. At the station Albert bought the tickets for Toulouse and a platform ticket for himself. In addition to Rudy and Robert, ten American airmen and one RAF pilot were to be escorted by guides from the escape organization to Toulouse. Five of the airmen were from the crew of the B-17 Flying Fortress 'Sarah Jane', which crash-landed near Vimy in Northern France late in 1943. They were Ernest Stock, Frank Tank, Russell Gallo, Eric Kole and Leonard Cassady.

The airmen wore black leather boots, blue, grey and black overcoats and blue French berets, and some carried *musettes* (knapsacks) slung over their shoulders the way French labourers would carry them. Rudy and Robert were introduced to their group leader, code name 'Jacques', and informed they would get more information when they arrived at Toulouse station. After the war Rudy learned that 'Jacques' was actually Jacques Rens, an important man in the Dutch-Paris Line.

The next day they got off at the Gare Matabiau in the old part of Toulouse near the Canal du Midi. In small groups they were taken to a restaurant by the name of Chez Emile at the Place St Georges in the middle of Toulouse. The restaurant still exists and today is quite famous. Here they had breakfast, with little or no conversation as there were eyes and ears everywhere. Details were important. Jacques warned the Americans to use knife and fork in the European fashion, since the American style was an easy give-away which had resulted in the arrests of many airmen.

Jacques then escorted Rudy and Robert to his hotel, which was one used by the Dutch-Paris Line in Toulouse. Here they were given water-resistant clothes to wear under their raincoats for their walk across the Pyrenees. Then they were led to a two-storey brick house with boarded up windows. In one of the rooms they joined four of the Americans they had met earlier at Chez Emile: the small, dark-haired Leonard Cassady, and the blond James Hussong, who was nursing a wounded leg, navigator Charles (Chuck) Downe and Ernest Grubb, a Marauder pilot.

Escorted by two guides, they returned to the station, only to be told that Rudy and Robert's group would leave later on another train. Back they traipsed to the boarded-up house, which the Americans decided was an old brothel. Here Rudy and Robert were given more clothing and berets so they would also look like travelling French labourers.

They were introduced to their guides, 'Palo' (Etienne Treillet) and 'Mireille' (Henri Marret), who arrived in the late afternoon to take them back to the station. Once again bad luck overtook them. As they arrived, the train was already pulling out, with the result that Robert and Rudy's party of six escapers missed joining the others. Now they had become separated from the second group of Americans, who were the survivors of 'Sarah Jane'.

Rens and the two guides, Palo and Mireille, then decided the group had to overnight in a house in a small village. Here Rens took leave of the six and wished them luck.

Nothing so far had been going smoothly or easily. The next day they were again taken back to Toulouse station, where they waited in a large café, surrounded by Germans of all ranks, and bought bread rolls and beer with the food coupons Mireille had given them. Every now and then one would say, '*Merci*' or '*Merci beaucoup*'. This was considered a dangerous station because passengers were carefully watched by the French gendarmes as well as SD/Gestapo and the Vichy-French secret police. But when they walked through the station nobody was stopped and no papers checked.

Finally Palo and Mireille arrived to assist the now disguised 'French labourers' to board the slow train to St Gaudens. They were directed to use one of the last carriages, because the locomotives and carriages at the front always suffered the most when the Maquis (French Resistance) sabotaged a train.

Group leader Jacques distributed the fugitive airmen over several other carriages. They were strictly warned not to speak and to pretend to sleep most of the time. All the while they endeavoured to behave in as French a fashion as they could.

They alighted at the village of Cazères, where after a walk in complete darkness they arrived at an incomplete two-storey safe house, where they stayed a couple of days with four of the American airmen. The Americans joked that they had decided that this house was also an old brothel. In fact, brothels were often used as safe houses by the Resistance, so they were not far off the mark.

From Cazères they took the slow train to Boussens, where they walked across a wide road to a café near the station, spread themselves out and waited for the bus that would take them further along their route. An ancient contraption finally arrived which, petrol being a scarce commodity, ran on coke gas. Palo joined them, and just as they were about to leave, an officer in his light-green *Grüne Polizei* uniform entered the bus and sat down in the front row reserved for German officials. Palo, alert to danger, got up, sat in the empty seat next to the officer, and started an animated conversation, laughing and offering him a cigarette. This diverted the officer's attention from the illegals at the back. He was suspicious, though, glancing at them from time to time, and Palo had to use his wits to keep the officer's attention, telling him in his basic German that he would be going back to work in Germany in a few weeks' time.

So danger was avoided, and they made their way to a basement café in Mane, where they fed heartily on eggs and fatty bacon. Here they were given provisions for their trek over the Pyrenees consisting of bacon, sugar cubes and a few slices of bread.

As well as instituting a curfew, the Germans had created a forbidden zone 15km wide adjoining the French-Spanish border where the locals were issued with special passes. The Germans, often with dogs, regularly patrolled the roads, villages and hamlets in the valleys of this *Zone Interdit* and they were authorized to shoot on sight at any illegals, as they often did. From observation posts the Germans also scoured the hills and mountains with binoculars, while ski-patrols were employed in the snowbound areas.

This is extremely rugged country on both sides of the border and impassable for the most part. The guides were forced to lead escapees from mountain ridge to mountain ridge, spending as little time possible crossing the valleys and avoiding the occasional hamlets, farms or woodcutters' huts.

The escapees could not believe how busy and crowded this route was, as they met up with others heading south. Here all were divided into smaller groups. So as not to draw attention, each small group started at different times and followed different paths.

It was nearly nine in the evening when the group of four Americans – Leonard Cassady, James Hussong, Charles (Chuck) Downe and Ernest Grubb – and two Dutchmen, guided by Palo and Mireille, started their dangerous three-day and two-night walk across the foothills and high ridges of the Pyrenees to the Spanish border.

The first stage from Mane was over route D13 to Arbas, an approximately 12km walk on a tarred road, and they made good time. At around one o'clock in the morning they reached a barn and here they slept under hay to try and keep warm. They were woken at 0400 hrs in pitch darkness and off they went again. There was light rain falling, which eased up when they reached a hamlet, most likely Sarrat De Bouch, where they were given breakfast of bread, butter and sausages.

This was the heart of winter. There was no moon that night, since for safety the guides preferred to travel in the dark. They knew their goat trails well and could not risk being spotted. The rain made the narrow mountain track slippery, and it got worse, much steeper and narrower, as they walked to the Pic de l'Aube. Light snow started to fall, and as they climbed higher they were trudging in deep snow. The going was tough, particularly as the men were weak from lack of exercise after hiding for many days, or even months, in lofts and barns. They pulled themselves up, at times crawling on hands and knees, all the time encouraged by Palo. Fingers and toes were numb with cold. Many escapees suffered from vertigo on these climbs, as they had to walk along narrow paths with *cirques*, sheer drops, on one side that could be thousands of feet to the valley below. Danger abounded everywhere, with the narrow-winged Henschel 126 scout planes making regular swoops above the better known paths, the airmen sweeping the terrain with their binoculars and not hesitating to fire if they spotted escapees on the run.

The higher they climbed, the colder and thinner the air became. Every breath was a struggle, and one slip could send a man plunging down into a ravine. Some of the granite peaks were as high as 11,000ft. They could not stop and had to keep moving in the mud and icy slush. Along the way men ate their meagre rations of hard biscuits, cheese and dried fruit. Occasionally a canister of water was passed along for men to take just one sip. Torrents of water called *gaves* gushed down from fissures in the cliffs, making a thunderous noise. Up they went, round hills at dizzying angles, through gaps, until they noticed they were descending more than climbing.

At about 5,000ft above sea level they crossed a ridge and zigzagged down a footpath on a tree-covered slope to the south. Below was the fairly level area of the pass known as Col de Portet d'Aspet, near which stood a hut, today called 'La Cabane des Evades'. Inside they ate a piece of bread and fatty bacon, had a swig of cognac and a few lumps of sugar for energy. Later they were told that here at this hut, only eleven days after their stop, the Germans ambushed a large group, but Palo and Mireille had been able to make their escape.

They enjoyed a brief rest, before setting out again. The weather had become foul, and the wind had increased, with sleet and snow blowing horizontally into them. A more unpleasant and dismal night could not be imagined. All the while they were climbing again, occasionally taking a break to turn their backs into the blizzard and catch their breath.

Boots were wet through, socks were soaked and nearly frozen, and finally, stumbling over small rocks and stones, blinded by the blizzard, they crested a mountain ridge to take refuge in another hut. Into the shelter fell the bedraggled men, shivering from the icy wind. Nobody spoke for a few minutes. Rudy took off his boots, which had now split open, and rubbed his toes to restore the circulation. He then put his wet socks back on and pulled out a pair of walking shoes he had packed in his rucksack. He had heard that putting on even wet socks helped prevent frostbite.

Then it was back again on the trail, walking Indian-file, often with one hand on the shoulder of the man in front, to avoid falling behind or losing the way in the darkness. Rudy writes that images of that ascent to the Cabane du Gauch and the descent in the bitter night and icy cold dawn are permanently engraved in his memory as one of the most harrowing experiences of his life.

By daybreak the gale-force wind had abated and they had descended well down the now wooded slope leading to the valley of a small river called the Maudan. There was a bridge guarded by a blockhouse, which housed German soldiers, and this they crossed silently, crouching over, praying they would not be spotted. Luckily they weren't seen, as the Germans were probably still asleep. After a short rest they had to climb the looming slope of a dark mountain ridge.

'We must be over the top before 0830 hrs, otherwise they can detect us through their binoculars and alert the ski-patrols,' warned Palo.

They made it, grasping at branches, sometimes crawling on hands and knees, and with their lungs stinging at every breath. The group had hardly reached the crest when Ernie Grubb collapsed in the snow. Weakened by his long period in hiding, his physical fitness had deteriorated. Yet he had bravely made it all this way, in pain and without a complaint. Mireille quickly made him a mixture of cognac and sugar lumps, and after ten minutes he was hoisted to his feet. From then on he had to be assisted to walk the rest of the way.

Finally, with everyone in a state of exhaustion, ahead of them Palo planted his stick in the knee-high snow.

'This is the frontier.'

It was half past twelve on the afternoon of 26 January 1944.

As they descended the mountain they finally left the snow line and made their way on sore and swollen feet to the village of Canejan. At the police station an elderly woman made a fire to help dry their soaked clothes and socks and brought them water and hot coffee. Here they were told that they were to stay in *residence forcé* (house arrest) at a hotel in the nearby village of Les. After a hearty meal of soup, meat, rice and herbs, and a fairly large quantity of port, Rudy and the American Ernie Grubb collapsed and the others carried them up the stairs to a bedroom. They didn't wake up until well into the following day.

Some of the other groups were not so lucky in attempting to cross this frontier, and many men whom Rudy met in the foothills had the misfortune of encountering German patrols. These were mostly Alpine troops in their white uniforms, camped in huts along the routes, equipped for the freezing conditions and determined not to let escapees through.

Ernie Grubb and Charles Downe were able to contact the American embassy in Barcelona. Robert asked the embassy to contact the Dutch Consul and report the arrival of Robert Piet van Exter and Pieter Rudolph Zeeman and to take the necessary steps to inform the Spanish authorities.

Rudy and Robert were detained by the Spanish police, who took them for questioning to a jail in the town of Lerida. This detention did not last long, and they were soon released, put up in another hotel and given a new set of clothing and shoes, paid for by the Dutch Government.

From Lerida Rudy wrote a postcard to his parents in Amsterdam. It read:

Dear friends,
How are things? I have not heard from you for ages, hopefully you are all well. I am fine, although I still have a sore throat, caused by a cold I caught last week. My work is progressing well. Yesterday I finished a painting and I am now busy with a city view of Lerida. I think I'll go to Madrid or Barcelona, in a few weeks' time, in order to spend some time in a large city again. Lerida is not what you would call a large town although we have seven cinemas here. They show American and German movies, synchronized in Spanish.
Meals in my hotel are good and my favourite fruits, bananas and oranges, are in plentiful supply. Comparing Spain with Holland, according to your letters, we do not notice much of the War. My dears, I am going to light a 'Lucky' and have a nip. Do write. Adios, Rudy.

Rudy then had second thoughts about whether the postcard would ever reach his parents and decided to play it safe and send a telegram. It read:

HEARTIEST CONGRATULATIONS WHY DON'T YOU WRITE BACK HOTEL MUNDIAL, LERIDA HOPE ALL WELL GIVE MY BEST GREETINGS TO ALL – RUDY.

Both items passed the German censors and duly arrived at 96 de Lairessestraat in Amsterdam, embellished with German eagles and swastika stamps.

Rudy and Robert spent thirteen days in Lerida, much of the time lounging on chairs on the sidewalks on the Plaza de Jose Antonio or Avenida Blondel, drinking good coffee and watching the girls go by.

Finally, they were escorted by a good-natured member of the Guardia Civil to Zaragoza, where they were held in a waiting room at the police station. That night they were taken to the station and given first class tickets to Madrid.

Once in the Spanish capital, again they were handed over to a police station and there took their leave of their friendly 'Guardia'. The Security Police issued them each with an identity document, which stated that they had entered Spain illegally. They were instructed to report to the Direccion General de Seguridad on the Puerta del Sol every Saturday and were released into the custody of the Dutch Diplomatic Service.

At the Dutch Embassy they were interviewed by Captain Edmond (Eddy) Hertzberger, and the first question he put to them was to ask why they wanted to get to England. Rudy states he was completely taken aback by this idiotic enquiry, but he gave a civil answer anyway.

The two spent six days in Madrid, hanging around the bars and eateries near the seventeenth century Plaza Mayor and enjoying small tapas served with sherry, which they could afford on their limited allowance from the Dutch Embassy. The horrors of the Inquisition and the executions on the Plaza Mayor have long since faded from memory and are only kept alive in history books. Today the plaza, situated in the middle of the city, has a ring of old and traditional shops and cafes under its porticoes and is always a popular spot for visitors.

Rudy and Robert also managed to fit in a visit to the Museo del Prado, famous for its paintings by Velasquez, Goya and El Greco. Two of the most famous are Goya's 'The Naked Maja' and 'The Clothed Maja'. The former was actually banned at one time as it was considered obscene. It was the first time a female nude had been painted with pubic hair! Rudy, with his interest in art, found this to be an inspiring visit.

They were told that their departure would take place on the afternoon of 24 February and at this news they celebrated in style.

All were aboard the train, when about five minutes before it was due to depart, a flustered Jack Bottenheim (another *Engelandvaarder*), accompanied by a consular official, ran up the platform and jumped aboard. It appeared that in a bout of drunken revelry some of his party had, amongst other things, swung like Tarzans from the overhead telephone wires of no less a building than the Department of Foreign Affairs. Jack, when arrested, had talked his way out of the situation and was released. He was the only member of the group who could speak Spanish.

At the station they also came across a large contingent of Poles, and all were then packed like sardines on to a train that would take them across the border to the Portuguese coast. Robert and Rudy shared their compartment with the future Chairman of the *Engelandvaarders* Association, Frans Dijckmeester, and others. Their train crossed the Portuguese border late the following morning and continued through extensive cork tree groves, finally arriving at a small fishing town by the name of Villa Real de San Antonio. Here they boarded a ship of about 1,000 tons with large tarpaulins covering what appeared to be deck cargo. When they were about three miles off the coast the tarpaulins were pulled off, to reveal a small cannon and anti-aircraft guns. They were on the corvette HMS *Tenderfoot*.

Even this short passage, in rough seas, was not without danger. Near the Spanish coast sleek, speedy German E-boats with Spanish crews patrolled the coastal waters. They could stop any vessel they found suspicious and board her, arresting anyone they thought to be illegal. Then there were the U-boats. By 1944 these were fitted with a *Schnorkel*, which enabled them to 'breathe' fresh air when submerged. This air-ventilation apparatus, which stuck out above the periscope, allowed U-boats to remain underwater for many weeks and made detection far more difficult. This resulted in an increase in the number of Allied ships torpedoed. In the so-called 'Battle of the Atlantic' just under 3,000 Allied and neutral merchant ships were sunk by enemy action between 1939 and 1945, with a heavy loss of life.

Fortunately, there were no U-boats around that day. Closer to Gibraltar, though, were British patrol boats, their officers keeping an eye out for the enemy vessels that frequented the strait.

The ship safely entered the inner harbour at Gibraltar early in the morning, the giant rock dominating the passage between the Mediterranean and Atlantic offering reassurance to the travellers. HMS *Tenderfoot* approached one of the steel piers and eased to a stop.

Here, in this British stronghold with its labyrinth of illuminated tunnels, a large military base, complete with barracks, offices and a well-equipped hospital, Rudy was finally safe. Rudy's group made up the second batch *of Engelandvaarders* to reach Gibraltar in a matter of weeks, bringing the total number to 130. This was the largest group of *Engelandvaarders* assembled in one place until the annual reunions after the war.

Many others were not so lucky and spent more than a month in the Campo Miranda del Ebro, which was mainly used for captured Republican Spaniards. The reason for this rather harsh treatment was that, while Spain was officially neutral, its government was friendly and co-operative with the Nazis because of the assistance Germany had given the dictator, General Franco, during the Civil War. Numerous escapees were handed over to the Germans by Spanish officials who were sympathetic to the Nazi cause. Because of this pro-German tendency, 'neutral' Spain was actually a dangerous place, and all escapees and their guides had to stay on their guard at all times. It was only after the D-Day landings in Normandy that Spain relaxed its hunt for illegals and escapees, because the Spanish authorities had begun to realize that Hitler was not going to win the war after all.

Rudy and Robert were issued with British uniforms, woollen battledress embellished with a shoulder patch showing the Lion of Orange emblem with the word '*Nederland*' and other standard issue items. While they were waiting in Gibraltar they were interrogated by British Intelligence officers and housed in a white-painted stone building known as the Moorish Castle.

Just over a week later, Rudy and Robert, together with American air fugitives, other escapees and a large group of *Engelandvaarders*, which included Jack Bottenheim, boarded the SS *Orduna* and in a convoy of nineteen ships set sail to Liverpool. At the centre of the convoy was the battleship HMS *Warspite*, escorted by a host of minesweepers, corvettes, destroyers and a cruiser. HMS *Warspite* was returning to Britain for repairs, having been damaged by enemy fire off the Italian coast near Salerno.

Rudy Zeeman was thus one of the several *Engelandvaarders* who made it safely across the Channel with Henri's assistance. The number of *Engelandvaarders* varies in different sources. Rudy, who kept in touch with *Engelandvaarder* organizations after the war, estimates that there were about 1,600, maybe even 1,700, who made it to England, including 48 women. How many didn't make it, we do not know, but most likely thousands. Many were arrested and died in prison. These were exceedingly dangerous journeys, with double agents and traitors everywhere, who betrayed the escapees while pretending to be helpers. A large number of these German collaborators were only identified after the war when the escapees, Allied airmen and *Engelandvaarders* made their reports to the Allied authorities. Some of these traitors foiled the escapes of dozens of people, with *V-Mann* René van Muylem, being one of the most successful.

The stories of other *Engelandvaarders* connected to Henri are similar to Rudy's and they include the experiences of Alexander (Lex) Gans, (Bob) Bram van der Stok and Jack Bottenheim, all famous brave men.

Lex was an author who had been deported with his parents to Westerbork but was able to escape in October 1942. He travelled on false documents given to him by Henri, under the name of Hiddema. He eventually reached Paris just a few days later on 21 October, stayed at the Hôtel de Medicis with the others and later made it to England. It was established that Lex was assisted by Henri, as Rudy Zeeman has mentioned this in his memoirs and in emails. Unfortunately, beyond those notes by Rudy, not much is known about Lex, except for his stay in one of the Paris safe houses.

There is more information available on the famous Bram (Bob) van der Stok, who became the most decorated aviator in Dutch history. Bob studied medicine at Leiden University and was an enthusiastic sportsman, focusing on rowing and ice hockey. In 1937, while continuing his studies, he joined the Reserve of the Netherlands' *Luchtvaartafdeeling* (Army Aviation Group) – a precursor of the Royal Netherlands Air Force, training on a Fokker D.XXI.

When the Netherlands and Belgium were attacked on 10 May 1940, Bob scored his first victory by shooting down a Luftwaffe Messerschmitt while on patrol over De Kooy airfield. He made three unsuccessful attempts to leave the Netherlands to join the Dutch Government-in-Exile in London. On the fourth attempt he was successful, landing in Scotland in June 1941 – a stowaway aboard the *Saint Cerqu'*. Following a refresher RAF course he was posted to its 41st squadron in December 1941 and up to April 1942 scored six confirmed kills, which qualified him as a flying ace (five were required to achieve this). On 12 April 1942, during 'Circus 122' on operations over occupied northern France, he was shot down while flying a Spitfire. After bailing out from his stricken aircraft he parachuted down safely at Saint-Omer in the Pas de Calais. Unluckily, he was immediately captured by a Wehrmacht patrol and subsequently sent to the newly built Stalag Luft III.

Bob made three escape attempts. The first was inadvertently spoiled by another PoW, who drew attention to the escaping van der Stok while retrieving a stolen German cap from the roof of a hut. The second attempt was thwarted when the German guards noticed the date had expired on a forged pass he was using to get past them. His third attempt, on the night of 24 March 1944, was part of what later became known as 'The Great Escape', in which he was number 18 of a total of 76 prisoners who staged a mass break-out from the camp. This became the subject of the acclaimed war movie.

Only three participants in the Great Escape ultimately succeeded in getting clean away. Bob van der Stok was one of them. Like most of the *Engelandvaarders* he travelled west, finding safe hands in the Dutch Resistance. Whether he was one of the several *Engelandvaarders* Richard Scharrer remembered as having visited their house in Amsterdam in need of assistance is not known. So we are not sure whether Bram was actually assisted by Henri. What is known is that van der Stok reached Breslau train station and then went on to Dresden, travelling on forged papers. We are also not sure whether these forged papers had been arranged by Henri. All we do know is that it was possible.

In Brussels he was given the papers of a Belgian and headed south, missing the dangerous Van Muylem KLM false line trap, to Paris, where he met Albert Starink, and then on to Toulouse. Here he was put in touch with a small group of evaders consisting of two Americans, two RAF pilots, a French officer and a Russian. They continued south, with guides helping them over the treacherous Pyrenees to Lleida in Spain, reaching Gibraltar on 8 July 1944. He was then transported by air to Whitchurch airfield at Bristol three days later, just three months after his famous escape from Stalag Luft III.

Bob van der Stok was awarded the Order of Orange Nassau from the Netherlands and the British MBE. He qualified with a degree in medicine, moved to the United States, set up a medical practice, married Petie and had three children. In 1980 he published his wartime autobiography entitled *Oorlogsvlieger van Orange* (War Pilot of Orange).

Rudy, Robert and Bob were fortunate to have Albert Starink, an exceptional young man, to look after them in Paris. Albert's resistance work started early in 1943, when he had joined the organization headed by Jan Strangers. Here he was introduced to Wyssogota-Zokozenski (a Polish member of this cell) residing then in Paris. Shortly afterwards, Albert met Mathijs (Thijs) van Roggen (alias van Rijswijk), another member of the organization who was staying with Wyssogota. Through his contacts with Resistance leader Strangers, Albert worked with Wyssogota for about three months. One brave young woman in this group needs mentioning, the famous Anika (Neis) Neyessel.

Wyssogota and van Roggen were arrested at one of the German controls on the train between Toulouse and Pau, taken to Biarritz prison and from there deported to Germany. We know that Wyssogota survived the war. We have not been able to establish whether van Roggen did.

In a report by Albert Starink to Sergeant Koekemoer at the Grand Hotel du Palais Royal on 25 July 1945, he states that as soon as he heard of Wyssogota's arrest he and another Resistance man, Chris Lindemans ('King Kong'), immediately broke into Wyssogota's house in order to dispose of any incriminating documents. These were handed over to Wyssogota's secretary, Eva Vassias, aka Mme de Clichy, at her apartment in Paris.

In November 1943 Strangers was also arrested by the Gestapo and deported to Germany, while Albert continued to work with the organization. In the same month, Albert was introduced by the leading woman operator, Catherine Ockhuizen, to John Weidner, chief of the Dutch-Paris Line in France. It was from this time that he started to work with the Dutch-Paris Line and Victor and Albert Swane, two young Dutchmen from 's-Hertogenbosch. The Dutch-Paris line became the most successful of the escape lines.

Wyssogota's secretary, Eva Vassias (Mme de Clichy), continued working for the organization until her arrest by the Gestapo on 12 February 1944, when they raided her house. Unfortunately, Albert was also present in the house at the same time. He was arrested, but with his usual good luck succeeded in breaking away, despite being fired at twice. Other members of the organization were immediately warned. Albert decided it was unsafe to stay in Paris and left in haste for the Netherlands. Sadly, the brave Eva Vassias died in a German prison camp.

Rudy reports in his memoir, *Luck Through Adversity*, that in 1977 he met up with Albert in Paris in an emotional reunion and they had a great celebratory dinner. At this time Albert told Rudy that he had published a short memoir which referred to all his experiences, including his association with Henri Scharrer, 'Monsieur Henri' or 'Sandberg'. We have been unable to find a copy of this memoir.

According to a memo dated 26 June, 2009, from Rudy Zeeman to Megan Koreman, an historian in Paris, after the war a special report was written on Albert Starink by Lieutenant A.B. Charise of Allied intelligence:

M. Albert Starink
Capt. Weidner says that he was very courageous and one of the lucky ones who got away when the organization was betrayed by Suzy Kraay.
At one time suspected of treason, but that was found to be absolutely wrong.
He performed dangerous missions to Holland for the Capt. Also conveyed groups and transmitted information, messages. Did everything the Capt asked with punctuality and precision.
Capt. Weidner has Starink as agent in the 'Paris Group' who's [*sic*] lodging was 'Gaestel', point of contact, M.J. Mohr and Leo Cok.
In Suzane Hilterman folder it is stated that once Mr Laatsman asked Starink to warn Brussels not to send airmen – Starink fell [*sic*] to do so and the airmen arrived in Paris. PS. See Lt. Bottenheim's report in this folder.'

Albert Starink was one of the most highly decorated of the men associated with the Dutch Resistance and was awarded France's highest military honour, the Croix de Guerre, for his valiant work during the war. He subsequently lived a long and happy life.

The hair-raising escape of another intrepid *Engelandvaarder*, Jack Bottenheim, took a great deal longer than those of Rudy, Robert or Bob van der Stok. These details and his help from Henri were documented in Jack's statement to the Allies after the war.

Jack was on the run for all of six months. His escape was dangerous and physically demanding; it also makes a fascinating story of courage and determination as we shall see later.

Chapter 4

The Initial Fiasco

We now leave for a while the stories of the escapees Henri Scharrer helped, in order to take a look at the workings of the Dutch Resistance, because none of his work could have happened without the organization. The history of this Resistance movement is not as well-known as that of the French, but is particularly interesting and different in many ways to other underground organizations.

A little scratching beneath the surface and it is not difficult to find out how it all worked. The Dutch Resistance cells, the helpers along the escape routes and those who hid Jewish people and Allied airmen in safe houses were part of a bigger organization and were unusually well financed. This is not surprising when you recall that the Dutch Government-in-Exile and royal family had access to substantial funds. When they beat a hasty retreat to London just before the German invasion in May 1940, they took their treasury and bullion with them. Only what could not be carried was left behind.

Once established in England, they moved into action fast. A special London-based organization and a Dutch Government-in-Exile was set up. Winston Churchill, who had been campaigning with as much passion and oratory as he could muster against the Nazi threat to Europe and the United Kingdom, wasted no time in setting up the SOE (Special Operations Executive) in 1940. Their objective was to 'set Europe ablaze' and to assist the Resistance movements in occupied countries. Few people knew of its existence, and it went under different names – one being 'The Baker Street Irregulars'. Nevertheless, it was a powerful organization. At its peak it employed thousands of people, organizing finance, running agents, breaking and creating codes, collecting intelligence, making payments, broadcasting via the BBC and arranging resistance and sabotage behind enemy lines.

With backing from Downing St and the cabinet, it fast developed into an organization that enjoyed many successes in France and other countries; but it had failures too. Unfortunately, of these, the early failures in the Netherlands run by Section N were by far the worst. Records show that poor leadership of the Dutch section of SOE-N sowed the seeds of a disaster that almost sabotaged the whole creation of the Dutch Resistance. It almost did not get off the ground.

The person at the head of the Dutch section in the beginning, and who was responsible for setting it up in the Netherlands, was Major Charles Blizard, working under the codename 'Blunt'. He was later replaced by Major Bingham, who bore the brunt of much criticism after the war, when the failures and sheer ineptitude of Section N became common knowledge.

The story of this near-disaster is also well documented in the book by Leo Marks, *Between Silk and Cyanide*. Marks was head of the codes office at SOE, and his book gives the inside story of the Bletchley Park code breakers and the Enigma machine. Towards the end of 1941, the SOE's 'Plan for Holland' was ready to go into action. Agents trained in espionage and radio codes and briefed in London were to be flown across the Channel and then dropped by parachute into the Netherlands. These agents were mainly escapees who had made it to the United Kingdom or former Dutch military men based in Britain. Vital intelligence from members of the Resistance was transmitted to London as the control centre, and this was specially coded in such a manner that London would know whether the message was genuine or false. The critical element was that true radio messages would carry a special code. False ones, sent under German duress, would not.

What nobody in London realized was that almost right from the beginning the entire Dutch SOE operation was compromised on the ground in the Netherlands, and the Germans knew practically every move.

This is how it happened. A number of agents, who all had vegetable code names ('Parsnip', 'Cabbage', etc.), were dropped into the Netherlands. The first two agents under this plan were parachuted in at a designated place, on a cold November night, and taken into hiding by the Resistance. They were Thijs Taconis, a trained saboteur, and his wireless operator, Hubert Lauwers. Initially, all seemed to be going well and their confidence soared.

'Now we can start to get our own back against these dreadful people jackbooting it around our streets as if they owned us!'

A number of others were also dropped, and according to Leo Marks' book, these included Ebenezer, who had a radio transmitting set, and another person named Abor. But this initial undercover operation only lasted four months. The German security police had no problem in being able to penetrate the embryonic Dutch underground and rounding up all the 'vegetables'. Stool pigeons were present in every nook and cranny, and one earned his stripes by informing on Lauwers, who was captured early in March 1942.

Once in custody, Lauwers was forced by his captors at gun point to transmit encrypted messages to England. He did this according to his training and purposely failed to include the vital security code; he was thus confident that SOE in London would immediately be alerted to the omission and realize that the message was false and being sent under German duress. Unfortunately and incredibly, the London operatives did not notice the missing security check, and even more astonishingly, were not to do so for a long time. In fact, they assumed that Lauwers was being careless in not including the code, or maybe believed he had been poorly trained. Leo Marks, however, states in his book that he started to feel uneasy about the Dutch messages at an early stage. But despite the missing security codes and other anomalies, at first he couldn't put his finger on what it was that bothered him.

Shortly afterwards, the SOE-N sent a message to Lauwers to advise him that he was to receive another agent. Agent number three, 'Watercress', arrived later in March 1942. He, too, was immediately captured. Horrific as it may sound, this process was repeated time and again, as many more agents arrived in the Netherlands in ones and twos, all as a consequence of Lauwers' false radio messages dictated to him by his German captors.

The total betrayed in this manner amounted to a staggering 56 highly trained Dutch agents – most of whom were arrested. The lack of radio security checks in all of Lauwers' transmissions was completely ignored by London, something which many observers later found to be not just negligent but inexcusable. Unbelievably, London was even irresponsible enough to radio back, 'You ought to use your security checks', thereby alerting the Germans to the fact that such checks existed.

Now it was not just any German intelligence operation keeping track of these parachuting agents and supplies. This was the number one German counter-intelligence operation, working mainly in the Netherlands but also in France and Belgium, and it was brilliant. It was code-named *Englandspiel* (England game) and its leading light was no less than the man considered the most successful of all German counter-intelligence operatives – Abwehr Major Hermann Joseph Giskes.

Englandspiel was described as an enormous operation and one of the most successful German counter-intelligence campaigns in the west. Giskes, also referred to in many documents as 'Dr German', played a prominent role in this story and had an impact on several operations, as we shall see. He was a larger than life character: confident, cynical and clearly in possession of a sense of humour.

After the war he told his story in a best-selling book, *London Calling North Pole*, quite a clever title considering how he operated. The main purpose of his operation (besides the capture of agents, thus preventing them from joining the Resistance and causing harm to the German forces) was to get information on when and where the Allied forces were going to land in Europe. That was the critical piece of missing intelligence. For the German forces to prevail it was vital they received this information.

Giskes reported daily to Admiral Canaris, the head of Abwehr intelligence. His associate Josef Schreieder, alias Sepp, another senior German counter-intelligence officer, however, reported directly to Reichsminister Himmler. So we see that the management of these reporting lines was rather intricate and kept separate. A key Dutch agent in Giskes' operation was the notorious SD man, Anton van der Waals, described as one of the most dangerous of the agents and a notorious traitor. Anton also plays a part later in this story. René van Muylem, the boss of Anna-Maria Verhulst-Oomes and others, also reported to Giskes.

Giskes was not just the German counter-intelligence leader in the Netherlands, he was a brilliant super-spy. This penetration only became known to British intelligence on 1 April 1944, and the man largely responsible for uncovering it was Leo Marks – the SOE cryptographer. However, even then British Intelligence could not believe that the Dutch connection had been contaminated and infiltrated.

The full extent of the damage inflicted on the early Dutch Resistance by *Englandspiel* only became known after the war. As a result, a political scandal erupted when the news was leaked to the press. And quite a story it was. British Intelligence had sent dozens of trained Dutch activists to the Netherlands, only to have the great majority arrested; some died mysteriously on arrival, and most of the others died in prison.

The Dutch were outraged. A three-volume report weighing about 12kg was published in July 1950 by a Dutch Parliamentary Inquiry Commission, which investigated the wartime conduct of the Netherlands Government and British Intelligence in London. In the course of this investigation, Dr Donker, the secretary of the Commission, interviewed ten members of the London organization directly involved in sending these brave agents straight into German capture and a doomed fate. How could they have repeated this error dozens of times and not realized there was a problem?

The files reveal that, up to October 1943, of the 56 agents London SOE sent to Holland, as many as 44 were given a 'reception' by the Germans. Of the total number of agents arrested only eight survived the war. Thirty-six of those captured were executed in September 1944 at Mauthausen concentration camp. Eleven RAF aircraft were shot down in the process of dropping the agents, resulting in many more casualties and arrests. For a tightly knit intelligence organization, this was a disaster on a considerable scale.

The Parliamentary Commission strongly criticized the Netherlands Government-in-Exile and the British for their mistakes and negligence. They particularly highlighted the shocking fact that nobody in London had paid attention to the glaring omission of security codes in all the encrypted radio reports sent to them, under duress, from the Netherlands.

The British attempted to salvage their reputation. On the positive side, the report did reject the frequently aired theory that there was treachery on the British and Dutch sides of this debacle. It came to the conclusion that, despite the capture and death of so many good and highly trained agents, the Germans still failed to obtain the answers to the important questions they were urgently seeking. They knew the D-Day invasion was being planned and that its launch into Europe was inevitable. But when it finally did happen, the Normandy invasion came as a complete shock to them. They bought the false leads sent out by British counter-intelligence and expected the invasion to be at Pas de Calais, where they had concentrated their forces.

While Giskes failed to get accurate information on the invasion, his *Englandspiel* did benefit his Berlin masters in another way: up until D-Day they succeeded in thwarting most attempts to build an efficient, highly trained and equipped Dutch Resistance movement that could work effectively with Allied plans and provide support when the Allied forces landed. The Dutch Resistance was seriously compromised by the loss of so many trained agents and so much arms and equipment, all of which they desperately needed.

One of the Dutch Resistance leaders on the ground in the Netherlands did grasp what was going on and realized that messages were compromised. He was Major Kas de Graaf, and he played an important role in the story of Henri Scharrer as he was the man in the RVV (Raad van Verzet) Resistance group to whom Henri reported. In effect, Kas was Henri's boss.

After the war, when the Dutch Parliamentary Commission was conducting its investigations into the wartime conduct of SOE officials in London, de Graaf wrote a report under the pen name Noel de Gaulle, on operation *Englandspiel*. He was in an excellent position to write about it, since after escaping from the Netherlands and making it successfully to London he had been appointed Acting Head of the Bureau for Special Assignments. It was in this capacity that he interviewed many of the Dutch escapees who arrived in London, so he personally knew a number of the agents who had been parachuted into waiting German hands.

In this report he referred to a plot in which Major Bingham, the Head of this British Special Intelligence operation, was said to have collaborated with Josef Schreieder, senior German counter-intelligence officer in Holland, who worked with Giskes in the Hague. Major Bingham was so incensed by this allegation that he threatened to sue de Graaf.

There is considerable correspondence on this in the files, but Bingham was finally persuaded by the Allied authorities to leave well alone. The matter was highly sensitive politically, and Kas de Graaf had every reason to feel angry and betrayed by the negligence that had been shown. Also he had been one of the first people to alert British and Dutch SOE officials that something was seriously amiss with the delivery of agents into the Netherlands. For this vital information he had not been given immediate recognition, as initially the British believed his allegations were either exaggerated or untrue. It simply wasn't possible that the Germans knew the details of the delivery of agents into the Netherlands! Impossible! And meanwhile, Giskes was laughing all the way.

In the aftermath of the scandal, when this failed SOE-N operation became public knowledge, an important letter dated 6 March 1949 was written by Admiral Sir John Godfrey, the director of naval intelligence during the first half of the war and a one-time candidate for chief of the SIS (Special Intelligence Service). It is addressed to Sir Hartley Shawcross, the Attorney General in the Attlee government, and refers to an article that had been published in the *Manchester Guardian*. This article reported the speculation in the Netherlands that the success of *Englandspiel* was the result either of treachery in London or a 'grave mistake' on the part of British intelligence.

This was a serious, public condemnation of the SOE Netherlands operation in a highly credible publication. Sir John's letter declares that he believes neither allegation to be true:

> The real explanation is one which can hardly be published. There is always an element of oblique collusion (not co-operation) between belligerents who indulge in double agent work, especially if both sides know that he is double-crossing one of them. And yet the skilful use of such a man, a direct pipeline into the enemy's most secret counsels, can be of inestimable value so long as his original employer does not reveal his knowledge of the double agent's duplicity . . . At no time did SOE drop agents knowing that they would fall into enemy hands, nor did they use any of them as double or treble agents.

Despite this disastrous start to SOE's Dutch organization, urgent attempts were made to set matters straight. The situation was corrected with great urgency, and in a short time the Dutch Resistance was at full strength, with five groups and nearly 500 top agents.

This new, reorganized British operation did not please Giskes at all. The flow of Dutch agents into his hands had all but petered out. He was so irritated that he sent a cable to London, uncoded, advising them he had a great welcome for the SOE chiefs should they come to pay a visit. This is what he sent London – uncoded:

> To [the SOE section chiefs] Messrs Blunt, Bingham and Succs Ltd, London. In the last time you are trying to make business in the Netherlands without our assistance, Stop, we think this matter rather unfair in view of our long and successful co-operation as your sole agents, Stop, but never mind whenever you will come to pay a visit to the Continent you may be assured that you will be received with the same care and result as all those you sent us before, Stop, so long.

Chapter 5

Restructuring the Dutch Resistance

It could not have been easy for Henri and other Resistance cell leaders to work with a dysfunctional operation in London. They were promised trained agents, money and equipment that often never arrived.

In the aftermath of the initial debacle, SOE-N finally worked out how to set things straight. They sat in their smoky, wood-panelled committee rooms, on green leather chairs with brass studs. Portraits hung on the walls, all needing restoration. There were boards to work on, covered with diagrams, names and arrows. Plans were proposed, discussed and rejected. Tempers flared.

'No, no. We can't do that! Too complicated!'

Then, finally, consensus. An SOE memo on the Dutch Resistance of May 1943 states:

> The sabotage organization as planned is now complete. It comprises five groups containing sixty-two cells and totalling some 420 men. These groups are now well equipped with stores and are ready for action.

These five groups consisted of the following:

> The LO (*Landelijke Organizatie voor Hulp aan Onderduikers*). This was the main group, with 12,000 members, and is credited with helping over 200,000 underground activists. Over 1,200 of its members died in the course of their work.
>
> The KP (*Knokploeg* or 'Strong Arm Boys'). Each large town had a KP, so there was a KP Amsterdamse, a KP Alkmaar and so forth. They did the tough and dangerous work on the ground in their regions and their numbers were around 400. Henri did work for various KPs.
>
> The OD (*Orde Dienst* or Service of Order) was a small group preparing the way for the Government-in-Exile to return.
>
> The RVV (*Raad van Verzet* or Council of Resistance) also referred to in a number of reports as Bureau for Food in Wartime. Kas de Graaf was a leading member of this group, to which Henri Scharrer belonged.

The main groups acted completely independently, though all reported to the Intelligence Services of the Dutch Government-in-Exile in London. For ease of understanding, I will refer to these groups in future by their initials.

There were also a few small independent cells that did not directly fall under the SOE. An organizational diagram (see the plate section) shows that the RVV group communicated with the communist CS.6, a small independent cell, probably named after the address where they were based – Corellistraat 6 in Amsterdam.

According to the Dutch official state historian, Dr L. de Jong, the CS.6, although it had only forty members, was by far the most deadly of the Resistance groups, committing some twenty assassinations of top German officials and collaborators. Started in 1940 by the brothers Gideon and Jan Katel and 'Janka' Boissevain, its later leader was the leading Dutch communist and neurologist, Dr Gerrit Kastein.

You did not want to be in the sights of CS.6 if you were a senior German official or collaborator in the Netherlands. They targeted only the highest ranking German officers and most notorious Dutch collaborators and traitors. Then, as happened so frequently, CS.6 in turn became the victim of the most dangerous Dutch traitor and spy in Giskes' counter-intelligence organization, Anton van der Waals.

So who were some of these twenty odd German and pro-German unfortunates who fell foul of CS.6?

At the top of the list was no less a figure than the head of the Dutch SS-Legion – General Seyffardt, a particularly unpleasant character. They also managed to assassinate an assistant minister, Reydon, and several police chiefs, and attacked the Utrecht police station amongst others. Their planned assassination of the best known Dutch traitor and collaborator, Chairman of the National Socialist party Anton Mussert, was delayed and could never be accomplished by the CS.6, much to the regret of its members. He was too heavily guarded. The Allies did round him up, though, but only after the war. Then there was the 'accident' involving the vehicle of Austrian-born Lieutenant General Hanns Albin Rauter, the highest ranking SS and police officer in the Netherlands. He narrowly survived, but the other passengers in the vehicle were killed or seriously injured.

In the British National Archives is an Allied Forces diagram showing a connection from CS.6 to Kas de Graaf, and the connection between him and Henri Scharrer. This is corroborated by Kas de Graaf's own reports made later in London and now in the Military Archives. Among the many reports signed by Kas de Graaf is one which is specific about Henri and the RVV organization, dated 25 July 1944.

This important report clearly positions Henri Scharrer in the hierarchy. It refers to the questioning of a KP man, Balder, on the workings of the RVV. The background to this report is that Kas de Graaf was disagreeing with a statement by Balder that the RVV had no escape routes to England.

I, however, had direct contact with the Head Group of the RVV and knew that this organization had at least three escape routes, as follows:

a) The organization SCHARRER
b) The organization SCHRADER
c) The organization VAN TIENHOVEN

He goes on to state:

> Capt Klijzing, who had indirect contact with the Muller organization, fully agrees with the opinion that the RVV is one of the most important Dutch resistance and sabotage organizations.

So there we have it. Kas de Graaf, Acting Head of the SOE-N in London, himself expressed the opinion that the RVV escape organization was one of the most prominent Dutch resistance and sabotage organizations and that the Scharrer line was one of its three escape routes.

The 'organization Schrader' refers to Anton Schrader – known as 'The Man with the Boats', while the 'organization Van Tienhoven' refers to a prominent Dutch family involved in the Resistance.

So now the Dutch Resistance had a brand new structure and could hopefully escape the contamination of being infiltrated by Giskes and his counter-intelligence organization. Finally it could start to make its presence felt and continue to expand.

Three years into the occupation, the Resistance was now a force to be reckoned with. The actual number of Dutch people assisting in the hiding or helping of people on the run (*onderduikers*) was estimated at being anywhere from 60,000 to 200,000. The marked disparity in these figures may be because many of these underground helpers were ordinary citizens simply playing their part, and the larger number includes landlords, caretakers and farmers who made up the bulk of the numbers. The 60,000 figure represents the more highly active members, of which we know that 12,000 were members of the LO group. By the autumn of 1944 as many as 300,000 people were believed to be in hiding across the Netherlands. If this number is correct, it represents an extraordinary feat for a small country under widespread, vigilant and often brutal Nazi occupation.

The official war historian Dr Louis (Loe) de Jong of NIOD (Institute for War Genocide & Holocaust Studies) described several categories of Resistance members, because some did dangerous work, while others did not. For example, helping people in hiding (*onderduikers*) was not considered a Resistance activity, nor was non-compliance with German rules, because these were regarded as passive acts. Even sabotage at German-run companies, although rife, was dismissed as not being real resistance, since it was relatively easy to do.

While it is true that many of these activities could be regarded as 'easy', the reality is that thousands of people in all these 'non-resisting' categories were arrested by the Germans, often jailed for months, tortured, sent to concentration camps or killed. More recently, historians have had another look that these more passive categories; today they are regarded as being part of the main Resistance and their numbers help make up the higher total of approximately 200,000.

Communication was essential to the movement's success. Besides the SOE and the work of the Dutch leaders in London, also keeping the Dutch Resistance alive and growing was the BBC's programme, Radio Oranje, fulminating against the Nazis. Listening to the radio was, of course, forbidden. The Germans reacted to Radio Oranje by issuing a new decree for the confiscation of all Dutch radio receivers. The Dutch reaction was immediately to move as many as half of the existing sets underground.

A 'black' telephone system was set up in September 1944. The Germans controlled the telephone service, and only approved people were given telephones. However, telephones were handed out clandestinely, and Resistance sympathizers in the telephone exchanges helped people contact each other and relayed messages.

The underground press, too, was highly active, with nearly 1,100 titles. Of these several still exist today, such as *Trouw*, *Het Parool* and *Vrij Nederland*.

It cost money to run these Resistance organizations, especially the big ones. So the NSF (*Nationale Steun Fonds*) was set up to receive money from the exiled government. The principal figure here was the young banker, Walraven van Hall, whose activities were discovered by chance by the Nazis and who was shot at the age of thirty-nine. He succeeded in raising as much as 50m guilders, much of it from scams involving the Dutch National Bank, forged bank notes and other activities. He is referred to as the 'Banker of the Resistance'.

It took some 55 years for the Dutch Government to give van Hall the recognition he deserved, as his work within the Resistance is considered to have been of the utmost importance. A monument was erected in his honour near the Nederlandsche Bank on Frederiksplein, Amsterdam in September 2010.

It is a felled tree in bronze – representing a fallen giant.

Chapter 6

The Escape Lines

Henri spent a great deal of time on his escape lines and safe houses. A route would work for a few months, and then a collaborator would betray it to the Germans. So Henri would have to take off, using his press credentials to travel, and work to set up a new route. This was a dangerous undertaking, as there were traitors everywhere.

It was one thing to quietly sneak people into hiding and keep them supplied with food, warmth and clothing. Many hid for the whole duration of the war. But as more people went into hiding and more Allied airmen were shot down and needed assistance, things became dangerous. Nosy neighbours could easily notice if a house had an unusual number of visitors, too much garbage or if there was other suspicious evidence. Nobody could be trusted. Plans had to be made to pass people along to escape groups and get them away to safety. Besides, the airmen wanted to get back to their bases and into their aircraft to continue the fight.

The result was the creation of the more formalized escape routes. Until recent years much about these remained classified, but we are in luck today, as new information is becoming available about the escape lines.

While there were many different escape routes, there were four primary lines that impacted on the routes of the evaders Henri Scharrer assisted. It was a fluid situation, because as one line was discovered and shut down, its operators joined up with other lines.

The main escape line that has been extensively researched is the Dutch-Paris Line, started by John (Jean) Henri Weidner. It was the largest route of all, based in Paris, with some three hundred members, including the well-known Suzanne Hiltermann-Souloumiac. This line helped a couple of thousand people, either hiding them or helping them move on, and delivering money and false documents on a regular basis.

The famous Jean Weidner was born to Dutch parents. He had been living in Paris at the outbreak of the war but had to abandon his business and start up again in Lyon. His escape group was led by Dutch people, with the main network being French – hence the name Dutch-Paris.

Weidner was assisted by Jacques Rens, Edmond Chait, Herman Laatsman, Albert Starink and others. In February 1944 a young female courier was arrested and handed over to the Gestapo; under extreme torture, which included near-drowning, she revealed a large number of key names. The result was that many members of the Dutch-Paris Line were arrested. Among these was David Verloop, a bright law student who co-ordinated the Dutch-Paris Line from Brussels and who is mentioned in papers on Henri Scharrer. Before the Germans could interrogate him, however, he committed suicide so that he would not betray his colleagues under torture.

Jack Bottenheim, an *Engelandvaarder* assisted by Henri, recalled in his statement that his representative of the Dutch-Paris Line in Paris was Johan Hermann Laatsman; he also referred to Catherine (Okky) Ockhuizen. They were assisted by Anne-Marie Hilterman and a Romanian by the name of Pierre Mermignaux.

Henri's activities are revealed in another report dated 28 July 1945 by Albert Starink and given to Sergeant Koekemoer. Albert lists the names of Dutch people who were taken up by the Dutch-Paris Line and known to have stayed at 56 Rue Monsieur-le-Prince, Paris; it even mentions the number of days they stayed.

Most of these names are connected to the story of Henri Scharrer and appear in Allied reports. The list states that they are:

September to October 1944, all from Amsterdam, Capt de Graaf – 10 days; Lieut. Celosse – 10 days, an associate; Lt. de Braan; Lt Greidaniges – 4 days; Sgt. Gans; Lt Tuts – Oct 44; Sgt. v. Exter Jan 45; Tusenias – Oct 22; and Lt. Cuit –Jan 45 from Fargo.'

In 1943, the Dutch-Paris merged with Herman Laatsman's line, and for a short while with the Wyssogota line led by a Pole, Andre Wyssogota, who was shortly thereafter arrested. He was the incredible 'Gotha' of the Visgotha-Lorraine Line, and is one of the lucky few to have survived the war. Much has been written about Andre in war archives.

Toulouse was an important stopover on the escape route south. The Dutch-Paris chief in charge of organizing Toulouse as the concentration point for the passage into Spain of Dutch civilians and Allied airmen was Salamon Chiat, aka Edmond Moreau. In his report he states that when there were heavy snow falls in the Pyrenees escapees had to stay in Toulouse until it was possible to travel. The groups consisted of between twenty and forty people. Salomon must have had a whole string of safe houses across the farms and hamlets in the area. How he kept the pro-German sympathizers at bay is still a mystery, but this he did successfully, and his cover was not blown. Maybe a few assassinations did the trick, but that is speculation. His group was assisted by guides referred to as 'Palo' (Etienne Treillet), 'Mireille' (Henri Marret), 'Charbonnier' Baserques and Barrere. Salamon estimated that about 100 people were able to cross over into Spain under his direction – an enormous achievement which demonstrated the effectiveness of one man. Even more miraculously, his main guides, with the exception of Charbonnier Baserques and Barrere, all survived the war.

Like most of the escape lines in other regions, the Dutch-Paris was infiltrated by pro-German sympathizers. One researcher has commented that Jean Weidner unfairly blamed Suzy Kraay for betraying the organization. She had been arrested and subjected to a heavy-handed interrogation, which finally resulted in her revealing names and addresses. After the war, she wrote a horrifying report on her interrogation.

The second important escape line was the one that went across the English Channel organized by 'The Man with the Boats'. We know that at least two of Henri's escapees were sent by that route. The boatman was twenty-six-year-old Anton (Tonny) Schrader, who had arrived in the Netherlands from Indonesia shortly before the war.

In the abbreviated RVV organizational chart (see the plate section) the three RVV escape routes and food distribution organizations listed are: de Graaf, Scharrer and Schrader (Tonny). Special mention should be made of Tonny Schrader. He was a colourful, optimistic personality and had landed an important job as supervisor at the Bureau of Raw Materials which made it possible for him to travel around. He had permission to use one of the cars of Queen Wilhelmina, complete with her chauffeur, Gerard Bryne; all the royal family's cars had been confiscated by the Germans. This freedom of movement made it relatively easy for Tonny to organize an escape route over the North Sea.

There are several amazing stories of Tonny's narrow escapes. Rudy Zeeman, in his memoir, describes one incident that occurred when Schrader was collecting Allied crewmen. After picking up New Zealander Cyril Mora at Utrecht-Tuindorp, the car was halted at the town of Woerden by German soldiers. Asked whether they could give a German general a lift to the Hague because the general's car had broken down, Schrader replied, '*Selbverstandlich*' (Of course).

The general took a seat in the back next to Schrader and started an animated conversation. When dropped off in the Hague, the *Herr General* invited Schrader to come and have a drink at his place soon. All the while, the New Zealander had remained fast asleep in the front seat next to the driver. The general never found out about the unusual company he had been keeping that morning. The New Zealander, on the other hand, on his return to his base in England, could tell the gripping story of how he had travelled in a car with a German general and a few Dutch Resistance men, amongst whom was the former chauffeur of Queen Wilhelmina! He definitely will have made the most of it, despite being fast asleep the entire trip!

It is believed that Tonny organized seven crossings for groups of escapees. His sixth crossing failed in August 1943 when the Kriegsmarine intercepted the boat and the crew were arrested by the Gestapo. Several days later, under torture, one man gave away Tonny's name and address. By the time the Gestapo came calling for him, they were too late. He had organized a seventh voyage, which he joined, and successfully reached England. Here he joined the American OSS (Office of Strategic Services), for whom, after being parachuted back into the Netherlands, he did much sterling work. On the personal recommendation of General Eisenhower, Anton Schrader was awarded the Silver Star for outstanding services rendered.

Henri's escapees also on occasion made contact with the Strengers/Starink line. This line later joined forces with Andre Wyssogota and the original line started by Victor and Albert Swane, thus making a new line. Paris-based, this line also linked up with the Dutch-Paris. Victor did not survive the war, but Albert Starink and Andre Wyssogota did.

No story about the escape lines would be complete without reference to the important Comete Line in Belgium. A number of Henri's airmen and *Engelandvaarders* were given refuge by this line, including Jack Bottenheim, whose story is told later.

The original founders were the three Ds: De Jongh, De Bliqui and Deppe. Soon Frederic De Jongh's daughter, a pretty young Belgian girl by the name of Andrée De Jongh (Dedee), also became involved. Her father was executed by the Germans towards the end of the war. Dedee worked in the advertising department of the SOFINA company, and one of its directors was Baron Donny, a Belgian Resistance man who was also executed.

Dedee joined forces with Arnold Deppe and they worked out a route through Bayonne to Spain. Deppe undertook the first reconnaissance trip to Spain to establish the contacts and safe houses and met up with the chief of the Spanish mountain guides. Their contact in Spain was the British Consul at Bilbao, who assisted escapees who might otherwise have been arrested by unfriendly Spanish authorities and handed over to the Germans.

Like most escape lines, however, it was infiltrated by collaborators, and many members of the Comete line were arrested, including Arnold Deppe. After this setback Dedee fled to Paris, from where she continued to help escapees. She herself was finally arrested, and the new leader of the Comete Line became Jean Francois (Franco) Nothomb, who fortunately survived the war, even though he had been arrested and sentenced to death. Franco's aunt was Cecile Van Nerom-Duickers, the last treasurer of the Comete Line. She also had a close association with Jan Strengers. Cecile was one of those arrested, and she died in prison in Germany.

The smaller lines which feature in the story of Henri include the Witte Brigade in the north, the Smit-van der Heijden line, the Elsie Boon escape group, the Piet Felix line and, in the early years of the war (before he turned collaborator which is another extraordinary story), the Chris Lindemans line, and others.

What did all this undercover organization and structure achieve? There were three areas in which the Dutch Resistance excelled.

Firstly, it was extraordinarily good at hiding people, especially Jews and Allied airmen.

Secondly, it made its mark by supplying important intelligence to the Allies. It was the Dutch Resistance that informed the Allies that the German SS IX and X Panzer divisions were in the region of Arnhem in September 1944. The Allied leaders made a major blunder in ignoring this key piece of information. There had been so much trouble with radio messages from the Netherlands that they did not know which ones to believe. Consequently, they committed their paratroopers and gliders to the Battle of Arnhem ('A Bridge Too Far'), resulting in the biggest failure for the Allies in the Western European area of operations.

Thirdly, no stone was left unturned to get underground operators and escapees to safety. This involved by far the greatest risk, as anywhere along the line there could be slip-up or betrayal. This happened frequently. As we have on record, 278 or so Allied airmen in the escape group known as the KLM were arrested on escape routes by Giskes' counter-intelligence operation *Englandspiel*, with operator Van Muylem the champion hunter of escapees.

After the war, because of the secrecy and the closed nature of networks, it was difficult for Allied intelligence to sort out the Resistance hierarchy in the Netherlands. To gather information for their records they interviewed numerous people who escaped to the United Kingdom during and after the war, many of the interviews being conducted by Kas de Graaf. They also investigated survivors and Resistance fighters in the Netherlands. So it is not surprising to discover that many of the reports contain somewhat conflicting and erroneous information, including incorrect spelling of personnel and place names and addresses.

The most reliable and revealing reports on the Dutch Resistance have come from the escapees themselves, many of whom wrote about their experiences after the war in letters, articles and books. It is here, in these emotional and real stories of the survivors, that we find the true story of Henri Scharrer and the Dutch Resistance.

Chapter 7

Henri Scharrer, his Operation

Before we go too far into the Resistance work of Henri Scharrer and his brave helpers, the treacherous double agents and those who betrayed him, we should pay a visit to the Scharrer residence in Amstelveen and their later apartment in Amsterdam near the Amstel River. It was here that so many downed and lost airmen stayed, sometimes for a few days, sometimes for a great deal longer. The Scharrer household was only one of countless safe houses that operated in the Netherlands during the war, and is probably typical of the many others.

When they first married, Henri tried a number of jobs, finally settling on translation work because of his talent for languages. He was a French citizen, and besides French, could speak German and Dutch well and had good English. This led to his career as a journalist and correspondent for a number of French publications and press bureaux. The family home was a happy one, filled with laughter and friends whom Henri would help entertain by preparing special French dishes in the kitchen.

At weekends he would take his sons sailing in his small boat on the Kager Plas, near Lisse. He taught them to fish and tried to teach them English. Raymond remembered that he occasionally visited his father's busy press offices and was fascinated by the telex machine that was always clacking away, spewing out tapes. He also recalled that Henri was never a stern, strict father, but a relaxed, kind man. Sometimes his father sent him on small errands, to deliver a note or to buy a packet of cigarettes. Henri would quite frequently bring home publications and show them articles with his byline, and the boys believed they had the cleverest father in the world.

Henri had an adventurous nature and enjoyed new sights and experiences, so before the war, when time and money allowed, the family travelled. When they did so, Henri always took along his sketch book, canvases, pencils and paints, and would do small oil paintings and sketches, which are still in the possession of the family. He enjoyed mimicry and acting parts for the amusement of others. He could take off accents in Dutch, from the drunken sailor to the aristocrat, and perform the same feat in French and German, although we are told that his strong French accent would often creep into his other languages.

Visits to the Concertgebouw in Amsterdam were frequent, as Henri and Truus shared a love of classical music, especially the works of Handel, Bach, Beethoven and Wagner. This enjoyment of music was passed on to their two sons.

Even now, in the middle of the occupation, the family were fortunate. Henri had access to large quantities of fake food coupons, the printing of which he helped organize and which he handed out to those in the Resistance movement who needed them. His printer was the talented Theo Koersen, who also printed the PBC (*persoonsbewijzen*, or identity cards) and *Het Parool*, an underground publication, which later became an important Dutch newspaper. Some have claimed that the fraudulent coupons, identity and travel documents Henri arranged were so good they could have been the genuine articles. But fraudulent they definitely were, as is proved by samples in a number of war archives and in the possession of Professor Doeko Bosscher of the University of Groningen. Moreover, Robert van Exter's documents from Henri Scharrer are in the Verzetmuseum (Resistance Museum) in Amsterdam, and we know how Henri made them, from the details in Rudy Zeeman's memoir, *Luck Through Adversity*.

On this evening, then, there are no hidden visitors at 21 Emmakade, Amstelveen, which was a small village near Schiphol airport outside Amsterdam. Geertruida (Truus) Scharrer had prepared *snert* – a split pea soup with ham – for her two sons, Richard then aged fourteen and Raymond aged twelve. Truus was a pretty, slightly plump woman, and a devoted wife and mother, even though life with Henri in wartime could not have been easy. Indeed, most families in occupied Europe were leading stressful, disrupted lives.

The weather had been warming up after a cold, dark winter of fear and tension. The house was an attractive street corner building, two-storey, built of red brick with woodwork painted white. The table had been laid for three, as Truus did not expect to see her husband that evening.

In fact, she had not seen him for weeks. Inside the dining room, in the pale electric light, all was cosy and relaxed. In the fireplace was wood that had been delivered by wood cutters who, by the end of the war, had cut down practically every available tree in the country. Outside, a German military vehicle occupied by heavily armed soldiers was carrying out a slow patrol down the street, hoping to catch anybody who was late for curfew. So we have a typical family scene in the Netherlands in May 1943, during the middle years of the German occupation and before the horrors and starvation of the '*Honger* (hunger) *Winter*'.

The family was aware that Henri was involved in dangerous, illegal activities, because of the downed airmen who stayed in the attic from time to time. Although they knew little, it was sufficient for them to feel anxious and unsafe from time to time. Truus would also have realized that Henri might be engaged in dangerous activities against the Nazi occupiers, given his adventurous nature. Exactly what Henri was doing, she did not know. How he received the food coupons was a mystery. He explained it was safer she did not have information on his activities, as when anyone was arrested on suspicion of underground work, after interrogation and often torture, their families would be pulled in to supply more information and put pressure on the suspect. Not a pleasant prospect!

Henri's family background gives us insight into this audacious man and his talents for disguise and playing different characters – be they French, German or Dutch.

We can also observe the possible conflict of loyalties within families and groups of friends that was also typical of Holland at this time. There were people who first assisted the Dutch Resistance movement but then turned traitor when put under pressure, tortured and had their families threatened. It is also fair to say that there were German officials who turned a blind eye to Resistance activities. So under the surface things were often not what they seemed.

Henri was a slight man, balding, slim, with penetrating brown eyes and always impeccably dressed. His demeanour was calm, and he did not display any aggressive tendencies. He enjoyed fun and humour, spoke quietly and convincingly, fixing his eyes unwaveringly on the person to whom he spoke. He could charm most people, and conducted his business affairs with a brusque efficiency.

Once the German occupation began, Henri's whole relationship to his family changed. While he continued his journalistic work, he had also started reporting undercover to the British and Free French intelligence services.

'The war changed everything,' Raymond Scharrer said many years later. 'From then on he was always away.'

Henri was a product of his background and upbringing. His grandparents were Jean Scharrer and Marguerite Martin, both from Metz – an historically German-speaking city in north-west France on the border of Germany in what was then French territory. His father was Henri Scharrer, also born in Metz in 1878, in what by that time had become the German territory of Alsace-Lorraine, annexed by Bismarck after France's defeat in the Franco–Prussian war in 1871. His mother was Johanna Decoo, the daughter of Jean Baptitse Decoo.

The Scharrers were of German descent, the family originating in Bavaria. Henri's parents arrived in Metz some years before the Franco-Prussian war, and the new generation had become French-speaking, while at the same time keeping up their German language and traditions. According to Richard Scharrer, the family owned an exclusive shoe shop and were reasonably well off. The first Scharrer to settle in Alsace-Lorraine was by all accounts an officer in the Prussian army who had become entangled with another's man wife and had fled when challenged to a duel by the wronged husband. That was how Prussian officers sorted out such matters in those days, but the Scharrer concerned avoided the duel by beating a hasty retreat. There is, however, no evidence to support this colourful story.

By the turn of the century, Henri and Johanna Scharrer had moved to the coastal town of Oostende (Ostend) in Belgium, where Henri was born on 23 April

1900. When he was twelve years old the family moved to the Hague. He had a sister, Maria Jeanne, and a younger brother, Emmanuel. Maria Jeanne first married Henri Vittecoq, the French military attaché in the Netherlands, who died of cancer. She then married an officer in the French armed forces by the name of Henri Viallat and moved to France.

Quite unexpectedly, while researching this book, some information came out of the blue by way of an email from a Belgian researcher by the name of Robert Courtois, who lives in Brussels. Was I in any way related to Henri Scharrer, he wanted to know? Once Robert knew who I was, he sent me the story of the controversy surrounding Henri's younger brother Emmanuel. According to his memoir, my late husband Richard believed that Emmanuel was also in the Resistance and was killed on 17 April 1941 in the Ardennes forest when in the process of warning an underground group by radio that the SS forces were on to them. Robert Courtois sent me newspaper reports describing the finding of the body of a man in the forests, identified as Emmanuel Scharrer. But here lies a completely different tale.

Robert wrote that Emmanuel was shot by a Belgian Resistance group that included his (Robert's) great-uncle, Georges Dumont, because they believed that Emmanuel was a German agent. There is some indication also, Robert reports, that he might have been a member of the Verdinaso, a Belgian right wing party. He pointed out, however, that there is no documentation to confirm this.

There is no doubt from the scans received that Georges Dumont was a distinguished man. The Belgian Government had awarded him the Knight's Cross of the Order of Leopold with palm, the War Cross with palm in 1940 and the Medal of Resistance. So clearly Georges was an honoured hero of the Belgian military.

Georges and his accomplices were arrested by the German administration in Brussels a couple of months after the death of Emmanuel, and accused of his murder. They were tried and found guilty. Georges was first detained in the prison of St Gilles and then sent to Essen in Germany, where he was sentenced to six years hard labour. He was last seen alive in the Buchenwald concentration camp a few days before the camp's liberation in April 1945.

All this creates grave doubt as to whether Emmanuel was a member of the Belgian resistance, as the family had believed. Is it possible that Emmanuel, with his Scharrer German background, felt more closely associated with the Germans, in spite of his older brother's strong opposition to the Nazis and the German occupation of France, Belgium and the Netherlands. However, there were other anti-Nazi activists in the family. Emmanuel and Henri's uncle – Truus' brother, Kees Compter – was an active member of the Dutch Communist Party. The Dutch communists, including one of their leaders by the name of de Geuzen, were amongst the first to be arrested by the German occupation forces. Kees was rounded up with the other communists, sent away to a prison camp and finally died in Buchenwald.

Could Georges Dumont have been misinformed? On the balance of all the information, it would appear that this was not the case. It also seems likely that Emmanuel might have been a double agent. He easily could have been, given the family history. His army record, which is not favourable, also sets a big question mark against him since it records a desertion. So although information is limited, there is evidence that there was a cloud over his character and reputation. As most human resource experts will tell you, a poor army record is not a good indication of excellent character. Attempts to contact Emmanuel's surviving family also did not bring any favourable results.

But where did his real loyalties actually lie? Nobody knows for sure.

It was some time in the warmer months of 1928 that Henri and Truus were married. She was then twenty-nine and he was a year younger. Without university training, he appeared at first to have struggled to find his feet, working in a number of different positions. However, it didn't take him long to find his role in life. The year following his marriage, he was appointed translator in the Hague offices of ANP (*Algemeen Nederlands Persbureau*) – a position ideally suited to his talents. He was responsible for translating all incoming information in French and also checking any outgoing French bulletins. With his connections, he also served as a sounding post and adviser to the French ambassador in the Hague from that time.

In no time at all he established himself as a leading expert in French affairs, especially politics and economics, for which he had a natural talent. Within months he was overloaded with work. In addition to his daily news reports, he was responsible for a French news bulletin broadcast every evening on the NDJ (*Nouvelles du Jour*) and for supplying news from the Hague to the *Belgische Telegraaf Agentschap*. He would be back at the office at half past nine the next morning to work on the more financial/economic orientated afternoon editions.

What comes across most clearly is that Henri loved being a journalist. He was a complete workaholic and on occasion would drive himself to exhaustion. He was described in several reports by people who knew him from his Resistance contacts as a brave and highly intelligent man, who found it thrilling to pull the wool over the eyes of the enemy and outwit them. As time went on, he became more and more confident. In fact, one family member commented that he became over-confident.

Life was going extremely well, and Henri's career was prospering. Truus and Henri now had two sons, Richard born in 1929 and Raymond a couple of years later. Then suddenly the world changed on the fateful day of 3 September 1939, when the British Prime Minister, Neville Chamberlain, in a broadcast to the nation announced that a state of war existed between Britain and Germany. This was in the fulfilment of Britain's obligations to Poland, following Germany's invasion of that country. It was at this time, nine months after he started work at the ANP, that Henri was appointed a correspondent for what appears to be another but associated Belgian agency, *Agence Télégraphique Belge*. Because his previous experience as a journalist was somewhat limited, it was agreed that his work would be carefully monitored to ensure that quality standards were upheld. It was soon realized, however, that Henri did not require any monitoring. He was a natural born journalist. This meant an extra work load. When his work with NDJ was completed at ten o'clock in the evening, he would then spend an hour telexing the Belgian edition. A working day of fourteen or sixteen hours was not unusual.

Had Henri at that time applied for Dutch citizenship alongside his French nationality, he would have spared himself a great deal of the trouble that was about to descend on him. Unfortunately, he did not.

It was barely seventeen months after Henri joined the press bureau that on 10 May 1940 German troops entered the Netherlands with their huge army of 750,000 men, the Luftwaffe attacking the small Dutch Air Force. This terrifying blitzkrieg came as a shock to many Dutch citizens, as the Dutch had not engaged in war with any European nation since 1830.

The occupation of the Netherlands by German forces was now underway, and with their usual brusque efficiency they quickly took control of all areas of commerce and government in the country, right down to village councils. The influential press bureau was certainly not overlooked.

Henri's boss was H. H. J. van de Pol, whose stepfather, Dr P. H. B. Libourel, was the notary for the ANP. Dr Libourel's daughter Carry (Caroline), a lawyer, also worked at the press bureau as the Director's secretary. In the course of her day she assisted Henri with his radio bulletins for the NDJ and other work. With the war creating havoc in many relationships, and the long working hours away from home, it was almost inevitable that Henri and Carry would become lovers. This was no discreet office romance on the side. There was nothing casual about the relationship; it is clear this was a serious affair.

From the beginning, Henri and Carry's conversations were in French, although Henri spoke excellent Dutch, with a French accent. His memos to the directors were also mostly in French. Carry, whose ancestors had settled in the Netherlands in the wake of Napoleon's occupation, took pleasure in speaking French. She would take over Henri's work not only for the NDJ but also the *Agence Télégraphique Belge* when Henri was absent on vacation or other activities.

What is interesting about the character of these two lovers' relationship is that it did not in any way affect Henri's sense of responsibility and love for his wife and family. There were no unhappy demands made on each other.

It appears that, from that time, Henri's life was split into two, and he tried to manage this double life as best he could. Dutch historian Professor Doeko

Bosscher wrote that this situation was fairly common during the war, considering the dangerous work many people did and the pressures they were under. Carry even showed a remarkable sense of care and responsibility towards Henri's family, as we shall see.

What kind of person was Caroline Libourel, whose life became interwoven with the Scharrer family? What we do know is that she was an exceptional woman for her time. A free thinker and highly intelligent, she led her life in her own way. She is described as a liberated woman with a strong and powerful personality.

Her daughter, Linda Morison Libourel, also confirms that Carry assisted Henri by providing a safe house for Allied airmen in her own apartment in Delft. She has a strong recollection of her mother telling her about a young American airman who stayed a short while in her apartment; he was so young that he had travelled everywhere with his teddy bear as a kind of mascot, and even took it to bed with him.

Carry was a career woman, which at the time in the Netherlands was unusual. The Dutch were a conservative society and women were expected to get married, then look after their house, children and husband. Carry was almost the opposite in nature to Truus – the conventional and loyal housewife, who even though she must have suspected there was another woman in Henri's life, kept her thoughts to herself. Richard did not remember arguments or discussions in the home about Henri's other woman, although he knew that his father had this romantic relationship. He related that it was one of the unusual circumstances in his early teenage years that made him feel insecure. So it would appear that in the Scharrer household Henri's relationship with Carry was known, but not discussed.

As the occupation got under way, van de Pol was ordered by the new German authorities to reorganize the press bureau. He had to fire twenty-one journalists and give them eight days' notice. These included all the British, French, Belgian, Norwegian and Polish citizens and the Jewish editors. So it was due to his French citizenship that Henri was forced to resign from the ANP, because Germany was at war with France.

All foreign journalists in the Netherlands suffered under these restrictive German decrees; they could not find new employment within their professions, as the Germans were now in full control of the industry. Most companies had no option but to retire their Jewish and foreign personnel, leaving many people without income and other important perks of employment.

Shortly after being axed from the press bureau, Henri received another message of impending trouble. Sacked journalists were all instructed to report to the German Foreign Affairs offices. Here Henri and the others were identified, and once it was established how many people were affected they were advised of the address at which they would be interned. Henri was sent to the prison camp at Schoorl, north of Amsterdam, where he was incarcerated for several months.

Schoorl was originally built for the Netherlands army, and was taken over by the Germans on capitulation. At first it was used by the German army for their own troops, and then for internees – mainly British and French. Henri now found himself behind barbed wire. It was a bad omen of things to come. But the living conditions were bearable, and being a reasonable artist, he kept himself busy with sketches and drawings, which are still in the possession of Professor Bosscher.

Truus visited him to start with, but after July, even as Henri's wife, she was not allowed to see her husband. So it was an anxious time for the family.

What we do know is that during this time, and despite the German censorship, Henri and Carry corresponded frequently. They did not write in French as they would have preferred, but in German, hoping that this would provoke less censorship. On 25 August she wrote to him saying that French citizens would soon be released, but that it was in her better judgement that they must not cherish false hopes. She was only allowed to visit him once, in July, and thereafter all visitation rights were cancelled.

The new French government led by Pétain finally capitulated in September 1940, with the result that French citizens were no longer considered to be enemies of the state by the German authorities. Shortly following this, Henri was released from Schoorl prison. The British internees, however, did not fare so well, as they were sent from the reasonable conditions at Schoorl to the harsh regime of a camp in Upper Silesia.

It is quite clear that it was during his months at Schoorl that Henri became a member of the Dutch Resistance movement. Soon his Resistance work began to grip him, and his absences from home grew from days to occasional weeks at a time. His hatred of the occupation forces and the Nazis, whom he tried to obstruct at every opportunity, now started to become the focus of his life.

Having had no income for many months, Henri now immediately started looking for journalistic work. He had already in a short space of time developed a good reputation as a result of his work with *Agence Télégraphique Belge* and the ANP, which people were now referring to as '*Adolf's Nieuwste Papegaai*' (Adolf's Newest Parrot). Within three months of being released from Schoorl, Henri was appointed correspondent at the SPT *(Schweizer Press-Telegraph)*, which had its headquarters in Bern, Switzerland. This opportunity put him in a dynamic environment working with top quality journalists.

His new boss was Oscar Mohr, a former colleague and the previous editor of the ANP. Mohr had resigned his position at the bureau on the day the Dutch capitulated, then signed up with Rudolf Noesgen and became the editor of SPT. Oscar tried to keep the news reports balanced and accurate, but ultimately landed in trouble with the German authorities. His resignation letter to Noesgen described his lack of motivation. Noesgen, who had held him in high regard, replied that he hoped that in the future he could call on his services again. Shortly afterwards, Oscar Mohr was arrested for having contacts with the Resistance group under the control of van Hattem. His position at SPT was taken over by Henk Beishuizen, who was no less a patriot than his predecessor and surrounded himself with the same calibre of journalists that Oscar Mohr had employed. Henri was working with the best in the business; he was with STP for two years and again in the second part of 1943.

While under cover as a journalist, Henri was now also sending reports to the British MI5, to Free France in London, and the BCRA (*Bureau Central de Renseignements et d'Action*) of DB (Deuxième Bureau) through the Secret Service Netherlands. In these new Resistance circles he worked together with one group around Resistance fighter, Carel Bos.

By the time Henri was working for the Swiss newspaper, he was considered a leader of the Dutch Resistance, his own escape organization within the RVV Group being now well established.

Carry's daughter, Linda, who today lives in the Hague, remembers her mother telling her that there were times when she and Henri were walking in the street carrying guns or other incriminating items and papers. On a couple of occasions they came across Germans conducting a raid, performing control checks or arresting people. Instead of trying to slip away unnoticed, Henri would make her join him, go over and watch what the Germans were doing, as interested bystanders. Henri would ask the Germans questions about what was happening, and so the couple were never taken seriously. Had they behaved in any other way, Henri cautioned, they could have been stopped and searched. Carry had said that she found this a frightening thing to do, when all instincts were to flee and get as far away as possible. These were the situations that Henri enjoyed most, putting the fear of danger behind him and living on adrenalin. When it came to the basic urge to fight or flee, Henri's character was to fight and address the problem head-on.

Linda also remembered that Henri painted a beautiful large mermaid on the inside of Carry's bath.

We know that during this time, Henri's name and his aliases ('Sandberg', 'Henri Dupon', 'Monsieur Henri', even 'Henri Dubois' according to one source) start to appear in reports on Resistance activities written by individuals who survived the war and the Allied interrogators who investigated these activities. Such investigations were not only conducted for the sake of historical records, but also to track down, arrest and prosecute traitors, double agents and collaborators.

Carry stated in a report to the Allied military after the war that she did not know when Henri started working for the Resistance, although it is obvious from their close working and romantic relationship that she knew perfectly well. She seemed to have preferred to take the discreet route of disclosing as little as possible about Henri, even to the Allied investigators.

But we do know that Jan Lowey-Ball from Delft played an important role in Henri's Resistance operation, and his story is well worth telling, particularly as he was such an interesting and adventurous character.

Jan and Henri met in 1943 as a result of his relationship with Carry. Jan, who also lived in Delft, was a house friend of Carry, and it didn't take long before she introduced Henri to Jan and his friend, Hugo van der Wiele. Hugo had set up an underground information service in Delft which had been given the code name 'Rolls Royce'. Lowey-Ball, a handsome Indo-European, had already experienced a number of amazing escapes following arrest. Together with fellow students at the Technical University, including Rudolf de Vries and Ben van der Wiele (Hugo's brother), they were active Resistance men seeking out tasks and projects that would help the Allied cause and hinder the Nazi occupiers.

So we know it all started in earnest in 1943 after that introduction. Initially, Jan and Henri worked together on Henri's idea to print travel documents that could be used by escapees. This developed into a large project that produced hundreds of false travel and identity documents for Allied airmen and *Engelandvaarders*. These three men (Jan, Ben and Hugo) were to be among Henri's important and trust-worthy allies over that dangerous period.

They created the pseudonym 'Sandberg' for Henri and worked on their own escape route that would lead from Amsterdam to Spain. In France their route led to Paris. Two important hotels were identified: the Hôtel de Noailles on the Rue de la Michodière, their anchor address, and the Hôtel Monsieur-le-Prince on the Rue Monsieur-le-Prince. These were used by Rudy Zeeman and other escapees.

On the Boulevard Montparnasse they also established a residential address at the Hôtel de Medicis. Another hotel they identified and which appears in a number of stories is Hôtel Des Deux Hémisphères on Rue des Matiers. The planned route for most travellers from Amsterdam to Paris would involve staying at one of these hotels. From here they would travel via Toulouse to the small village of Boussens in Roquefort-sur-Garonne in the South of France. The next destination would be Pau, then with the help of a guide they would follow one of the routes up the Pyrenees that would take them over the border. This trek might take them down to Donostia, San Sebastian or Caneja, depending on circumstances, the presence of German patrols and other security factors.

As time went on, the dangers brought on a growing tension between Henri and Jan. This was aggravated by a disagreement over how much Henri charged his clients for the documents, plus travel and accommodation costs on the Spanish route; this varied from 200 to 300 guilders. This disagreement, however, did not result in a break between them, as the two men sat down and discussed the matter thoroughly. Henri was not a man to let disagreements simmer. It was an expensive business to get escapees safely to England, and it was important that Jan should understand the expenses involved. Often help had to be bought and paid for.

When it came to the art of escape, Jan Lowey-Ball could outwit the most ruthless pursuers. He had attempted to escape via Spain in order to reach London and assist the Resistance movement from there, but was arrested in Carcassonne. The SD in Toulouse at first tried to break him, but he was able to convince them that his trip through France was only an attempt to gain freedom. He comes across as a cool customer under pressure, and for a while the Germans actually believed he was one of their agents. As a former student of the aerodynamic engineer, J. M. Burgers, he was, with German approval, able to obtain a position in the established Toulouse company Ateliers d'Aviation, and he was expected to supply the Germans with intelligence about the firm. This position allowed him to have a special train pass, which he used to return to the Netherlands and his hometown of Delft.

Jan is also referred to in a file marked 'Secret' written by Mr E. B. Stamp, who was actually investigating double agent Chris Lindemans at the time. This report is dealt with more fully later, but it does refer to Jan Lowey-Ball, Henri Scharrer and an escapee they helped, a student by the name of Phillipus Christiaan Tuts, a friend of Lowey-Ball.

Phillipus told Stamp in an interview that Jan had introduced him to Henri Scharrer, who arranged to get him documents and proof that he was employed by the SD. He stayed with Jan while the documents were being prepared, and then they went to Paris where they stayed at the Hôtel Des Deux Hémisphères. Here he met Kas de Graaf, Jack Bottenheim, Alexander (Lex) Gans and Nicolaas Celosse, all of whom had papers prepared by Henri. Jan felt it was important too that Phillipus meet another head of the organization, so he took him to the Hôtel des Medicis to introduce him to Albert Starink. It was here that Tuts first came across Christiaan Lindemans, as Chris and Albert were working together at that time. Tuts was another *Engelandvaarder* and travelled south via Toulouse, eventually arriving in Liverpool in March 1944.

Jan Lowey-Ball was clever enough always to put on a friendly façade for the Germans, and because he had a long association with double agent Christiaan Lindemans, and seemed to get out of jail with ease, many thought that he too was a double agent. His record is, however, completely unblemished. He has been acknowledged as a loyal friend of Henri and Carry, and a brave and highly effective Resistance fighter.

We are fortunate that there are many individual stories of how Henri touched people's lives in times of danger. A number of those he helped save, and even those whose escapes were betrayed, went on to tell their stories in memoirs, reports and letters after the war. So we have Frank Hart's letters, the memoir written by Rudy Zeeman on his hair-raising escape, the detailed debrief reports to the Allies by the brave Jack Bottenheim, and the reports on the downing of Jim Davies' Lancaster bomber. All these and many other reports tell the personal stories of those who survived one of the darkest periods of history.

Chapter 8

Engelandvaarder Jack Charles Bottenheim's Lucky Escape

There were a number of *Engelandvaarders* who landed up at the Scharrer house and travelled on Henri's escape route. Among them was Jack Bottenheim, a colourful and rather jolly person.

It appears that the story of Jack Bottenheim was at one stage considered highly sensitive for reasons of security. There is one report on his assistance to two Jewish families that is stamped 'Closed until 2031'. A number of Allied military reports relate to him. A couple are interviews and debriefing sessions, while others are reports of interviews with people who were associated with him. One long, detailed report is stamped 'Closed' on the front page, and many of the names and places involved have been blanked out. What remains, however, still gives us an outline of the story of how he too made it to England with Henri's help, and fortunately there are other shorter reports which have helped to fill in details of most, but not all, of the classified material.

Jack was a Dutch citizen and the son of a textile manufacturer, Jules Bottenheim. He took a two-year textile course at Manchester University and was employed in the Midlands as an apprentice. He returned to Belgium, where he continued his studies and finally joined his father's firm in the Netherlands in 1938. Photographs show him with a mop of dark curly hair and an infectious smile. He was also a man with a wide circle of friends.

In November 1940, under the racial laws then introduced into Holland by the German occupying forces, Bottenheim, being a person in charge of a large commercial undertaking, had to prove that he was Aryan. The twenty-three-year-old succeeded in doing this after a journey to Antwerp to search the town records. Exactly how he obtained the evidence is not clear, since he later admitted that his Belgian mother was Jewish; she originally had the surname Hartzog and had changed this to Happe shortly before the war.

He began his Resistance work around September 1942, when the Germans started deporting Dutch workers; much to his dismay, this included people from his own factory.

The ever increasing exploitation of the Dutch people angered him. He incautiously made it clear that he would help any of his employees who were unwilling to go to Germany, and told them that if they needed to hide, his firm would take care of their families. About eight or nine employees took advantage of this offer, and he was able to procure for them identity and ration cards. We do not know where he obtained these cards, but he did not have any trouble laying his hands on them to help those in need. He assisted Dutch students to escape their obligation of compulsory labour by finding billets for them in South Friesland, and provided them too with ration and identity cards. He also found ration and identity cards for two Jewish families he had helped. The information about his work connected to these Jewish families remains classified, and so we have no information about this part of his anti-German activities.

The scope of his resistance work until 1943 was limited to helping people duck, dive and hide, and providing ration and identity cards. It was during this year that living and working in the Netherlands started to become more dangerous, with the Germans applying more pressure on the Dutch population in the form of restrictions, curfews, draconian decrees and terror tactics.

In the summer of that year, Jack received a visit from an old friend, who told him that he had escaped from a train near Oldenzaal, in the east of the Netherlands, and was seeking refuge. What he wanted urgently was an escape line that could assist him to reach England. He had received a number of proposals, but frustratingly, all of these had come to nothing. Escaping to England was not an easy matter, and so far he had met with a great deal of talk and promises, but no action. Maybe Jack, with his many connections, would know of somebody who could help?

Unfortunately, Jack had to explain to his friend that he had no information on escape lines to England, and so sadly was not in a position to help. He had been far more concerned with his factory, his workers and the difficulties he was experiencing managing his business under German occupation. Empty-handed and disappointed, the friend had to try and seek help elsewhere.

Jack Bottenheim's life was about to change, however, and be overtaken by unexpected events. In September he received news that his grandmother, living in Antwerp, was ill, and so he made a dangerous clandestine crossing of the frontier to spend two days with her. On his way back home he passed through Brussels, where he met up with another old friend, Adolf Strassburger. Adolf had contacts in the Belgian Resistance, one of whom turned out to be another former acquaintance of Jack's.

The most efficient and successful escape line in Belgium was the Comete Line, which is known to have assisted Chris Lindemans and his common law wife, Gilberte (Gilou), Victor Swane and family and many others. A young Dutch girl by the name of M. A. E. (Matilde Adrienne Eugene) Verspyck was a well-established link between a number of escape organizations in Brussels. She was by all accounts highly active in the Resistance, endured three arrests, and died in Ravensbrück of physical exhaustion on 11 February 1945. It is possible that her name is one of those blanked out in Bottenheim's reports on his stay in Brussels.

This was Jack's first experience of the hard-core Resistance, and as a result of these connections and their guidance he was able to get back into Holland by illegally crossing the border undetected at Baarle-Nassau.

Jack was much relieved to be safely back home and imagined that his illegal adventures were over. Not so! He now discovered that the situation at the factory had taken a turn for the worse. There had been two unfortunate developments. One of these remains classified to this day, but the other concerned a report that one of his foremen, who had pro-German sympathies, had either gone or was going to the Germans to denounce Bottenheim for anti-German sentiments. A surprising number of people in the Netherlands actually used denunciation as a means of revenge or to get rid of people they did not like. Although the Germans were well aware of this unpleasant and frequent occurrence, they still felt duty bound to follow through on every report received, which they did with the usual Germanic thoroughness.

Jack's situation was not looking good. He realized that the Nazi investigative spotlight was turning on him. The heat was on and danger was closing in. He was in a critical situation, but as well as feeling fear, he came to believe that it was his duty to survive, escape and get to England. Carefully and cautiously he started making investigations as to how he could escape the enclosing net.

Although everyone he spoke to was most secretive and guarded, it did not take him long to make the contacts he needed. Almost immediately he found himself meeting a Dutch captain by the name of Greter, in the bar at the Park Hotel, Amsterdam. They had hardly ordered their drinks when the captain started grumbling about his own failure at planning an escape and his lack of any progress in this matter. Jack suggested that they should cross into Belgium by his own newly discovered route at Baarle-Nassau. Captain Greter shook his head. He was not interested in the Baarle-Nassau route. After sharing the little information they had, the two promised to keep in touch.

They met up again on 10 October, and Greter advised Jack that an acquaintance had given him the name and an address of a dentist called Van Nagel in Rotterdam at 176 Noordsingel. This looked promising. Wasting no time, and with a sense of urgency, the next day the two travelled to Rotterdam by train.

At the dentist's home they knocked on the door, trusting that they were not walking into a trap. They were admitted by a young woman, and Greter asked if they could see a Mr Lindemans, which was the name of a Resistance man he had been given. Shortly after this, a young man aged about twenty joined them. He introduced himself as the brother of Chris Lindemans and asked to know the purpose of their unexpected visit. After preliminary and careful fencing around the point, they finally declared their intention of seeking an escape route.

Now that their cards were on the table, the young man left them, and they could hear quiet talking in the background. After a short wait, Christiaan Lindemans, known as 'King Kong', walked into the room. He was a big, imposing man – hence the nickname. Bottenheim noticed that he limped on his right leg and had a crippled left arm, which was the result of an accident. Lindemans seemed to fill the room with his personality. He was a strong, lively character who exuded confidence and an air of bonhomie. He confirmed that he was working with the Resistance and could probably help Jack and the captain, as he had already helped a number of Canadian airmen to safety.

He explained there would be a fee involved to cover expenses. This would be 100 guilders each, to supply them with Organisation Todt papers. (Todt was a civil and military engineering organization named after Fritz Todt, who became Minister of Armaments and Munitions. After his death in a plane crash in 1942, Todt was succeeded by Albert Speer.) Lindemans assured them that the Todt papers would get them to the Spanish frontier, where they would be met and conducted by experienced guides over the mountains into Spain.

After everything had been explained and discussed, it was arranged that they would meet up again in about a week. Lindemans also advised them that he was not working alone and that he had other connections in the Resistance network. He mentioned the names of Baron Johan van Heemstra and another aristocrat, Jonkheer Verspijck – the chairman of Unilever in Paris. Bottenheim later commented that he had the impression that Lindemans had done this bit of name-dropping to give his proposal weight and credibility.

Jack was relieved that the plans for their first mission in Dutch Resistance activity now appeared successfully completed. Maybe this would all be far easier that he had anticipated. The two left Rotterdam and travelled back to Amsterdam. During the journey Captain Greter told Jack he was not satisfied with Lindemans' plan. He felt uncomfortable about it and he had heard of another escape line that might be worth exploring before they accepted the Lindemans proposal.

They wasted no time in following up this second proposal, and within days a meeting was arranged with Henri Scharrer at his home at 21 Emmakade, Amstelveen. Henri opened the solid wooden front door immediately after their knock, so that watchful neighbours would have less time to see strangers waiting outside. There was much coming and going at this house, and nobody could be trusted, not even long-standing friendly neighbours. They were hurried inside. Jack in his report described Henri as aged roughly forty-three and of medium height, dark haired but nearly bald and dressed in flashy clothes.

They entered the lounge, where Henri invited them to be seated. Jack noted that Henri spoke excellent Dutch but with a French accent. Henri's wife Truus arrived to offer refreshments and home-made Dutch biscuits. The children were nowhere in sight. In the course of the meeting Henri explained that he was, in fact, a French national and was employed as a journalist by the Swiss Press Agency in Holland.

After preliminary discussions his offer amounted to this: that at a cost of 300 guilders (more expensive than Lindemans) he would supply each of them with papers to enable them to reach the Spanish frontier without trouble. He explained that these would be papers of the Sicherheitsdienst and that they would be travelling disguised as senior SD officers. This was one of his favourite ploys, Henri explained. Lower-ranking German officers did not stop or question their superiors. Also there would be no problem with their Dutch accents, as the majority of officers in the local SS and SD were Dutch or Flemish citizens anyway.

After a long conversation about details and procedures, the two men thanked Henri and advised that they would have to think this offer over. It was decided that a further meeting would be arranged at a café in Amsterdam.

On their walk back to the train station, Jack told Captain Greter that he thought Henri's proposal carried too great a risk, and that it would be far less dangerous to travel with Lindemans' false Todt papers than false SD identities. The suggestion that they should pose as SD officers was something he found out of the question. This would be an impossible task with huge risks. It was a crazy idea!

Greter, though, wanted to play it safe and was in favour of getting both sets of papers. Reports on what happened next appear to contradict each other, but all confirm that the conversation between the two became heated. Greter then announced that there was a third proposal he would be investigating and he would accept this offer if the opportunity presented itself. There was one problem Jack had to realize. If Greter went with the third proposal, there would be no room for him. Jack would be on his own.

This dilemma provoked even more argument, but it was finally agreed that the two would once again visit Chris Lindemans in Rotterdam in the next couple of days. A day before they were due to go, Greter telephoned Jack to inform him that his third proposal had materialized and he had accepted it. Then, with his usual over-caution, covering all bets, he asked Jack to visit Lindemans again and organize a set of the Todt papers for him as a back-up, in case he needed them for travelling south from Paris.

Always the gentleman, Jack agreed to help his new friend and travelled by train to Rotterdam the next day. When he arrived at Van Nagel's rooms he was astonished to be told by the receptionist that the Lindemans had left two days before, and that their present address was unknown. They had disappeared. This was all rather sudden and curious, he thought.

These setbacks, however, did not deter him in any way. In spite of his initial concerns about the risk of Henri's plan, the sheer urgency of his situation compelled him to reconsider. He now had no other place to go and was at his wits' end. He felt that there was danger all around him and that at any time he could be pulled up and arrested.

He put his concerns aside and wasted no time in setting up another meeting with Henri which this time was held at the Park Hotel in Amsterdam. This stylish hotel is not too far from the Rijksmuseum with its vast halls of Dutch old masters, and the famous Dam Square, located on the site of the original dam on the Amstel River and now dominated by the Royal Palace and the Gothic Nieuwe Kerk. Here over coffee in the sumptuous lounge, where a number of German officers were relaxing with their Dutch girlfriends, he quietly requested that Henri urgently prepare the necessary papers for his escape to Spain, and also papers for another friend who would be accompanying him. Henri assured Jack that this would not be a problem and advised what was required in terms of photographs and other information. After a quick handshake they left the hotel in different directions.

On the morning of 13 November Henri and Jack met up once again in the bar of another hotel a short distance from the Dam Square. This time it was the ornate Hotel Americain. Jack was accompanied by another person by the name of Evers. The name Evers appears in at least one report as Jack's companion at this meeting but is blanked out in other reports, indicating that his identity was sensitive and that 'Evers' might even have been a code name. The photographs Henri needed were also handed over.

Later the same day, back at the Scharrer Amstelveen house, in exchange for the 300 guilders, Henri gave them two *Sonderausweise* (free passes) in the name of Bottenheim and two in the name of Evers. In each case one *Sonderausweise* was properly stamped and the other was blank. He also provided one *Personliche Ausweis* (personal pass) for both Bottenheim and Evers. These documents, printed in black on yellow paper and each bearing a photograph, stated that Bottenheim and Evers were members of the SD in Toulouse and requested that every assistance be given to them by the Wehrmacht.

Here again, just as in the case of Rudy Zeeman, we see that Henri preferred to disguise his escapees as senior Nazi personnel. Whatever apprehension Jack had felt previously seems to have disappeared in the urgency of the situation. This was the disguise technique about which Henri was the most confident, and which so far had always proved to be successful. Furthermore, because of the store of German uniforms and other German military paraphernalia at his house, he found this part of the plan easy to execute.

The third document for each of them was a *Grensbescheinigung* (frontier certificate) for the Belgian-French frontier and the demarcation line in France between occupied and Vichy zones.

Henri then gave Jack and his companion detailed travel and accommodation instructions. These, too, were reinforced by briefings as to how to respond and what attitude to adopt when questioned by German officials. They were given the general background information they would need to present themselves as authentic members of the SD, including the names, places and ranks they would need to know. Streets, buildings, tram stops, railways stations, restaurants in the vicinity of their 'so-called' offices had to be remembered. This was an important briefing. Time and time again they were taken through the procedures, how they had to walk and stand, even the right expressions on their faces and the exact words they had to use. They had to appear arrogant, unafraid, dismissive at all times, no matter what occurred. The important thing was they had to intimidate, or at least be somewhat dismissive of, anyone who spoke to them or wanted to see their papers.

Once he felt satisfied with their performance, Henri, always the actor, demonstrated with some exaggeration how they were to behave at German checkpoints. There was much laughter all round, and a few 'Heil Hitlers' and clicking of heels, which eased the tension.

Now they were on their way. Later the same evening, as instructed, Jack and Evers travelled to Maastricht. Though they passed a number of German patrols with beating hearts, they were not stopped. They marched into their specified hotel at Maastricht, their nailed boots clacking loudly on the floor boards, and demanded immediate service, which they got. Everybody scurried around to serve them and show them up to their rooms.

The next morning, they took the *S. F. Zug* (a special troop train making a daily journey from Maastricht to Paris). There were two German controls en route, which they treated with bored disdain, producing their papers and behaving in the stern and confident Germanic manner they had practised with Henri. Quick salutes, and the papers were handed back. Reaching Paris at 1900 hrs, again following Henri's instructions, Jack and Evers went straight to the Hôtel Des Deux Hémisphères, which was one of the hotels Henri and Jan Lowey-Ball had originally identified for use on their escape line. Here they were in safe territory within a Resistance group.

Bottenheim's activities and the names of people he met in Paris are mostly blanked out as classified. However, we know Jack did have two addresses which Christiaan Lindemans had given him previously. One was the address of Jonkheer Verspijck, chairman of Unilever in Paris, and the other was the home of Baron Johan van Heemstra at 3 Rue Lord Byron in Paris.

On 16 November Jack and Evers arrived at Van Heemstra's address, where they were received in a most cordial manner by Van Heemstra himself. Jack described him as a fattish man of average height. The visit, though, was in vain as Van

Heemstra told them that he was unable to assist because he was about to leave for Holland. The baron didn't abandon them on his doorstep, however, and took both of them to the Hôtel Venezia, on the Boulevard Montparnasse, where they were introduced to a Dutch girl believed to have been Anika (Melle Anna) Neyesel. Melle Neyesel was a Dutch-Paris Line helper, and her assistance to Allied airmen is well documented. Other Resistance fighters were also introduced to them, including Albert Starink, Herman Laatsman and Catherine (Okky) Ockhuizen of the Dutch-Paris line. Here they received a new set of instructions. Their stay in Paris lasted nearly a week, while further arrangements were being made to send them south.

Dressed again as senior SD officers, on 23 November Jack and Evers boarded the slow train from the Gare d'Austerlitz to Toulouse. They had hardly sat down when a large group of Germans came on board, taking control of the train. Jack and his companion were joined in their compartment by a jovial Luftwaffe officer, who became most friendly after they produced their SD papers. There was no control at the demarcation line and they reached Toulouse without incident the next morning.

The person they were to meet, however, did not appear, so after a few days Jack decided to return to Paris and find out what happened. By this time they had become confident in their role as SD officers and played their high-handed arrogance to the hilt. Who would dare question them? They reached Paris safely on the morning of 28 November, went straight to the Hôtel Venezia and again contacted Melle Neyesel. Everybody was mystified by the disappearance of their man in Toulouse, and it was only on 30 November that news came that a person by the name of 'Georges' with a group of escaping Dutchmen had been arrested on the train between Toulouse and Pau by the Germans; they were all now in prison at Biarritz or Bordeaux. Urgent new plans had to be made.

Much to Jack's frustration, nothing was moving swiftly and more time was going by. It was not until 5 December that someone new was introduced to Jack. The name of the individual has been edited out, but this person came from a different escape group, described as having a young Dutch woman as its leader. Her name is also blocked out and we can only speculate about her identity. There is a suggestion that she was Elsie Boon, a student at Leiden University who was a prominent Resistance leader. Elsie's story on its own makes a fascinating study and is told later.

With the help of this new group and the same SD papers they had received from Henri, Jack and Evers once again went back to Toulouse, where they were instructed to wait outside the station buffet for a young woman to make contact with them. They waited in vain, however, for she did not arrive. Most disappointed at this second failed rendezvous, Jack and Evers found lodgings at 3 Rue Alex

Fourtannier. Uncertain what to do after these failed attempts, Jack decided that the best course of action was to once again head back to Paris.

He now realized that trying to escape was actually a tiring and complicated business. They were going round endlessly in circles. At the Hôtel Venezia he was advised that there had been a misunderstanding: they should have met the young woman outside the station, not outside the station buffet. Another frustrating waste of time, and Jack was beginning to wonder whether at this rate his escape plan would ever succeed. The unfortunate reality was that such plans frequently went awry for various reasons, mostly to do with safety, security and arrests. Collaborators and suspicious people were everywhere, and if they could report a person to the authorities they would do so immediately. German sympathizers would do anything to score points.

By 19 December a bottleneck was developing in Paris as a large number of Dutchmen had arrived with Henri's papers and documents compiled by other escape lines. To avoid suspicion, the leaders of the organization had them broken up into smaller groups. Again names are blanked out, but most likely involved at this stage were Baron Abraham Boetzelaer, to whom Baron Johan Van Heemstra reported, Albert Starink, who was closely involved with Ruby Zeeman's stay in Paris, and John Weidner, originator of the Dutch-Paris Line. Bottenheim in a report refers to meeting 'George Wyssogota Lakczewski' in Paris, and this is probably a pseudonym for Andre Wyssogota. The names of these people and these escape lines crop up time and again during the Paris stopovers.

Jack and Evers were now dressed as French labourers, with berets and farm boots, and found themselves in a small group with a leader. They left Paris by train for Boussens, the first station on the line from Toulouse to Pau. Here they had a good meal and a rest, were supplied with provisions for their journey and introduced to their guide. They were told they could only travel by night and when there was no moon, so they had to wait until conditions were right. From here, just as Rudy Zeeman had experienced, they had to proceed on foot, off the beaten track in the direction of the craggy Pyrenean foothills a few miles ahead.

Jack took one look at the snow-covered 11,000ft granite and limestone peaks and his confidence left him. How were they ever going to be able to climb these mountains? He had lost his physical fitness from all the hiding and waiting around, and besides he had never been much of a mountaineer. But there was no turning back. All they could do was keep going forward, no matter how their muscles ached, and how their lungs strained with every step. Every now and then the guide cautioned them to duck and hide, or press against a rock face, to escape the binoculars of the German Alpine troops patrolling the area.

Jack soon realized that their clothes were insufficient to keep out the February cold. His boots became wet, his toes began to freeze, his fingers started to swell.

The icy damp seeped through everything. The higher they climbed up the narrow goat paths, the more laboured Jack's breath became.

'Keep moving,' the guide cautioned them. Then he called, 'Hide!'

A Henschel scout plane swept up the valley behind them, passing 50ft over their heads, before sweeping away. They waited with bated breath, and then the plane came back to double-check.

'Is this the moment I die in a hail of machine gun bullets?' Jack thought.

But the plane swept on out of sight, the noise of its engines fading away, until the only sound was the water gushing out of crevices in the algae-flecked granite face of the rock. Up they went, slowly and painfully, into freezing ice and snow, until just as daybreak started streaking the sky, they reached a lean-to backed up against a rock. Here they collapsed amongst a pile of old mouldy blankets on the floor. The guide passed around a flask of brandy, which warmed their stomachs, and handed out cheese, olives, and bread. They fell asleep almost immediately and didn't move until dusk.

The guide woke them and handed out more of the food rations and water. Jack felt as if his entire body had gone into spasm. His muscles could barely move. Then again in the darkening light they set out, struggling to put one foot in front of the other. Another shot of brandy each, which somehow seemed to help, and on they plodded, along the narrow paths on slippery rocks, ravines below, where many had slipped and fallen, crashing to their deaths on the rocks.

Jack started to seriously feel the effects of vertigo and was overcome with nausea and dizziness.

'Don't look down! Look ahead.'

Would the agony ever end? Just when he thought he could not put another foot forward, here was another hut offering another few hours of rest. It seemed he had hardly slept when he was prodded awake by the guide. Off they went again into the cold and darkness.

Then, with daybreak brightening the sky, they came through a gap and Jack saw one of the beautiful sights he had ever seen. Down below they could make out the foothills undulating towards a huge plain with vineyards and trees, and even a few houses. They had crossed the border in the night, in one of the most harrowing experiences of his life. Feeling weak and frozen to the core, Jack and his companions slowly descended the mountains, fingers chilled in wet, frozen gloves, toes freezing in their boots, but their hearts filled with joy and confidence as they knew they had made it.

Jack wrote that the sense of relief and happiness he felt when he sat on the ground against a gnarled fig tree at the bottom of the foothills was a feeling he would never forget.

There were other small groups crossing the border at the same time, and by coincidence in one of these was Rudy Zeeman. The underground contacts were waiting for them, and they were taken in an old cart to a farmhouse, where welcome hot meals and warm clothing were provided and they were left to sleep.

The next day, a motor vehicle collected them and they were taken to a Spanish prison to be interrogated by Spanish authorities in a not very friendly manner. Were they going to be handed back to the Germans? It was always a possibility.

As Rudy had also discovered, escapees could have a difficult time in Spain; they were often harassed and detained. The Dutch Consul soon came to their rescue, however, and they were sent via Vielle and Lleida to Madrid, where they were booked into a hotel and advised they had to wait until further arrangements were made. Here they could rest their aching bones and muscles.

Freedom at last! They were safe in a neutral, even if unfriendly, country. The escapees enjoyed sight-seeing in the capital, and after months of strenuous rations and bland food, especially enjoyed the good coffee and tasty Spanish tapas, fresh bread and delicious cured ham. On 23 February they were told that their departure from Madrid would take place the next afternoon. This news came as a big relief and was emotionally welcomed by all. A few escapees, including Jack, thought the occasion called for a last big party and celebration. Some, of course, in their high spirits and excitement would party too much!

The next afternoon, about five minutes before the train was due to depart the main Madrid station, Rudy Zeeman was surprised to see Jack, accompanied by a consular official, run up the platform and jump quickly on to the train. He told Rudy about the celebration which had got out of hand and ended in his group of escapees being arrested for swinging from the overhead telephone lines of the Department of Foreign Affairs.

Jack later explained his release to Rudy and the others by telling them that whilst he had enjoyed a few drinks, he had refrained from the telephone wire antics and was not playing Tarzan when the guards had appeared. The arresting officers corroborated his account of events at the interrogation. As a result, he could not be accused of any crime, was allowed to walk free and, accompanied by a Dutch consular official, go to the station to catch the train south.

The rest of Jack's party did not fare so well. Unable to speak Spanish, which Jack could do fluently, they were asked to sign a document which they were given to understand Jack had previously signed. In doing this they were admitting entering Spain to spy for a foreign power and to commit acts of sabotage and a whole string of other offences against the Spanish state. They had actually signed their own death warrant. It was believed by some that the authorities had purposely let Jack go because he understood Spanish, would have seen the trap and warned the others not to sign.

As a result of signing this false affidavit, the others had to spend four months in a hellhole of a prison, before the Dutch Consulate managed to get them transferred to the jurisdiction of a civil court, where a 'Not Guilty' verdict was passed.

The train from Madrid took Jack, Rudy and other escapees to the Portuguese coast, from where they travelled to Gibraltar aboard a small ship. Fortunately, they were left alone by any U-boats in the area and by the Spanish patrol boats seeking out illegals. Another couple of days were spent on the Rock with a large crowd of other *Engelandvaarders*, until they embarked on the SS *Orduna* for Liverpool.

Also on board this ship were the 'Desert Rats' and other troops from the North Africa campaign. Jack does not give much detail about his voyage to England. However, Rudy described it as unpleasant. They were packed in the hold, where oppressive heat and poor ventilation made it impossible to sleep, so most of them spent the nights on deck until the convoy reached the Atlantic and cooler weather. The latrines, he said, were indescribable, twenty toilets facing each other without partitions.

Travelling in these convoys was always a risk. This particular convoy was made up of nineteen troopships, with the damaged battleship HMS *Warspite* in the centre. Jack does not report seeing any Luftwaffe planes or any sign of U-boats.

One of the evenings was to remain unforgettable for anyone who was on deck: thousands of men on the SS *Orduna* and other ships sailing nearby spontaneously burst into song. Rudy writes that it pulled at the heart strings to listen to 'It's a long way to Tipperary,' 'Over there' and 'My Bonnie lies over the ocean,' whilst the convoy sailed under the clear, bright night sky. Six days after leaving Gibraltar, and sailing a wide arc around Ireland, just after a cold dawn their ship arrived in the roads off the Mersey River. Jack gives the date of their arrival in England as 16 March 1944.

Like all the escapees from the Netherlands, Jack had a debriefing interview with the Allied authorities, and his story was investigated and proved to be accurate. It was decided he could go free as he would not be a danger to the Allied war effort.

Jack's escape, which started in September, took all of six months. His report illustrates just how time-consuming, frustrating and dangerous escaping could be, and why so many thousands of people who attempted it, failed. Also it explains why only about 1,600 to 1,700 Dutch people actually succeeded in making it to England, according to Rudy Zeeman's memoir.

It is an intriguing fact that Evers' name is fully blocked out repeatedly in one long and important Allied report on Jack. In some reports he is simply referred to as 'the companion'. Was Evers a code name, an important individual, or even a woman? One can only speculate.

From a number of written comments it appears that Jack's acquaintance, Captain Greter, made it across the Channel after deciding to accept the third proposal of an escape route. In notes written by Matilda Verspyck's mother, she states that after her daughter's arrest she hid a 'well-known equestrian', Captain Greter, at the home of Joseph Schaar, and the next day he hid at the home of Master Andre

Vaes of Antwerp. From there, she says, he was sent to England. In a letter to Jean Weidner, a Mr E. S. Chait writes that Greter and Pahut went through the '*Panier Fleuri*' – an Annecy link in Dutch-Paris.

Who was Captain Greter exactly? His name occurs in a completely different report on the Belgian resistance: J. J. Greter, who had been an aide-de-camp to Queen Wilhelmina, is reported to have made it safely to Brussels from Amsterdam, assisted by helper Simone Cambrelin. In Brussels he was destined to be taken over by the Dutch-Paris Line. The aide-de-camp is possibly the same person as Jack's friend and could be the same person known for his riding ability. However, this is not known for certain.

After the liberation, Jack would have been one of the first to make it home to the Netherlands. There is a happy photograph of him with friends at a party in Wassenaar in 1945. In her statement to the Allies, Carry Libourel reported that she had met with Jack Bottenheim after the war, so somewhere on his long journey their paths must have crossed. It is possible that her name is also one of those blanked out.

In this same report on Carry the interrogator states that the following names, notorious or otherwise, were included in or had a connection to Henri's organization: Lindemans, Domine Ten Carte, Brothers Verloop, Jan Strangers, Van Heemstra, Louis de Bray, Andre Wyssogota and Baron Van Boetzelaer.

More fascinating stories of these men later.

Chapter 9

British Airmen Down

Henri and his cell group dealt not only with *Engelandvaarders* who were Dutch citizens, and American aircrews, but also with British airmen and other nationalities who fought for the Allies. Richard Scharrer, in his essay about his father, refers to two RAF crewmen who stayed at their house in Amstelveen on a particular occasion, and there is some anecdotal information about this visit. There is also a signed witness account in British military records of two RAF aircrew being handed over to Henri Scharrer by Fritz Conijn at Alkmaar. One of these airmen made a statement to the Allied authorities after the war; this is his remarkable story of how he came to be helped by Henri.

James (Jim) Davies was an ABC (Air Borne Cigar) Operator. He could speak German and, operating his ABC device, was able to contact Luftwaffe ground control, giving them false information and causing disruption in radio contact between planes and ground. That was his area of expertise, and he did the job well.

He was from 101 Squadron, flying in an Avro Lancaster heavy bomber. This plane, powered by four Rolls-Royce engines, had become the central weapon in the RAF night-time bombing campaign, following its successful first flight on 9 January 1941. It was later modified to equip 617 Squadron to carry the 'bouncing bombs' designed by Barnes Wallis for Operation Chastise, which was the attack on the Ruhr valley dams made famous by the film *The Dam Busters*.

Efficient a bomber as this plane was, it was an extremely dangerous machine to be in if the crew had the great misfortune of having to bail out as a result of being hit. This was because the escape hatch measured only 22ins by 26½ins, not an easy space to get through if you were a large man wearing a parachute. There are figures suggesting that, compared to a 50 per cent success rate for crews bailing out of the American Liberator, only 15 per cent of the Lancaster crews managed to bail out successfully. A shocking statistic!

Jim's plane was only one of many Lancasters that took off that night of Saturday, 19 February 1944, heading for Leipzig, home to over 700,000 inhabitants and the factories making the Messerschmitt Bf 109 fighter planes. Their take-off time from Ludford Magna on the east coast of England was 2338 hrs. These missions were part of an attack on Leipzig known as 'The Big Week'.

It is reported that the RAF executed twenty-four raids on Leipzig between 1942 and 1945, causing large numbers of civilian casualties and destroying the city

nri Scharrer, 1900–1944.

ertruida 'Truus' Scharrer.

Richard Scharrer, Henri's elder son.

Christiaan Lindemans, alias 'King Kong', double agent.

illiam Pons, double agent.

k Bottenheim (top of stairs) at
ssenaar, Holland, 1945.

(*Above*) *Engelandvaarder* Jack Bottenheim (right), with Prince Bernhard of the Netherlands.

(*Left*)Anna Maria Verhulst-Oomes, double agent. Photo taken after her arrest.

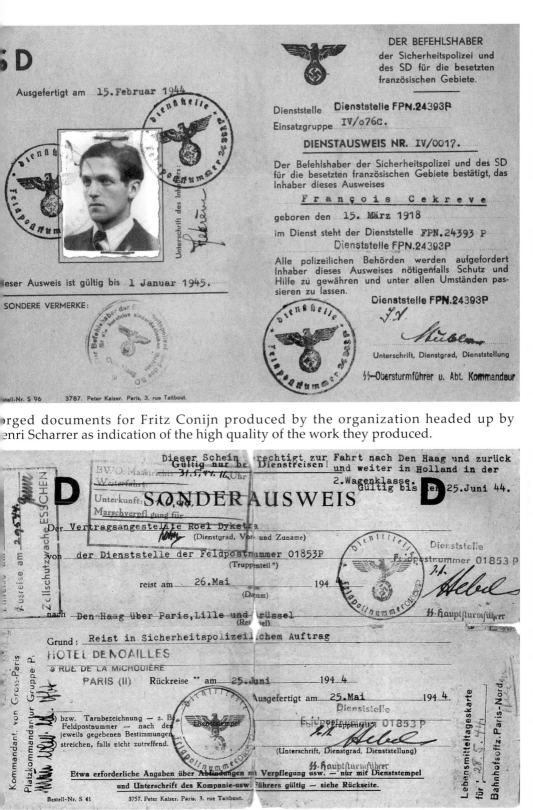

forged documents for Fritz Conijn produced by the organization headed up by Henri Scharrer as indication of the high quality of the work they produced.

REGEERINGSPERSDIENST
DEPARTEMENT VAN ALGEMEENE ZAKEN

'S-GRAVENHAGE,   10 Mei 1940.
PLEIN 23
TELEFOON 117296

De Regeeringspersdienst verklaart dat houder
dezes, *de heer* H.J. Scharrer
verbonden is aan het Algemeen Nederlandsch Persbureau
en dat zijn /haar aanwezigheid op het bureau van
het A.N.P. (Lange Voorhout 26, den Haag) in 's Lands
belang onontbeerlijk is.

De Chef van den Regeeringspersdienst
Administrateur aan het Departement
van Algemeene Zaken,

(A.J. Lievegoed).

(*Above*) Henri Scharrer's press ID.

(*Left*) Raymond Scharrer, Henri's youngest son.

Wie kan inlichtingen geven over
Henry Scharrer. Geb. Ostende 23 April 1900
Franschman. die zeer goed Hollandsch spreekt.
gevangen genomen 18 Augustus 1944. eerst gebracht naar
Scheveningen, toen ± 23 kwartier naar Amstelveensche
weg. Amsterdam, daarna op 4 of 5 September naar
Weteringschans en vermoedelijk op 5 September naar
Vught getransporteerd. Heeft iemand ergens met hem
gevangen gezeten, hem op transport gezien of weet
of hij in Vught is. Iedere gebruik [...] Daarna alle berichten
hoe oogenschijnlijk onbelangrijk ook [...] Rivierenlaan
16" Amsterdam; of [...] Oude Wega 253. Alle
kosten worden vergoed.

This was formerly De Gekroonde Valk, the café where the ransom meeting was held wi
William Pons.

Emmakade, Amstelveen, the Scharrer residence.

Caroline 'Carry' Libourel,
Henri Scharrer's Dutch underground
colleague and mistress.

Doeko Bosscher

Haast om te sterven

Het korte leven
van verzetsman
Fritz Conijn

PROMETHEUS · BERT BAKKER

Cover of Doeko Bosscher's book,
published in 2015.

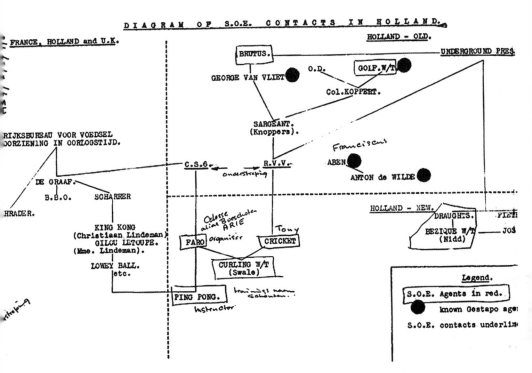

DIAGRAM OF S.O.E. CONTACTS IN HOLLAND.

FRANCE, HOLLAND and U.K.   HOLLAND - OLD.

BRUTUS.   UNDERGROUND PRES

GEORGE VAN VLIET   O.D.   GOLF.W/T
                                      Col.KOPPERT.

RIJKSBUREAU VOOR VOEDSEL
OORZIENING IN OORLOGSTIJD.   SARGEANT.
                                      (Knoppers).
                                                          Franciscus
                    C.S.6   R.V.V.   ABEN
DE GRAAF.   onderstreping   ANTON de WILDE
    B.B.O.   SCHARRER
HRADER.   HOLLAND - NEW.
                                                                    DRAUGHTS.   PIETI
            KING KONG   Odesse
            (Christiaan Lindeman) alias Boeschoten   BEZIQUE W/T   JOS
            GILOU LETOUPE.   ARIE   (Nidd)
            (Mme. Lindeman).   FARO organiser   CRICKET Tony
            LOWEY BALL.
                etc.   CURLING W/T
                               (Swale)   Legend.
                                                   S.O.E. Agents in red.
                    PING PONG.   training! nm
                                 Schouten.   known Gestapo age
                    Instructor.   S.O.E. contacts underlin

(*above*) Diagram of SOE (Special Operations
Executive) and the Dutch Resistance movement
an Allied interrogator. The link between
harrer and de Graaf is shown.

(*right*) American airman Frank Hart.

This certificate is awarded to

Henri Jean Scharrer

as a token of gratitude for and appreciation of the help given to the Sailors, Soldiers and Airmen of the British Commonwealth of Nations, which enabled them to escape from, or evade capture by the enemy.

Air Chief Marshal,
Deputy Supreme Commander
Allied Expeditionary Force

1939-1945

Citations of 'gratitude and appreciation' for the sacrifices of Henri Scharrer signed by General Dwight D. Eisenhower, Supreme Commander Allied Expeditionary Force, and his Deputy Air Chief Marshal Arthur W. Tedder of Great Britain.

The Weteringschans Detention
Centre in Amsterdam.

Major Hermann Joseph Giskes,
Head of Counter-Intelligence.

(*Above*) A National Socialist Movement rally in the Hague, with the crowd giving the Nazi salute.

(*Left*) Leading Nazi Hermann Goering committed suicide before he was due to be executed by the Allies.

...ight concentration camp in the Netherlands, where Henri Scharrer and hundreds of Dutch ...esistance fighters were executed.

...me of the wartime escape routes over the Pyrenees into Spain used by downed airmen ...mongst others.

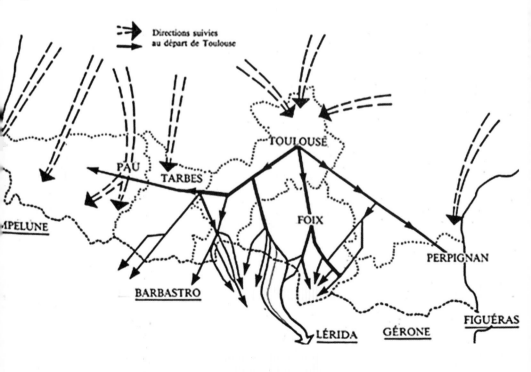

Directions suivies
au départ de Toulouse

German soldiers practising goose-stepping.

A group of armed Dutch Resistance fighters before going on a mission.

centre with a fire storm caused by incendiary bombs. This night, however, it was the RAF that would suffer many casualties. According to Bob Baxter's website article on Bomber Command losses, during this particular night-raid on Leipzig over forty Lancasters were shot down, either by night fighters or anti-aircraft fire, and most of their crews died. Baxter's website lists the names of every crew member who survived and every one who died.

The other crew members besides Jim consisted of the pilot, John Laurens from Cape Town, Cassian Waight from Belize, Leslie (Crash) Burto, Ronald Aitkens, William (Billy) Kibble, William Bolt and Albert Royston.

Their flight followed a similar pattern to the one that American airman Frank Hart and his crew experienced in their Liberator bomber. Once over the Channel, the night sky was lit up by flak explosions. There were German night-fighters winging around like mosquitoes. These were mostly Messerschmitts specially modified for night flying, often with radar and all with special systems enabling them to land in the dark, as runways could not be lit up due to enemy attacks.

Many of the pilots of these German night fighters were aces, credited with shooting down five or more enemy aircraft. The leading Luftwaffe ace of the war was Erich Hartman, with 352 victories. The leading night-fighter ace was Major Heinz-Wolfgang Schnaufer, nicknamed 'The Spook of St Troud', who had 121 night victories.

These figures are astonishingly high, and it is said they were due to the fact that the German fighter pilots kept going until they were killed, captured or collapsed from exhaustion. The top RAF ace was South African Marmaduke (Pat) Pattle with an estimated 40 victories, mainly in the North African campaign, while the top American ace was Richard I. Bong, also with 40.

Facing these German night fighters was a frightening experience, as they often flew head-on towards the slow, heavily loaded bombers, firing straight into the cockpit to kill the pilot, before veering off. Every man prayed that they would make it through the night, as they had done on previous occasions.

This time their luck ran out. The Lancaster took a serious hit from a night fighter, with debris and flames flying everywhere. There was no time for pilot John Laurens to turn the plane round and get back to base. The blow to the aircraft was fatal, but he struggled to keep it flying for a short while so that the men could try and get out of the escape hatch. When their altitude was below 15,000ft, with at least 30 per cent oxygen level, it was considered safe enough to jump through the hatch – some had to be pushed from behind. There were terrifying air battles all around them, with bullets and artillery shells blazing tracer across the sky. The airmen let themselves fall for as long as they could, so as to avoid being hit by machine gun fire, and opened their parachutes only at the last minute. A tricky piece of timing!

They came down in northern Holland, near the village of Niebert, between Marum and Tolbert, about 17km from the city of Groningen. Three of the crew, Cassian Waight, William Bolt and John Laurens, who was the last to leave the aircraft, did not survive the crash. Waight died of a broken neck, and his body was only later found at the town of Noordijk. The bodies were picked up by local residents and all three are buried in the churchyard at the Tolbert Protestant church, where a large memorial tombstone was later erected.

The five airmen who survived knew they had to get away from the vicinity as fast as they could, to escape German search parties. The fate that awaited anyone who was caught would be heavy interrogation, followed by incarceration in one of the notorious German PoW camps. Albert Royston was the first to get caught, as he had the misfortune to knock on the door of a Nazi sympathizer; he landed up in prison shortly thereafter.

It was about an hour or two past midnight when Jim Davies, shocked and shivering, knocked on the door of the nearest darkened house, waking up the occupants. The door was finally opened by a concerned elderly Dutch couple, dressed in their night clothes, who could not speak English. They understood the situation immediately. After pulling on an overcoat and boots against the winter cold, the man hurried Jim through the dark to their neighbour, Jan Veen at Idsings Zee. It was almost pitch dark outside, and Jim could barely make out the leafless trees along the road side, their branches moving gently in a winter breeze.

Jan Veen already had much experience as a Resistance helper and knew exactly what to do. He wasted no time and gave Jim civilian clothing and his sister's bike. The two pedalled through the cold night on small country roads in the direction of Siegers Woude in De Wilp, to the house of Jan's brother-in-law, Hanje de Jong, and his wife Roelfke, who were not surprised to be woken up in the middle of the night. They had become used to late night calls for help.

Here Jim and Jan were given hot food and extra warm clothing, together with 'safety instructions' for the rest of the journey. Then off they pedalled, this time to the farmhouse of Mr Sietse Wijkstra in the Heineburen hamlet, slightly tucked back from the narrow road. Safely delivered, here Jim could at least get some sleep under a goose-feathered eiderdown, while Jan now had to cycle the long way back home as fast as he could through the bitter winter weather. There was a reason he had to get home before dawn. It was Sunday, and it was vital that he be seen in church for the morning service, as his absence would be regarded as unusual and suspicious. Also he didn't want anyone to see him coming home on his bicycle in the early hours. Telling tales on people was a popular pastime for pro-German sympathizers. Fortunately, the sun rises late in the Netherlands in February.

A few hours later, Jan Veen parked his bicycle at his house, tidied up and, accompanied by his wife, calmly entered the church dressed his Sunday best, greeting everybody politely and hoping nobody would notice the dark circles under his tired eyes. But his work was not over. Not yet! A Mr Bijzitter approached him on the church steps to whisper quietly in his ear that he had a pilot in his house and ask for assistance. The man had just shown up at his door, and he did not know what to do!

The 'pilot' turned out to be Sergeant Ronnie Aitken. So having had hardly a wink of sleep, Jan went off again on his bicycle, accompanied by a friend by the name of Johannes. This time they were cycling in daylight and had to watch out carefully for the 'Moffen' (Jerries) who were searching the countryside for the crews of the many crashed Lancasters that had come down over the Netherlands during the night. Once again they arrived at the Wijkstra farm to deliver an airman. Here the two friends and crew members were happily united. They could not believe their luck.

It was too dangerous for them to stay, as the Germans were undertaking house-to-house searches for Allied airmen, who they knew were hiding in the area. So the next day Jim and Ronnie were moved to the safer house of Piet Dijkstra at Garip village. The branch of the Resistance taking care of them at this time was the Witte Brigade. Usually it was a matter of days before airmen were moved on, but for some reason not clarified, Jim and Ronnie lived with Piet Dijkstra for around three months, lying low. Jim's debriefing report states that they were waiting for the required false identification documents and food distribution cards, which were coming from a branch of the Resistance operation in Amsterdam. These he says were being organized by a man called 'Sandberg', which as we know was an alias of Henri Scharrer.

There is another report in the files drawn up by the Headquarters European Theatre of Operations in 1946 that also contains the Stichting documents for the file on Henri Scharrer. This report is signed by Pauki Schuur Bidot and dated 1 March 1946. It testifies to the fact that in May 1944 Henri Scharrer travelled to Alkmaar and at the train station picked up two RAF pilots from Fritz Conijn – only twenty-one years old and a close associate of Henri's. Henri escorted these two pilots by train to Amsterdam and then the Hague, where they stayed for some time. The RAF pilots in this witness statement are not identified by name – only the names of Henri Scharrer and Fritz Conijn are mentioned, but all the facts point to the strong possibility that these two were Jim Davies and Ronnie Aitken, as the timings fit, and Richard Scharrer did tell his family about the two RAF pilots who stayed at their house briefly.

Finally, Jim reports that the Resistance moved him and Ronnie out of the Netherlands to Antwerp in Belgium. Here another wait ensued, until Jim and Ronnie were introduced to an attractive girl who was only referred to as 'Anna'. She asked him and Ronnie to follow her to an address where they would be handed over to the head of the Witte Brigade who would be organizing their trip to France. Naturally they were keen to meet this important person.

Anna took them to an apartment in Antwerp. Jim does not state the address but it was most likely 17 Van Eycklei, the house often used by Abwehr agent René Van Muylem, when he had airmen who had unfortunately landed up on his false KLM line.

After the formalities of greeting, the Witte Brigade representative offered cigarettes and chatted happily in excellent English with an American accent. He explained that as the head of his group he was concerned that many of the Resistance groups did not know what the others were doing, and this led to confusion. One of his tasks was to centralize some of these movements. Another important matter he had to sort out was the compensation due to the helpers along the routes, many of whom were assisting Allied airmen, providing food and clothing and paying for the false documents out of their own pockets. The Resistance organization wanted to organize this compensation, as they had more than enough funds back in London.

So, with a smile, he asked Jim if he was able to help the people who had so bravely helped him. Perhaps he could give him their names and addresses and so be sure they received repayment of their expenses. Jim apologized profusely and told him that he couldn't help at all because he had only travelled in the dark, everybody used false names, and he had no idea who they were. He would try to be of assistance, though, and perhaps after the war he could attempt to contact his helpers and assist with their compensation.

After a few more minutes of polite conversation, Jim writes that he was told that the Witte Brigade needed to move him and Ronnie to France, which was the next leg of the escape route. So they were escorted to a vehicle parked outside with a civilian driver. After the expression of many thanks and best wishes, Ronnie and Jim were waved away by a smiling Anna and the Witte Brigade man. Ronnie and Jim could not believe their luck. At this rate they would soon be back at base in England. Everything had been working so smoothly.

The vehicle, however, took a different route. Not to France, but to the German prison in Antwerp. Jim and Ronnie had had the misfortune to land in the clutches of the same Anna Maria Verhulst-Oomes who betrayed Frank Hart and Piet Felix's party of escapees. They were only two of the 278 airmen, René van Muylem reported, that he had trapped on his notorious KLM Line. This betrayal was all part of the operation *Englandspiel* of the counter-intelligence expert, Abwehr Major Hermann Giskes, or 'Dr German'.

It was now 10 August, and Ronnie and Jim had been on the run for about six months since their take-off from England. Here in Antwerp they were interrogated, although Jim in his report does not give much detail. From Antwerp they were sent to the prison of Saint Giles and from there were transferred to

Stalag VII – Brankau Kreulberg. They both survived the war but remained in confinement until the camp was liberated by Allied forces.

Jim Davies lived a long and happy life after the war. He died in North Wales in 2007 but not before he had visited the graves of his three fellow crewmen in the churchyard at Tolbert in Groningen Province and paid his respects.

During the last flight that Jim Davies and Ronnie Aitken made, on that night of 19/20 February, residential areas in the south (Connewitz) as well as residential and industrial areas in the south-west of Leipzig, Schleubig and Grobzschoche, were hit. In total, about 970 people died, most of them during the British night raid. During the following day the Americans destroyed 65 per cent of the Erla Maschinewerk in Heiterblick, which produced the Messerschmitt Bf 109 fighter planes. Several months later, the factories had still not recovered from the bombing raids.

Winston Churchill when setting up the SOE organization, stated that they would 'set Europe ablaze'. This the RAF and USAF certainly did.

Chapter 10

Other Amazing Escapes

Historical reports have highlighted a number of the high-profile escapes and assassinations in the bigger picture around the Resistance organization for which Henri Scharrer worked. No account of the Dutch Resistance would be complete without a description of some of these extraordinary events and the fascinating characters involved.

One of the prominent names in assassination incidents is Resistance fighter Nicolaas (Bob) Celosse, code name 'Faro'. Born in Java, he was twenty-five years old when on 22 October 1942 he took part in the attack on the Utrecht police station. His deeds appear in a highly classified report and are not easy to recreate because so much information is missing. What we do know is that after this attack in Utrecht, which proved his worth, he was accepted as a member of the small communist assassination group CS.6 and had an instructor with the codename 'Ping Pong' reporting directly to him.

This acceptance into the CS.6 took place nine months after the assassination of Head of the volunteer Dutch Waffen-SS Legion, Lieutenant General Hendrik Seyffardt, and at the time when the student Jan Verleun, who had carried out the shooting, was arrested. His capture was a blow to the Resistance movement and put considerable pressure on the CS.6. Kas de Graaf, a prominent member and the man to whom Henri Scharrer reported, now had to escape to England before Verleun talked under interrogation. This would leave a hole in the leadership which CS.6 believed would be best filled by handing over de Graaf's responsibilities to Celosse, who had been a most valuable new recruit.

While de Graaf went into hiding at a safe house before trying to reach the United Kingdom, it was decided by the leadership of the RVV that Bob Celosse should also pay a visit to the UK. This would entail making personal contact with the official SOE authorities there, and would obtain greater recognition for the RVV arm of the Dutch Resistance movement. It would hopefully also result in closer cooperation with the SOE Dutch unit in Britain.

As Celosse prepared to leave, he made contact with Henri Scharrer through a Dutch journalist by the name of Hans Hoetink of Deventer. They had a meeting at which Henri issued him with his travel documents and went through the usual briefing. When he finally reached London, Celosse described in a statement what happened next. Using Henri's documents and following his instructions, he made his way safely to Paris, and while staying at the Hôtel Des Deux Hémisphères he was joined by two other Dutchmen who had just escaped Holland with the assistance of papers which had also been issued by Henri. They were Marinus van Heukelsfeld-Jansen and Willem Kremer. Bob Celosse met up with them again in Bordeaux, and the three continued their journey towards Spain in the company of other escapees. At some stage the group broke into two, so as to be less conspicuous.

Celosse, Heukelsfeld-Jansen, Kremer and three Frenchmen made the perilous and exhausting climb up the mountains to reach Spain on a freezing Christmas Day in 1943. Like so many before them, they were briefly detained by the Spanish authorities and transferred to a small town via Pamplona, famous for the running of the bulls. Here Bob Celosse met up with Kas de Graaf, who had been making his escape with another group. They then travelled together to Madrid, where they stayed at the Hotel International for nearly a month, awaiting further instructions from London. At the end of January Celosse travelled to Portugal, where he embarked on the SS *Saymaru* for Gibraltar, joining a large group of *Engelandvaarders*. From there he flew on to England, arriving in Chivenor a few days later. Safe at last!

Celosse assumed that the second group, who had separated from them before climbing the mountains to the Spanish border, must have been arrested, as he never saw or heard from any of them again.

He didn't stay in the United Kingdom for long. He had several meetings with the Dutch arm of the SOE, explained the RVV's plans and took briefings. Once the business had been concluded he was parachuted back into the Netherlands at Wieringermeer with four other Dutch agents. The plan was to continue the work de Graaf had originated. Here he often worked with Henri and other escape lines. Unfortunately, like so many other agents who were parachuted back into the Netherlands to continue the fight, Celosse was betrayed, arrested, detained and executed at Vught on 5 September, a notorious day known as '*Dolle Dinsdag*' (Crazy Tuesday).

De Graaf had better luck. His first priority on arriving in London was to warn the SOE-N that all their Dutch radio contacts were under the control of the German counter-espionage unit led by Hermann Giskes. He was interrogated, as were all arrivals from the Netherlands, and it was established that his story was unfortunately absolutely true. He became a leading Resistance figure in London, was appointed second-in-command of the SOE-N and at one point its acting head. His English assistant was the attractive Dodie (Door) Sherton.

He remained in the United Kingdom for the duration of the war, as it was considered too unsafe for him to return to the Netherlands. Many reports of Dutch escapees being interrogated in London were signed off by Kas de Graaf, who conducted the interviews. By the end of the war there was a large contingent of Dutch escapees living in London, where the Dutch royal family and the Government-in-Exile was closely involved in looking after their well-being and accommodation. To be invited to tea with Queen Wilhelmina was a much sought-after special treat.

De Graaf returned to the Netherlands after the war and Door followed him. They were married in 1946 and had four children. However, their marriage failed in 1960. Not much information is available on Kas de Graaf after their divorce. Door de Graaf, however, became a prominent figure in Dutch mental health care. She founded the *Clientenbond* and spent the last twenty-five years of her working life teaching at the *Relatiestudio* Psychotherapy Institute in Ghent, Belgium. She died in 2011, leaving children, grandchildren and great-grandchildren.

The Dutch Resistance was not a male-only organization. There were many women who played active roles. Henri's girlfriend Carry Libourel went on dangerous missions with him and had airmen stay in her Delft apartment. Another woman who played a long and successful role, and who had an astonishing escape, was Elsje (Elsie) Boon – after her marriage, Elsje van Loon.

Elsje came from a politically active family and in the early days of the war, while still a student at the University of Leiden, helped many Jews find shelter. She did not stop there, however, and continued to work, helping people escape over a period of at least two years. She set up three escape routes – one being the route at the border town of Baarle-Nassau used by Jack Bottenheim. The escapes of a large number of people have been attributed to her assistance.

Everything had been going well when, like so many others, she had the misfortune to meet up with Christiaan Lindemans, who had all the apparent credentials of a leading Resistance fighter. Like so many others he betrayed, she had no idea that by this time he had turned double agent. The sad reality is that nobody knew this until the end of the German occupation. Lindemans played his cards most carefully. Once they had established contact and had met on a couple of occasions, during which time Christiaan obtained her trust, she arranged a further meeting with him. The purpose was to introduce him to a Dutch radar officer, Isbrücker, who was on the run having escaped from a PoW camp and desperately needed assistance.

Fully prepared and accompanied by Isbrücker, she went to the meeting full of confidence. After waiting a while she became concerned when Lindemans did not show up. After all, he knew how important this escape was and how much was at stake. Thinking that maybe she had the incorrect address, she decided to go to another little café nearby to try and find him. As she walked along the street she was suddenly arrested by no less a person than the head of the Secret Military Police. When she got into the police van, she discovered that they had also arrested Isbrücker. Lindemans was nowhere to be seen. Elsje was an important catch and they interrogated her the whole day. There were three officials in the room, one playing with his revolver in an intimidating manner. Following her arrest, she was confined for a month at St Gilles Prison in Brussels, before being transferred to Vught prison camp.

The train that was taking her to Vught had guards armed with machine guns in every carriage. Anyone who wanted to go to the toilet had to seek permission, and the guard would stand watch outside the door. As the train slowed down, she pleaded with the guard that she needed to use the toilet because she was suffering from diarrhoea. He allowed her to enter the compartment while pointing his gun at the middle of her chest, then stood outside the door. Elsje, who fortunately had a slight figure, immediately climbed on to the toilet seat and managed to squeeze through the window while the train was still moving slowly. She landed on the stony ground below without suffering serious injury and fled the scene as fast as she could, before the guard had noticed that his bird had flown.

When the train was safely in the distance she cautiously approached a house and knocked on the door. Hopefully, the person who answered would not be one of the many German sympathizers around and be suspicious of this stranger in need. Nobody answered, and she spent the rest of the night hiding, cold and uncomfortable, in a garden she later discovered belonged to a man from the *Grüne Polizei*. That had been a narrow escape! The next day she wandered around the countryside, keeping her eye out for German patrols and seeking a friendly person, until finally, through the kindness of somebody she met, she was able to find safe, temporary shelter.

The fact that Elsje had such a narrow escape concerned the Resistance. She had been such a prominent person in the movement that the Resistance decided that she had to be protected and spend the rest of the war in hiding. After the war she married, became well-known as Elsje van Loon and rose to a prominent position. She qualified as an attorney, was elected to the Leiden city council and became chairman of the board of Madurodam, the famous miniature city tourist attraction.

It is worth noting that many women in the Dutch Resistance, such as Elsje van Loon, Door de Graaf and Caroline Libourel, achieved prominent positions in the Netherlands after the war. It is a testament to their strength of character, resilience and intelligence.

STORIES OF ENEMIES AND TRAITORS

Chapter 11

The Gestapo, SiPo, SD and Waffen-SS

In order to understand more fully the bravery and brilliance of the people in the Dutch Resistance, and to appreciate how extraordinary a feat it was to have survived so long doing such dangerous work, we need to examine the mighty power that Henri and his associates were up against.

The German military machine was frankly awesome; a big and efficient organization with vast manpower. It had various sections: the Waffen-SS (*SchutzStaffel*), which in turn controlled the SD and the Gestapo, was under an organization called RSHA (Reich Main Security Office). These were the organizations the Resistance had to fight and outwit. It was a colossal task and not for the faint-hearted.

The Waffen-SS was created as the armed wing of the Nazi Party. Originally a purely German Aryan force, it gradually developed into a multi-ethnic and multi-military force. It served alongside the regular army but was never part of it. Volunteers came from all parts of occupied Europe. The Dutch and Flemish volunteers formed the SS Regiment Westland. In turn, this joined the Danish and Norwegian regiment and became the SS Division Wiking. Towards the end of the war, it consisted of thirty-eight divisions, with around one million men.

At the Nuremberg trials the Waffen-SS was condemned as a criminal organization, due to its participation in war crimes. Its officers and men did not receive the same lenient considerations after the war as did the men serving in the regular German army; the latter were professional German soldiers, not volunteers from the occupied territories.

The origins of the Waffen-SS lay in a grand plan by leading Nazis Heinrich Himmler and Reinhard Heydrich to bring all of the police and security apparatus into one structure. This would be under Himmler's ultimate control, while Heydrich would be the Operating Director. There was an Interior Minister, Wilhelm Frick, to whom Himmler should have reported, but he did not. Himmler only answered to Hitler and was a man with enormous power because of this connection. The SS was mainly under the leadership of Austrians, only too keen to prove that they were good and loyal Nazis.

The SD (*Sicherheitsdienst*), also referred to as the SiPo (Security Police), was another security branch. It was a state controlled political and criminal investigation agency made up of the combined forces of the Gestapo (Secret State

Police) and the Kripo (Criminal Police). Formed in 1936, it was an agency of the Waffen-SS.

The Gestapo was originally the Prussian police force, of which Herman Göring took charge in 1933. On 20 April 1934 it fell under Himmler's control and became the official secret police of Nazi Germany and occupied Europe. At its height it consisted of only 46,000 men. These were mostly professional policemen and investigative officers. They considered themselves the elite, and looked down on the Waffen-SS as mere amateurs.

The Gestapo had the authority to investigate cases of treason, espionage, sabotage and criminal actions against the Nazi party and Germany. The basic Gestapo law passed in 1936 gave it carte blanche to operate without judicial review – effectively putting it above the law. Throughout the war, SS Gruppenführer Heinrich Müller was the organization's chief.

The story of Henri Scharrer and the Resistance is filled with references to arrests by the SS or Gestapo. These followed a predictable pattern. They usually started with a denunciation by a member of the public to the SS authorities. This could arrive in the post, or be through a telephone call or personal visit. The arrests that originated in surveillance operations, tip-offs from 'official' informers or from information sent by local Nazi block leaders were actually less frequent than those resulting from these often anonymous tip-offs.

It was Gestapo policy to investigate every denunciation by members of the public, no matter how small. A great deal of time was wasted on accusations brought by people with personal agendas and grudges who wished to land enemies or ex-lovers/spouses in trouble. While this type of allegation was an irritating time-waster, all were examined by the head of the local department and key personnel. It was then decided who would be the best man for the job. The officer chosen would gather information, arrest the individual and conduct interrogations. The accused would be issued with a Temporary Arrest Order, or at least ought to have been have been. Correct procedures were not always followed.

Every arrested person who entered a Gestapo office was fingerprinted and photographed. Their file would contain statements made by the accused and by witnesses. Final decisions were then taken by the heads of departments, heads of regional Gestapo offices, state prosecutors, and more rarely, by the Berlin HQ, when it was a matter of particular importance. So although Gestapo officers could by law wield arbitrary powers, there was a defined bureaucratic framework within which they were supposed to act.

Torture was used by certain Gestapo officers to extract confessions during interrogation, although beyond prescribed punishments it was never officially sanctioned. The extent of torture is extremely difficult to estimate, but it was more common in the occupied countries such as the Netherlands than in Germany, although after the war nearly all Gestapo officers denied using it.

The most common officially sanctioned punishment was beating with a bamboo cane – up to 25 strokes to the buttocks administered by Gestapo officers, with a doctor present. Other 'unofficial' practices included water torture. This involved plunging a person into a bath full of cold water until he or she almost drowned. The testicles of male prisoners were often crushed with a device similar to a garlic press. Electric currents were wired to hands, and to the anus and penis of male prisoners. Exhaustion exercises and sleep deprivation were also commonly reported by survivors of these methods. Many prisoners were hanged by their hands for varying periods of time, until they confessed. Fingers were sometimes burned with matches. And we know from Tom Yardin Millord's experience that sometimes the soles of feet were beaten and beard hairs plucked out. We know that Henri was in need of medical treatment after his interrogation.

The more extreme measures were reserved for key political prisoners and Resistance members in occupied territories; each time a confession or information was not forthcoming, the torture would be escalated.

The policemen in Kripo (the Criminal Police Force) did not approve of this brutal treatment. They prided themselves on their working methods, which were based on forensic, scientific techniques and physical evidence to prove the guilt of an accused person. Those who gave evidence after the war felt that the Gestapo method of focusing on harsh interrogation was not designed to find the truth but only to settle cases with speed.

Not all Gestapo officers were brutal Nazi fanatics; indeed, the majority could be described as career policemen with right-wing leanings. Many were university educated, and many came to a sticky end. Unfortunately for the Dutch Resistance people who were arrested, the Gestapo and Waffen-SS offices at Weteringschans and Euterpestraat in Amsterdam contained quite a number of the more brutal officers. Let's take a closer look at these men.

After Hitler had approved Anton Mussert as 'Leader of the Netherlands' in December 1942, he was allowed to form a national body called *Gemachtigden van den Leider* (Agents of the Leader), which would act as a Dutch shadow cabinet. This would advise Reichskommissar Arthur Seyss-Inquart from the beginning of February. The body would consist of a number of deputies in charge of defined functions or departments under the administration. Three days later, the appointment of retired general and *Rijkscommissaris* (State Commissioner) Hendrik Seyffardt as 'Deputy for Special Services' was announced in the press. Seyffardt was already head of the Dutch SS volunteer group *Vrijwilligers Legioen Nederland*.

Because of these appointments, the Communist resistance group CS.6, under Dr Gerrit Kastein, concluded that this new Nazi institution would eventually lead to a National Socialist government, which would then introduce general conscription to enable the call-up of all Dutch nationals to the Eastern Front. That alarming possibility had to be avoided at all costs.

In reality, however, the Nazis merely saw Mussert and the NSB (Dutch Nazi party) as useful tools to further general co-operation. But the CS.6 took this development seriously, and after approval from the Dutch Government-in-Exile decided Seyffardt would be the first person within the new institution eligible for assassination. They would have preferred Mussert, but that was considered too dangerous as he was heavily guarded.

Within a couple of days, on 4 February 1943, the CS.6 plan was made. Student Jan Verleun, accompanied by Dr Kastein, was driven to Seyffardt's home in Scheveningen, where he knocked on the door. Verleun was in luck. Seyffardt himself opened the door and Verleun shot him twice, before rushing back to the vehicle and escaping. Seyffardt died a day later. It took the Germans many months to track Jan Verleun down, but with their usual thoroughness, find him they eventually did.

When German officials were assassinated there were always heavy reprisals, so the targets selected had to be considered highly dangerous to the Resistance movement and worth the cost in human lives. Not everybody agreed with this strategy. There were some Resistance fighters who believed that no assassination was worth the drastic reprisals involved.

General Hanns Albin Rauter, the highest ranking SS officer in the occupied Netherlands, initially worked out what he believed to be a 'fair' reprisal system: for every single Nazi killed, he would execute ten Dutch citizens. For every Dutch collaborator killed, he would execute three Dutch citizens. However, as the war intensified, he began increasing the numbers of people executed in reprisals, and these multiplied into the hundreds.

A notorious war crime occurred on 1/2 October 1944 in the village of Putten. A vehicle carrying personnel of the Wehrmacht – two officers and two corporals – was ambushed near the Oldenaller bridge by the Resistance. In the attack Dutch Resistance fighter Frans Slotboom was wounded and later died. One German officer, Lieutenant Otto Sommer, was also wounded and died the following day. The two corporals fled the scene, but the second officer, Oberleutnant Eggart, was injured and captured. Because of his wounds, the Dutch abandoned him in a place where the Germans would be able to find him, and he survived.

The next day, a large contingent of German military entered the village, where a brief firefight ensued in which a number of villagers were killed. The military separated the men from the women and children and took over six hundred men prisoner, practically every adult male in the village. They were sent to various concentration camps, but a few of the men were able to make their escape during the trip. During their imprisonment, due to mistreatment, malnutrition and other causes, a total of 552 men and one woman of the Putten prisoners died. Only 48 men survived the war, and a number were left crippled as they had been kept in small cages for long periods during their imprisonment.

Every 2 October, a memorial service is held in Putten at a monument known as the Lady of Putten which is attended by various leading members of the community and Dutch society. It is still a sad and melancholy day, reflecting not only grief and loss, but also the evil that so-called civilized men can inflict on each other.

The assassination of another senior official, H. Reydon, the Attorney of National Relations, and his wife took place on 7 February. His wife was killed on the spot and Reydon died later. Following this attack, Operation Silbertanne was ordered by General Rauter: 50 Dutch hostages were randomly rounded up at universities and executed in retaliation.

The gun used in the Reydon attack had been given to Gerrit Kastein by SD agent Van der Waals – a double agent, in fact. Kastein was tracked down and arrested on 19 February. Two days later he committed suicide by jumping out of a window while tied to a chair, so as not to give away information under torture.

Not long afterwards, on 6 March, there was an accidental attack on General Hanns Albin Rauter's car. Rauter had been responsible for deporting 300,000 Dutchmen to Germany as forced labour, and had sent over 100,000 Jews to Nazi concentration camps, so he was naturally a prime target. The CS.6 resistance members involved, dressed in German uniforms, had wanted to hi-jack a truck to go to a farm where cattle had been slaughtered for the Germans. By mistake they hit Rauter's vehicle instead.

While the others in the vehicle were killed, Rauter was seriously injured, feigned death, survived and was picked up later by a German military vehicle. He spent many months in hospital, where he stayed until his arrest by British Military Police after the end of hostilities. As a result of this attack, in a German reprisal 117 political prisoners were executed, plus 50 in Kamp Amersfoort and another 40 each in the Hague and Rotterdam.

Rauter was put on trial and pleaded not guilty to war crimes. He was found guilty by the court and executed on 24 March 1949 by firing squad near Scheveningen. His burial place remains a state secret to this day.

It was sheer bad luck that Henri Scharrer, Tom Yardin Millord and Fritz Conijn should have landed up in the hands of these ruthless men.

Chapter 12

Christiaan Lindemans ('King Kong'), His Early Resistance Work

While the greatest enemy was always the powerful German military machine, we know that Henri had a constant fear of people who turned traitor or were secret German collaborators. No story of our heroes would be complete without examining their many fellow Dutch citizens who were pro-German and who worked against the Resistance, betraying them to their enemies whenever they could. Here we find that while there are numerous reports of such activity, many are still classified, and those released are often heavily edited. This is not easy or clear territory to explore.

Fortunately, there is one man about whom there is a great deal of information, because he was particularly notorious, and his name keeps re-appearing in the background to the Henri Scharrer operation. This was Christiaan Lindemans. The relationship between Lindemans and Scharrer is opaque. What we do know is that one of Henri's closest associates, and a close friend of Henri's mistress Carry Libourel, was Jan Lowey-Ball, who in turn was closely associated with Lindemans.

Lindemans' name appears in many reports and is associated with many people. He worked with the 'Gotha' (aka 'Georges' Wyssogota-Lorraine) Line that was destroyed at the beginning of 1944. The false papers he provided to escapees who approached him purported to come from Todt, the German construction and engineering company. As we saw from his report, Jack Bottenheim was given the choice of Lindemans' Todt or Henri Scharrer's SD papers, and Lindemans was his first choice, until he disappeared.

Lindemans had a number of names. He was also known as 'Brand' or 'Freddi Desmet', an officer in the Belgian army and SOE agent, with security clearance at the Dutch Military Intelligence Division of the SOE. In some circles he was referred to as *Le Tueur* (the Killer) as he undertook missions to kill and was ready to shoot at the slightest provocation. There is speculation that Lindemans may have been a member of Colonel Claude Dansey's Z organization. Dansey was the ACSS (Assistant Chief of the Secret Intelligence Service – more commonly known as MI6). Lindemans, however, was best known as 'King Kong' because of his impressive size, and close comrades called him 'Krist'.

In the early days of the occupation of the Low Countries there is no doubt that Lindemans worked bravely for the Allied cause; he is believed to have been personally responsible for the killing of 27 Germans during guerrilla fighting in the outskirts of Antwerp. It was said that he was a natural risk-taker who did not know the meaning of fear. Unfortunately, neither did he know the meaning of loyalty.

In the SOE diagram illustrating the hierarchy of the Executive, Lindemans' name is listed immediately below that of Henri Scharrer. Lindemans was also the person, a couple of reports maintain, who was responsible for Henri's betrayal, but there is no direct evidence of this. Furthermore, after his arrest he was requested by the Allies to supply them with a list of the names of Resistance members he had betrayed, and Henri Scharrer's name does not appear on this list. It is possible that Lindemans might have wanted to distance himself from the Henri Scharrer case, just as he tried to distance himself from the Battle of Arnhem disaster, denying that he had anything to do with it. But of course we know, from the most reliable German sources, that with the latter he did. Some betrayals might have been too hot for even Lindemans to claim credit.

He was born in October 1912 in Rotterdam. In 1941 he married Gilberte Yvonne Letuppe, and they had two children. (Some reports state she was his common-law wife.) Before the outbreak of the war, he worked alongside his brother Jan as a mechanic at his father's garage in Rotterdam. In the summer of 1936 he was injured in a motorcycle accident, sustaining a cracked skull and injuries to his left arm and leg which left him with a deformed hand and walking with a lumbering gait. He spoke French and German well and some English.

According to his own story, he started to work as an informant for the British secret service in the spring of 1940, relaying shipping movements to London. In 1940 the garage where he worked was destroyed in the bombing of Rotterdam. By August he had found work as a lorry driver on the Lille to Paris road, carrying petrol for the Luftwaffe. He became involved in the Resistance the next year. By September 1942 he had established his own escape route in Abbeville, where he was arrested two months later and imprisoned by the Germans for five months. This gave him a certain credibility in Resistance circles.

By 1943 his popularity as one of the leaders of the Dutch Resistance was at its height. He had begun collecting jewels and other valuables from rich women to provide funds for the underground escape routes through occupied Belgium and the Netherlands into Spain and Portugal.

It was around this time that he first met Resistance member Jan Lowey-Ball at the latter's home, 8 Wijnhaven in Delft, the town where Carry Libourel also lived. Following this introduction, he and Lowey-Ball developed a close association, working together in assisting many escapees.

Lindemans served as a contact with Resistance movements, some with Communist tendencies, such as the RVV, which was engaged in both communications sabotage and the protection of *onderduikers*. He is believed to have been a member of the CS.6 group of Amsterdam, the clandestine sabotage and intelligence organization. The CS.6 had connections with the Witte Brigade, a resistance group in Belgium. One of the links with this group was a man by the name of Aart Entvald.

Lindemans worked with Henri's printer, de Geuzen, on *Het Parool* and did some work on the Dutch-Paris escape line run by John Henri Weidner in Paris, but was not a member of Dutch-Paris. In addition, he was a member of one of the twelve recognized units of the Belgian underground called *Les Affranchis* (The Liberated), founded by Camille Tromme, allowing him to remain in possession of a machine gun and a revolver.

He was a member of groups in Rotterdam, Brussels and Paris. In the early days of the war Lindemans did his most patriotic work with people connected to Victor Swane, Albert Starink, Jan Strengers and Baron Abraham van Boetzelaer in Paris, and with the amazing Matilda (M. A. E.) Verspyck and others in Brussels. All these people were connected to Henri in some way or other, as we see in reports from some of the people he helped save. So Lindemans' Resistance connections were impressively extensive.

In later Allied military investigations there were suspicions that the Scharrer escape route was operated for financial gain by Lindemans together with his associate, Jan Lowey-Ball. The reason for this was that escapees had to pay Henri certain sums of money in Dutch guilders, which Jan Lowey-Ball later reimbursed in Paris with French francs. It was alleged that on occasion, when Lindemans was involved, the money disappeared between the two. We do know, however, that Henri and Jan worked out any difficulties relating to the funds collected for the escapees. So there are only suspicions that it was Lindemans who might have been making off with money. He later claimed to have always been short of funds, and it would have been easy for him to have intercepted some of the money transfers to help fund his flashy lifestyle.

So it was that right up to the beginning of 1944 Lindemans was one of the noted heroes of the Dutch Resistance and completely trusted by all who worked with him. He worked and travelled with the same people who assisted Henri's line, helping escort groups of evaders to safety.

But things were about to change. As a result of one key meeting, Christiaan Lindemans overnight became one of the most dangerous of men to the Resistance cause.

Chapter 13

Christiaan Lindemans the Double Agent, and Other Pro-German Sympathizers

The number of German collaborators in the Netherlands was astonishingly high. There was actually a group called Henneicke Column, the members of which, for a price, sought out Jewish people in hiding and handed them over to the German authorities. Between 8,000 and 9,000 Jews were caught in this manner, indicating how successful and active the group was.

It is recorded that around 55,000 Dutchmen joined the Waffen-SS and worked for the German authorities. Of the Dutch police force, it was estimated that around 20 per cent were Fascist and 50 per cent afraid of assisting the Resistance movement in case they landed in serious trouble. Thus only around 30 per cent could be relied upon to help. Thousands of Dutch government employees continued in their posts, having attested to their Aryan status and ethnic ancestry by filling in the required forms, and now worked for new German superiors. The great majority of these civil servants were pro-German, especially those who worked in the transport system that transferred Jewish people to the extermination camps. In fact, there were so many that right across the Netherlands people avoided expressing pro- or anti-German views in the office, or anywhere else, as it was too dangerous a subject. Anyone who was known to have anti-German views could be denounced by a colleague or so-called friend and arrested for questioning.

How did Lindemans become a double agent?

It happened as a result of a number of potentially disastrous events, which put him under severe emotional stress. In February 1944, his younger brother Henk was arrested in Rotterdam by the SD and held captive in the Hague, awaiting execution for helping English people escape from the Netherlands. Then on 24 February his wife Gilberte (Gilou), a cabaret singer, who was three months pregnant, was arrested by two members of the Gestapo and four heavily armed German soldiers. Gilou had been a member of the Resistance cell headed up by Victor Swane. Victor, too, landed up being arrested, after which he was deported to Buchenwald concentration camp, where he died in October 1944.

At the time of Gilou's arrest, the Lindemans house was thoroughly searched and the SD found three ID cards, some *Kommandantur* (headquarters) signatures, a pass, some German employment documents, three revolvers and a box of ammunition. This was all highly incriminating. Gilou was taken prisoner, interrogated for eleven hours that first day, and struck with such force in the face that she fell from her chair. Still the brave woman refused to speak.

The Germans then moved her to Fresnes Prison, south of Paris, where she was manacled hand and foot with no food, no bed and only little water for four days. She was questioned violently a few times, hit in the face on each occasion and finally locked up for six months in solitary confinement.

Finally, she was released from prison and taken to a local hospice in Saint-Denis where she gave birth on 25 August 1944 to her second child – a daughter named Christianne. Only then was she released. This may well have been because of Lindemans' efforts, or possibly it was ordered by Abwehr Colonel Oscar Reile, who left Paris on 18 August. Her testimony about her treatment was later recorded by the Allied Information Service (AIS-SHAEF) and used as evidence at the Nuremberg trials of Nazi war criminals.

While all this was going on with Gilou and his brother, Lindemans was in a most anxious state. He had to do something urgently to save both of them. After a great deal of effort he raised 10,000 guilders to pay an intermediary agent for help in freeing his brother and wife. Through this agent he was able to make contact with the Abwehr and advise them that he had an important offer to make. It was agreed that he would meet 'Dr Gerard', sometimes called 'Dr German' (both pseudonyms for Major Hermann Giskes of Operation *Englandspiel*).

As a consequence of *Englandspiel*, the German penetration of the Dutch resistance was so complete that it sometimes seems Allied escapers from Holland were under German control. It would appear that many were actually assisted by the Germans in some way or other, with German officers occasionally turning a blind eye. There was also a strategy, to which Giskes later referred, of letting the small fish go in order to catch the big one later on. Besides, he was more interested in obtaining information on the Allied plans for the invasion which Germany knew would be happening soon.

The war was beginning to go badly for the Germans, and there was much intelligence buzzing in the background when the fateful meeting took place between Lindemans and Giskes. We actually know in detail what took place, as Giskes in his memoir, *London Calling North Pole*, described it in fascinating detail:

'May I ask you to explain what brings you here?' I started the conversation. 'I have heard it said that you have contacts with the Allied Secret Services, and I shall be grateful if you will tell me in brief terms who you are, what you want from us, and what you have to offer.'

CL replied in fluent German.

'If I am not mistaken,' he began, 'I am speaking to the head of the German counter-espionage. I wish to address my proposal to him alone, as I do not expect to get satisfaction from anyone else. My personal particulars as given yesterday to Herr Walter [Wurr] are genuine. I am Christiaan Lindemans of Rotterdam, and I have worked for the English Secret Service since the spring of 1940. For the last six months I have brought my youngest brother to assist in getting English airmen out of the country. He has been discovered, arrested by the SiPo, and is now under sentence of death pronounced by a German military court. I feel myself responsible for my brother's fate, since it was I who introduced him to this work. If you can arrange to have my brother freed, I am ready to hand over the whole of my knowledge of the Allied Secret Services . . .

. . . The men through whom we carried the Resistance during the first years of the Occupation have nearly all gone – dead, arrested or just disappeared. Of the remainder, there are only a few I can trust. Leave them in peace! I will guarantee that in due course you will learn a great deal about the plans of the Underground and of London. Hand me over my brother and then make use of me as seems best to you. King Kong, as they call me, is friend or foe.'

The above is only part of what took place at the meeting, since they also discussed Lindemans' wife. However, it does confirm that at this meeting, which took place early April 1944, Lindemans agreed to become a German double agent, on condition that his brother and wife were released. Henk was, indeed, released in due course, and Gilou later in August 1944, after the birth of her daughter.

From this time on, Lindemans worked for *Englandspiel* with the same passion and enthusiasm he had previously devoted to the Resistance movement. He apparently found this no problem at all. He was instructed to renew his contacts with Resistance agents and transmit back to Major Giskes information about Allied plans, especially invasion plans, and about the Resistance movements across occupied Netherlands, France and Belgium.

In return for this information he received large sums of money. His early denunciations resulted in a string of arrests, for which he was handsomely paid by Willy Kupp on behalf of the German intelligence service. Lindemans refers to being paid, among other amounts, 30,000 francs and 10,000 francs. On one occasion he was so flush with money that he took a girlfriend, Mia, out to the Royal nightclub, where he spent 4,000 francs in a single evening.

Working with him was Richard Christmann, also a most effective Abwehr agent. Christmann, together with Cornelius Verloop (aliases 'Nellis' and 'Bakker'), another Abwehr agent, accompanied Lindemans on his first important mission for the Germans. It was a tour of the Brussels-Paris escape line helpers. As a direct consequence of this tour, all helpers of this line were betrayed and arrested, and many later died. In a strange twist of irony, both these Abwehr agents (Christmann and Verloop) were themselves employed by the Allies after the war. Cornelius Verloop's main claim to fame is that he betrayed the infamous spy, Harold Cole, and eventually his own associate, Christiaan Lindemans, to the Allies.

Now Harold Cole was no small fry. This British sergeant has been described as one of the worst traitors of the Second World War. He double-crossed the British, French and Americans, betrayed many Resistance fighters and wore his Gestapo uniform until his arrest. He was imprisoned but escaped, and an extensive manhunt tracked him down hiding on the fourth floor of a bar in Rue de Grenelle, Paris. Here he was conveniently shot by the French police for resisting arrest.

One of the escape lines that Lindemans successfully penetrated was the Scharrer Amsterdam-Spain line, and all this information he handed over to Giskes, who in turn briefed his operatives in *Englandspiel*. This caused a domino effect, and several escape lines were hit, resulting in the arrest of no fewer than 267 Dutch and Belgian resistance fighters.

Around the end of April 1944, shortly after his meeting with Giskes, Lindemans happened to be in an office in Rotterdam where a pro-German woman employee thought he was a suspicious person and called the police. On their arrival, Lindemans was asked to produce his papers, and when he put his hand in his pocket, he was shot by a policeman who thought he was about to pull out a firearm. He was taken to hospital, and when the police arrived they were dismayed to find a document on Lindemans that proved that he was actually in the employ of the Abwehr.

Two attempts were made to get Lindemans out of hospital. The first was a failed attempt by his brother Jan and friends Bob and Roelof. This was immediately reported to Giskes, who was concerned that Lindemans' cover would be blown, and he instructed the German officials immediately to remove Lindemans. They did this in such a manner as to make it appear that he was being rescued by his friends in the Resistance. Giskes, though, knew that no more chances could be taken, as the real Resistance would soon find out that whoever had rescued Lindemans, it was definitely not one of them. So as a precaution he ordered that Lindemans be moved to Belgium, with instructions that he could no longer operate from the Netherlands.

Lindemans' task was now to be focused on obtaining intelligence on the Allied invasion, which the Germans knew was imminent. Lindemans, however, did not turn up any really useful information for Giskes. What information he received pointed to an Allied landing at Pas de Calais, a cunning British intelligence deception which Lindemans and the Germans fell for hook, line and sinker. It had the codename Operation Bodyguard and it was conceived to mislead the Germans as to the date and location of the main landings. Supporting the deception were numerous fake radio broadcasts and dummy military equipment. The Allies went to elaborate lengths to lay a false trial of evidence about the proposed landings, and in this they were remarkably successful.

Finally, it was on 6 June 1944 on the Normandy coast that the D-Day landings took place, under the Commander of Supreme Headquarters Allied Expeditionary Forces, General Dwight D. Eisenhower, with General Bernard Montgomery as Commander of the 21st Army Group.

Codenamed Operation Neptune, this was the largest seaborne invasion in history, conducted by 24,000 United States, British and Canadian troops. The operation was conducted over 50 miles of shoreline divided into five sectors: Utah, Omaha, Gold, Juno and Sword Beaches. The amphibious landings were preceded by an extensive naval and airborne assault on the German entrenchments in and behind the sand dunes.

The Germans and the slippery Lindemans, in spite of all his hard work and investigations, had no idea that the landings would be in Normandy, and they were caught off guard. Furthermore, British Intelligence at Bletchley Park, with their code machine, Colossus, had broken many of the German intelligence codes and knew a great deal more about the German troop movements than the Germans knew about the Allied invasion plans.

Outwitted by counter-intelligence, and totally believing his own intelligence sources confirming that nothing untoward would be happening soon, the commander of the German army in the region, Field Marshal Erwin Rommel, was actually in Germany. When the invasion started he was celebrating his wife's birthday. Needless to say, the party broke up, and he immediately summoned his vehicles, got back on the road and rushed to the front, as news of the invasion and its size filtered through.

It was not all plain sailing for the Allies, however. The beaches were strongly defended and the invaders faced heavy fire from gun emplacements on the shoreline, which was also protected by mines and other obstacles. It was only after a few days of heavy fighting that Rommel's additional troops that had been rushed to the area were slowly pushed back.

The Allies now had a foothold in Europe, and the forward advance into France commenced. This was the beginning of the end. From this time on, everything changed and German counter-intelligence stepped up its work. The pressure was on for the German army to hold their ground at all costs and protect the Fatherland.

Despite not cracking the intelligence on the Normandy landings, Giskes did appreciate Lindemans' skills and knew that he could still play a vital role in counter-intelligence. For a start, no one suspected him. He was highly regarded by the Allies and the Resistance, for whom he had proved himself by performing sterling work. So skilful was he as a counter-espionage agent that by September 1944 he had actually succeeded in becoming a member of Prince Bernhard's staff, as liaison officer between the Dutch Resistance and a British Intelligence unit commanded by a Canadian officer. Hoodwinking them all was an extraordinary feat on its own.

Lindemans' enormous value to the Germans as a counter-intelligence operative was to be demonstrated only a few months later, and in a devastating manner.

He is blamed in several reports for betraying the plans of Operation Market Garden to the enemy, and as a result contributing to the Allies' defeat at the Battle of Arnhem in the middle of September 1944. This loss probably prolonged the war by six months, and added considerably to the number of casualties. The other serious consequence was that it allowed the Red Army to enter Berlin ahead of the US and British forces. Evidence of Lindemans' involvement in betraying the Allied plans to the Germans is clear and well established from German sources, and is particularly well documented by his German boss, Hermann Giskes.

There is a record of two written reports Lindemans submitted to Giskes' office prior to the Battle of Arnhem, on the Allied plans to take the Rhine area.

One report dated 22 August 1944 was incomplete but in sufficient detail to allow the German High Command to pinpoint some of the enemy targets and the likely bridges at Grave, Nijmegen and Arnhem. With this intelligence, Field Marshal Walter Model, as a precaution, ordered the 9th SS Panzer Division Hohenstaufen and the 10th SS Panzer Division Frundsberg to the neighbourhood of Arnhem for refitting and upgrading.

Lindemans' second report, dated 15 September (two days prior the start of the battle), was written as two summaries – one contained general information and the other concerned prospective aerial landings. These he handed to Giskes, who immediately sent them to his Berlin HQ. As Giskes later reported in his book, *London Calling North Pole*, between Lindemans' reports and all the British air reconnaissance taking place in the Arnhem area, his superiors had more than a 'hint' of the attack that was about to take place.

According to the official history, *British Intelligence in the Second World War*, Volume 4:

> He [Lindemans] was asked by Giskes to stay behind in Belgium to try and penetrate the British Intelligence. He quickly obtained an introduction through the Amee Blanche to a unit in Antwerp working for IS 9. Probably about 12th September he was despatched on a mission to pass through the lines to Eindhoven and inform chiefs of the resistance there

that they were to stay quiet. Such Allied pilots as they had in their care were not to move as the Allied armies would liberate the territory shortly.

A high ranking Dutch intelligence official by the name of Oreste Pinto wrote a book about Operation Market Garden in which he claimed that Christiaan Lindemans was the man who betrayed the operation. In addition to this, a colleague of Giskes by the name of Hunteman stated in a report to the Allies in February 1945 that Giskes had told him personally that Lindemans had actually blown the Arnhem operation. Giskes last saw Lindemans at a meeting on 2 September 1944.

The Battle of Arnhem took place from 17 to 26 September 1944. Lindemans' dates were spot on. It was the largest airborne battle in history, with 35,000 troops taking part. It involved not only thousands of troops, but also gliders and aircraft with supplies and armoured vehicles landing them north of the Rhine, Waal and Maas rivers. Here they would have to hold out while a major force was marched up from the south. The main strategic idea was that when the two forces joined, Germany's hold on the Netherlands would be cut, and the Allies would then be able to move into Germany faster than otherwise anticipated.

Warning messages sent by the Dutch to England about the German panzer movements in the wooded region were ignored, most likely because of previous false radio messages.

So the Germans were prepared. As the operation commenced, the Allied para-troopers and their supporting ground troops were attacked and the planes towing gliders stacked with equipment were blown out of the sky. The bridge over the Rhine at Arnhem proved to be the final obstacle the Allies could not overcome, as was brilliantly demonstrated in the movie *A Bridge Too Far*.

The city of Arnhem was bombarded and evacuated. Hundreds of thousands of people were forced out on to the roads. They were taken into schools in many towns and villages, where they were housed in school halls on floors covered in straw. Many people took the refugees into their homes. The Red Cross provided help with blankets and food. Cat owners were afraid of letting their pets out of the house, for fear that hungry people would cut off their heads, skin them and sell them as 'roof rabbits'. Women travelled the countryside selling their silver, linen and other valuables, just to buy a bag of grain or barley to feed their children.

The Arnhem disaster was also responsible for delaying the liberation of the northern and eastern part of Netherlands by six months. Large numbers of people in these territories suffered in the resulting *Honger* (hunger) *Winter*, and many died of starvation, as food and fuel supplies were all now being shipped to Germany.

Arnhem was the only major defeat the Allies suffered in the North-west European campaign, and it demonstrates the terrible consequences and severity of Lindemans' betrayal. The success Lindemans achieved in obtaining information on Operation Market Garden shows the extent of his skill at espionage work, as well as his new dedication to the German cause, for which he was well paid. Another indication of his bold and brazen attitude is that he succeeded in reaching the British base in their sector of the Normandy beachhead area. Lindemans paid them a visit, soon won their trust and was recruited by IS9 (Intelligence School 9 aka 'Nine Eyes'). After all, Lindemans was a great Resistance hero.

Time was running out for him, however. This was his last mission. While crossing the lines, Lindemans was, ironically, arrested by the Germans. He revealed to his captors that he worked for the Abwehr and he was sent to Driebergen, where he was questioned by the commander of the Abwehr unit there, Major Kiesewetter, who checked on his counter-intelligence credentials. Afterwards he was taken to Eindhoven, where he stayed until the area was liberated a short while later.

Lindemans was then arrested by the Allies, who had been tipped off by an unknown person, was placed in custody and interrogated, but appears to have convinced the Allies of his loyalty. In October 1944 he was again denounced as a German spy by his own fellow Abwehr agent, Cornelius Johannes Antonius Verloop, who informed the Allies that Lindemans had betrayed Operation Market Garden to Intelligence Officer Kiesewetter a month before at the Abwehr station in Driebergen.

Records and reports appear to indicate that Cornelius Verloop can be best described as a triple-agent, but with clear leanings to the side of the Allies. His claim to fame is not only that he betrayed Lindemans to the Allies, but also that he betrayed the infamous British spy, Harold Cole and one of Cole's French mistresses, Madelaine Deram, to the Allies in the early days of the war.

On the other hand, Verloop is the same man who, together with his friend Richard Christmann, had accompanied Lindemans on his tour of the Brussels-Paris escape line helpers. These three were directly responsible for the betrayal and arrest of the Brussels-Paris members, many of whom later died. This might possibly be the same Verloop referred to by the interrogator in Caroline Libourel's statement – a man who assisted Henri while at the same time betraying him and passing information on to the Germans. He should not be confused with a David Verloop in the Scharrer escape line who was arrested and committed suicide before the Germans could interrogate him.

There is much more to the story of Cornelius Verloop. The fact that he betrayed the infamous traitor Harold Cole, Madelaine Deram and then Christiaan Lindemans, makes it clear that he was actually becoming more of a valuable agent to the Allies, because these were very big fish – two of them, Cole and Lindemans, being the biggest! His work for the Germans was far less significant and more than likely was only done to keep in their favour, as a cover.

When Verloop first started pointing the finger at Lindemans, it was seen as such a ludicrous allegation that nobody believed him. After all, Lindemans, that important Resistance leader, was safely ensconced in the prestigious entourage of Prince Bernhard of the Netherlands, in his new headquarters in Brussels. All the while, however, as we know, he was busy passing on information to our clever German counter-intelligence operator, Hermann Giskes.

The Prince, in the meantime, continued to believe that Lindemans was a Dutch Resistance hero. So despite having delivered important intelligence to the Allies, the unfortunate Verloop remained in Allied custody, because they did not believe he could be trusted. They had plenty of proof that at least in the early days of the war, he was known to have been an Abwehr agent – a *V-Mann* – which, of course, he was at that time.

Cornelius Verloop was able to make his escape, but was re-arrested a year later. As a result of extensive investigations, the allegations against him were dropped, and though he continued to be held in custody he was never charged. Finally, in recognition of the two dangerous spies he had brought in, he was cleared and released. His counter-intelligence skills were now far more appreciated, and he was once again employed in the Dutch intelligence services, where Carry Libourel, too, worked after the war. Verloop came to be regarded as a hero, lived a long and successful life and died in Germany in June 1996.

Needless to say, unbelievable as Verloop's accusations about Lindemans might at first have appeared, finally they were taken seriously. The fatal day for Lindemans was 28 October 1944, when the Allied military made an unexpected visit to Prince Bernhard's headquarters at Chateau de la Fougeraie outside Brussels.

Lindemans was taken by surprise and showed no resistance when arrested by British Security officer Alfred Sainsbury, of Special Forces Detachment. What Prince Bernhard's reaction was is not known, but it could be assumed that, just as he came to the aid of Jan Lowey-Ball, initially he would have protested that Lindemans was a brave Resistance hero.

Following an intense two-week interrogation by MI5 agents, Lindemans suffered several epileptic fits and consequently made a full and detailed confession. Once they had his confession, Colonel Stevens recommended that Lindemans' betrayal was so serious he should receive the death sentence. He was returned to Dutch custody in December, then held in Breda prison up to March 1945 in Scheveningen for over a year.

The game was up. One of the most dangerous of the pro-German spies, a man under the control of Hermann Giskes, was now revealed for what he was. He had been turned, and became a ruthless traitor to the Dutch and Allied cause.

Karst Smit was a Resistance man who worked with Lindemans for several weeks before Lindermans betrayed the members of his escape line, including

Karst himself. After the war Karst visited Lindemans in prison, while he was still awaiting trial. Lindemans now knew full well that the prosecution would be seeking the death penalty. Karst asked him point blank if he was responsible for the betrayal of Arnhem, as had been alleged. This Lindemans denied.

There follows a translation of a part of Lindemans' confession to the Allies dated 4 November 1944:

- I worked in the German Intelligence Service from June 1944 until the departure of troops from Brussels.
- Willy Kupp paid me 30,000 francs on behalf of the German Service.
- I gave information about the resistance in Belgium.
- Nelles and Willy promised to set free my wife in Paris and my brother in Holland.
- If there should be any cause, the Germans told me to ring the Wehrmacht *Befehlshaber* [commander] and ask for German [Giskes]. I rang him up to 30 times. I gave my information this way.
- I gave information about the military operations of the Resistance.

I am responsible for my actions.
(signed Christiaan Lindemans)

Lindemans knew, however, that all was lost, and he committed suicide by swallowing a fatal dose of aspirin in a psychiatric ward before his trial – although another report states that he took an overdose of sleeping pills, and a nurse (he was always the womanizer) whom he had befriended also took sleeping pills in a suicide pact. She survived.

The press report on 'The Death of the Spy Lindemans' was brief. It stated that he was suspected of betraying the Allies by giving information on the proposed landings at Arnhem. Another Allied report claimed that he died under suspicious circumstances and arsenic poisoning was suspected. This latter report appears to have been supported by a number of serious researchers who believe it to be true. So there remains the possibility that he might have been murdered.

Even in his death this colourful, larger-than-life double agent created lively interest in many quarters. There were rumours that he had escaped. These persisted until long after the war, and to put an end to this speculation, nearly twenty years later the Dutch authorities had his body exhumed. Dutch pathologist Martin Voortman positively identified the remains of Christiaan Lindemans.

There is still a lot more to his story to be revealed one day, since a number of important Lindemans files still remain classified at the time of writing.

Interesting information can be found in an Allied report on Lindemans dated 5 November 1944 with a signature that appears to read 'E. B. Staryn', sent to me by Michael Moores-LeBlanc. Michael has studied the False KLM line and the line of the counter-espionage agent, René van Muylem. The report is a poor scan, but it reveals the opinion of the Allies on Lindemans' work with the Resistance following his arrest. Some of the assumptions in these early reports are of course erroneous, especially as regards Jan Lowey-Ball, as more information emerged in later years which exonerated the latter. The writer of this report had been carrying out an investigation into Lindemans, and the name Scharrer appears several times in the report:

5.11.44

LINDEMANS

I have been studying the full reports of the characters who have passed through the I.R.C. and who have mentioned Lindemans, short extracts of which were contained in the files which we sent you.

The man Lowey-Ball figures prominently in the above reports. The greater part of our investigation regarding Ball comes from Phillipus Christiaan Tuts. Tuts had a friend in the shape of Lowey-Ball, a student of engineering who tried to reach Spain at the beginning of March 1943, was caught by the Germans, went to a concentration camp and then taken to Toulouse and agreed to enter the services of the S.D. as an informer at an airport. He was sent to Le Bourget Airport to obtain permission to return to Holland in August 1943 to work at an aircraft factory. He then, after a few weeks, left without permission and returned home to Wijnhaven 8, Delft. Thereafter, according to Tuts, he made a living by going to France on S.D. documents, purchasing cigarette papers there and selling them at a profit in Holland. On one occasion in October 1943 he took with him, one [?] Tjardus Koetter [name illegible] to Paris on forged S.D. documents, and on his return he told Tuts that the organization with which he put Koetter in touch, had passed him across the frontier to Spain. It subsequently transpired, however, that Koetter was arrested in France and divulged his escape contacts to the Germans. When Tuts became convinced that Ball was able to obtain false S.D. documents and had contacts in Paris, Tuts decided to try and leave Holland this way. Ball introduced him to Scharrer as Henri Dupon, a journalist who appeared to Tuts to make a living out of forging S.D. documents. Scharrer supplied Tuts with:

1. Sonderausweis for travelling purposes
2. A document for crossing the frontier
3. A proof that Tuts was employed by the G.B.

November 1943 until his departure Tuts resided with Ball and his wife and then set out with Ball by train for Maastricht where they spent the night and then by train to Paris. In Paris Tuts collected money from the Hotel St. Maria and him and his friends were put up at the Hotel des Deux Hemispheres. There he found de Graaf, Celosse and [illegible], all of which were unknown to him and most of whom had obtained documents from Scharrer in Rotterdam.

After arriving in Paris, Lowey-Ball took Tuts to meet a man he described as one of the heads of the organization who was to arrange their escape, namely [?] Starink [illegible] at a hotel in Paris. It is to be assumed that according to Tuts, Starink was in the habit of visiting Lowey-Ball in Delft at this house at Wijnhaven 8. [Next sentences illegible].

This enables de Graaf and Celosse to travel from Holland to the Pyrenees frontier. Furthermore, Scharrer gave de Graaf and Celosse a contact in Paris, namely Lowey-Ball. De Graaf stated further that the head of the Gestapo in Toulouse (Obersturnfüehrer [sic] Stubbe) was a man who employed numerous Dutchmen including Lowey-Ball to penetrate escape lines. In view of the fact that the documents carried by de Graaf and Celosse were obtained from the S.D. in Toulouse, there can be little doubt that they were provided by the Gestapo head. The significance of this does not need labouring.

Lindemans' connections with these sinister proceedings is not clear but in view of what Mr Pinto [an Allied interrogator] says and of the confession which has been obtained from Lindemans, it looks very much as though he was playing an active part in the penetration of the escape route from Holland through Paris. When de Graaf arrived in Paris from Amsterdam which they left on the 22.11.43, they went to the Hotel des Deux Hemispheres (referred to above) but were not contacted there. They then called at the Dutch Chamber of Commerce, as Scharrer had instructed them, to call on Jonkheer de Graaf. He was not there and they went to the Bureau des [?] Interous [illegible] but could obtain no assistance there as [illegible] and De Wit had been arrested. They were, however, called on by a Dutch Reserve Officer of Amstelveen called Kroone who had been sent to them by Lowey Ball. Kroone (no doubt at the instigation of Ball) told them to call on Albert Starink and Albert Starink brought them into contact with King Kong or Christiaan. It would accordingly appear that there is a connection between Ball, the Gestapo informer working for Obersturnfuehrer [sic] Stubbe of Toulouse. Futhermore, Lindeman took de Graaf and Celosse to the flat of Victor Swann who is probably identical with the man whose name is in the possession of de Bray [illegible] who was in turn penetrating the Dutch organization in Paris.

The possibility this Lindeman played a part in the original penetration of the escape route from Holland which linked to a series of arrests referred to above is possibly supported by the fact that Baron van Heemstra, well known for his work in Paris for that escape organization, is a contact of Lindemans. John Buys Laetsman connected with the Dutch Chamber of Commerce in Paris and employed at the Netherlands Consulate in Paris and one of the chief members of [illegible] organization, was likewise a contact of Lindemans.

The I.R.C. has been good enough to get out a note of Lindemans' known movements which may possibly be of value. They are as follows:

June 1943	In Holland
12.10.43	At the house of Mr [illegible] in Rotterdam
3.11.43	Was no longer at the house, having left 2 days earlier
Early Nov 1943	In Rotterdam
26.11.43	In Paris and living with Victor Swan in Heuilly
9–10.12.43	In Paris
16.12.43	Accompanied de Graaf and Celosse to Bordeaux.
28.12.43	Handed de Graaf and Celosse over to Henrietta Luret in Bordeaux.
Aug 44	Missing and believed shot.

As we see from this extensive report, whether Lindemans was worked for the Resistance, or later for the Germans, he did so with resolute determination for both causes, and was at all times a convincing confidence trickster and a dangerous man.

Chapter 14

The KLM False Line and Other Collaborators

Christiaan Lindemans and the Belgian René van Muylem were the two men who did the most damage to the Scharrer Amsterdam-Spain and other lines, succeeding in getting many of their helpers and Allied airmen arrested. A substantial number of these did not survive the fearful PoW camps.

René van Muylem operated the notorious false KLM Line from Belgium until August 1944. The KLM had been a genuine Resistance group led by (Victor) Marcel Daelemans, a former member of the Comete Line, who developed contacts throughout Antwerp province and a safe-house system in Antwerp staffed by genuine patriots. The trouble was that 'Victor' did not know that van Muylem was a *V-Mann* with the Abwehr III/f.

Michael Moores-LeBlanc, who has researched the KLM line extensively, discovered that a total of 235 escapees were caught up and betrayed on this line. Michael found out more about the KLM line when he and his two sons returned to the town of Hank in Holland, and for a month participated in the recovery of a British bomber, Halifax LV905; the remains of the crew were still in it. The plane had been shot down on the night of 24/25 May 1944, while returning from an operation against Aachen railway yards. One of the crew was his uncle, Joseph Thomas Lloyd LeBlanc. The month-long recovery of this bomber culminated in the erection of a memorial to the crew at Jonkerbos War Cemetery.

Michael established that many of the survivors of aircraft shot down on that night raid ended up being sent down to Antwerp into the trap of the false KLM line and arrested.

René, while working on an anti-saboteur case, came into contact with Victor Daelemans early in 1944 posing as an important parachuted British agent with access to arms, ammunition and funds. He discovered that Victor had two lines for evacuating airmen out of Holland. His German bosses, wishing to exploit this find, applied for and received a special licence from Berlin to penetrate the escape lines. This was not usual for the Abwehr III/f, since it was normally the function of the Abwehr III/c.

Over time René infiltrated his own small team into the 'Victor' organization. These included Mattis Ridderhof (aka Georges van Vliet), whose speciality was penetrating the evasion lines, and Prosper de Zitter, whose claim to fame was that he had succeeded in getting nearly 500 Allied airmen arrested in the course of his work. There were also three women: Anna Maria Verhulst-Oomes (who betrayed Frank Hart and others), (Pam) Pauline Vlaming and 'Simone' Marie-Louise DeMay. Mattis Ridderhof, to whom Abwehr agent Louis de Bray reported, was responsible for the arrest of Johan Herman Laatsman, member of the Dutch-Paris Line and head of a cell in Paris. Laatsman was the man who had assisted Jack Bottenheim in Paris and landed up in Buchenwald.

'Simone' only worked occasionally with René. She was employed primarily with 'Arno' Martin Peeters, an assassin, and like him she was described as a dangerous agent. Arno and Simone worked mainly against saboteurs. In early August René took a holiday, after narrowly missed being killed by Victor's other right-hand man, 'Marcel André' (André Rosseuw) at a café. René managed to turn the tables on him at the last minute, and 'Marcel' and his bodyguard, Joe Bille, were arrested on 27 July 1944. Three days later, Victor and his immediate entourage were arrested, but the safe houses in Antwerp were spared by the Germans so they could keep an eye on them. One of these was at 17 Van Eycklei, a special top floor apartment rented by Karl Helmer, alias 'Stahl'. It was also the home of Scholvin, alias 'Chopin'. It was here that they entertained unsuspecting escapees with food, wine and pretty women, hoping to make them drunk and talkative.

After the arrests of Victor and his cell, the German agent 'Arno' (Martin Peeters) took over the running of the KLM line.

Three men assisted by Henri, namely Frank Hart, Jim Davies and Ronnie Aitken, were among the many Allied airmen taken in this fashion by the false escape line. It was all part of Giskes' *Englandspiel* and managed by René van Muylem, who was without doubt a brilliant counter-espionage German agent.

In his book, *London Calling North Pole*, Hermann Giskes described exactly how the clever German sting operation worked, adding more colour to Jim Davies' account:

> In our military counter-espionage activity covering all possible sources of intelligence concerning the impending Allied Invasion, the III/F out-station office in Antwerp had come across a potentially useful line. This station had made excellent contacts with underground groups in Holland which were concerned with the collection and concealment of shot-down Allied Airmen which organized their onward journey thence to Belgium. Contact men from the Antwerp III/F office purporting to be members of the Belgium Underground would meet the airmen on the Dutch-Belgium Frontier and bring them to Antwerp. Here, a small number of language experts from the Abwehr staff occupied a large house which was known as the Antwerp airmen's pipeline and acted the part of a secret 'central committee' of the Belgian conducting organization.

On their arrival the airmen had to fill up a printed form in English, ostensibly in order to confirm their identity to London by radio. It was explained to them that this full description was necessary for protection against German informers who had tried to penetrate the organization in the guise of Allied airmen. If anyone of the escaping men should not be accepted by London as genuine he would come at once under suspicion of being an informer and could not then expect to leave the house alive. There was no doubt therefore about the care with which these questionnaires were completed and they provided good leads for subsequent serious interrogation. After a stay of two or three days in the house, the airmen were told that their onward journey to the French frontier would start the next day. As there were on occasions no more than two or three in the house, a close relationship was cemented by good eating, and better drinking in the company of young women 'friends of the house'. Interrogating officers from the Luftwaffe appeared disguised as Belgians and 'helpers of the committee' and the results of their conversations produced important intelligence about all aspects of the Allied war effort.

Transport for the men was provided in the form of a car with Belgian number plates, driven by an III/F man in plain clothes. A patrol of the GFP would stop the car on the Brussels autobahn and examine the papers of the occupants, who would be placed under arrest until their identity had been established. The airmen's speech naturally failed to correspond with the description of 'Belgians' on the document supplied by the 'Committee', and they had once again to supply accurate particulars of themselves so as not to come under suspicion of being spies. They were eventually taken over as prisoners-of-war by a Transport Group of the Luftwaffe.

Over one hundred and eighty Allied airmen passed through the Antwerp pipeline between March 1944 and the evacuation of the city in September. At this period the results of the interrogation carried out by the methods described above provided one of the best sources of the German military intelligence about the invasion.

When later interrogated, van Muylem modestly claimed the actual number of airmen arrested was only 177, three fewer than in Giskes' book. It was the most successful of the German counter-espionage operations, but not successful enough.

In actual fact, Hermann Giskes, although he claims to have obtained good intelligence from his sources on the Allied invasion, did not get much useful information at all. The Germans were taken completely by surprise by the D-Day landings, having been deceived by the many false reports. Not only did German

Intelligence fail to give their operational commanders a feel for where the invasion might occur, but they completely fell for the Allied deception under Operation Fortitude, believing that the site of the invasion would be in the area of the Pas de Calais.

There is a report by another of the collaborators who betrayed the Dutch-Paris line. Suzy Kraay described after the war how she came to supply information to the Germans about the Dutch-Paris line led by John Weidner. She had been arrested and charged with being a collaborator. This statement was previously classified and is attached to documents signed by Captain Weidner, with the title 'HEAD NETHERLANDS SECURITY SERVICE. Paris Office. Dated 14 November 1945'. An extract from Kraay's testimony reads as follows:

> I answered him that I knew very well that Van den Berg had betrayed my father. The Germans began to lose patience and self-control, and tried in a rude way to force me to answer. At about three o'clock in the afternoon, they stopped yelling, the interrogator exchanged some words with the officer, and they brought me downstairs, accompanied by only those two men. I had to wait with the interrogator in a small room, while the officer entered the next room. When he opened the door I heard a loud tumult and moaning. A moment later we entered.
>
> Stretched and bound on a big table lay an undressed man, four soldiers were occupied to beat him with a whip. The man was in a dreadful condition and his back was one bloody mess. Almost instantaneous I lost consciousness, but after coming to, they forced me to stand and to look.
>
> However cowardly it may have been, I can only say that I was sure not being able to persist. I must confess that I could not dominate myself any longer. I only felt extreme terror. Leaving this room the officer said: 'Now it is your turn, unless you have enough sense to tell the truth. By telling it now your father will be liberated. We shall get to know it anyhow, but if we have to beat it out of you, it has no value whatever.'
>
> I cannot remember what they told exactly afterwards. They asked me also if I would like my father to be exposed to the same kind of interrogation, And by bringing me into a similar room as left a minute before, I did the unpardonable thing to tell them everything and everything that I knew. It was rather simple for them to squeeze me out entirely. Laatsman was the first I betrayed, then followed the names and addresses of Miss Weidner, Miss Hilterman, Pierre, Miss Neuzler, Miss Raviol, and Mr Meyer. I explained the address Rue Jasmin noted in my pocketbook. I had indicated till then as being the address of a girlfriend in Liège. I did the same with the address Rue Franklin at Brussels. I also mentioned Panier

Fleuri. In short outlines I sketched them the work, done by the above mentioned persons. At ten o'clock I was transported back to prison.

When you read this you can almost feel her terror and understand why an arrest and interrogation almost inevitably led to more arrests, and why there was a rush to leave safe houses once it was known that someone had been identified.

Despite the numbers of important Resistance agents betrayed in this manner and who fell into German hands, in the end it was the superior US and British intelligence strategies that were behind the success of the Normandy invasion; in this they outwitted the Germans.

Deep in the background of the big movements of the war and the success of the Allies there were the many unsung heroes of the Resistance movements, helping people hide, moving people along escape lines and sending key military intelligence. This critical work was all done in the face of great danger to themselves, their friends and their families.

However, the key traitor in Henri Scharrer's story was the treacherous *V-Mann*, William Pons. The story of his betrayal comes later.

STORIES OF
PLOTS AND BETRAYALS

Chapter 15

The Ransom and the Plot

If it is true that Henri's arrest on the train was no accident, then SD Officer Herbert Oelschlägel's initial plot had succeeded beyond his expectations. When his men boarded that train, it is claimed that they knew from secret collaborator sources that Henri was their man and that he was on that train. This also would mean that his arrest was not the result of carelessness and over-confidence on his part, as has sometimes been suggested.

Whatever the truth of the arrest, it provided Oelschlägel with the opportunity to lay another trap. This one would be more elaborate and cunning. He wanted more than just one man; he wanted to roll up the whole 'Sandberg' Amsterdam network and with luck also the KP Alkmaar, another thorn in his side. This was not going to be easy. To get the job done he called in an unscrupulous Dutch *V-Mann* by the name of William Pons. The idea was that this man would be planted in Henri's prison cell – a common enough tactic!

William (Willy) Pons was born in Rotterdam in 1899 and later lived in Amsterdam, where he became a member of the NSB (*Nationaal-Socialistische Beweging*), the Dutch Nazi party. Brought up in a large family, he comes across right from his early days as an unstable character. After a spell in the Marines, he drifted from job to job. He was a barber and a salesman, a chauffeur and a café installer, even a builder. He married Dirkje Ketting and they had three children, though the marriage was not successful. When it broke up, his wife sought legal means to prevent him having any contact with the children. His records show he worked in twelve different trades and was involved in no fewer than thirteen motoring accidents.

In April 1942 he was arrested by the SD for creating a domestic scene. This was followed by a brief spell of civilian work for the Germans in the Soviet Union. He was returned to Holland and for a whole year, between January 1943 and January 1944, languished in prison. On release he went to live in Dordrecht, where shortly afterwards he was arrested for theft and put back behind bars. This unstable, amoral and criminal character was recognized by the Germans as an ideal candidate to recruit as a *V-Mann*. They put an end to his confinement, and for a few months he undertook training. Things were looking up for Pons, and so, motivated by money, his freedom and the promise of a good lifestyle, he began to work as a *V-Mann*.

First, however, his counter-intelligence abilities needed to be tested, and he was given a number of special missions for the SD. He was associated with the discovery of a secret weapons cache in a grass-drying factory, Veevita, in Badhoevedorp. The director of this establishment, and others, were later executed by the Germans. Another mission he was involved in was the betrayal of Resistance man Th. H. A. Nieuwendijk, who was executed in early September.

Having performed these tasks to his employers' satisfaction, Pons had proved himself, in Oelschlägel's opinion, the perfect confidence trickster to bring down the circle around 'Sandberg'. This would be his most important mission. His skills as a charmer and deceiver would be tested to the fullest. He received the detailed and high level briefing that always preceded these important undercover operations. His credentials in Rotterdam were set up, including an address, a workplace, favourite pubs, in fact everything that the Resistance might check if they became suspicious. He was given a new identity as 'de Bruin', a bona fide resident of Rotterdam.

Once satisfied that Pons was fully prepared, Oelschlägel had him placed in Henri's cell as a prisoner 'awaiting questioning'. Here he confidently introduced himself to Henri as 'de Bruin' from Rotterdam. His story was well prepared: an unknown person had denounced him and he had been picked up for questioning. In his conversations with Henri he described himself as a Resistance sympathizer – 'We all have to do our bit to get rid of the damnable Hun!'

He told Henri that this detention, however, would not last long as he had useful contacts with certain prison authorities. He expected to be back on the street shortly. It was all an inconvenient misunderstanding.

The tragedy of Henri and Pons' incarceration together is that 'de Bruin' was able to convince Henri that he was in a position to help, and that once released he would be able to take a letter to Truus. Not only that, he would also try to obtain medication for Henri to treat the injuries he had suffered during interrogation. Henri had been given 'the treatment', although exactly what this consisted of is unknown.

Precisely how Pons was able to convince Henri that he could smuggle letters and medication into prison and take letters out is unclear. He certainly knew how to be convincing. It should also be borne in mind that Henri had worked with many Dutch pro-Germans over the past two years who had proved to be 'helpful', and he knew that not all Germans were evil Nazis. In addition, there is Henri's own background and German ancestry. So it would be fair to consider that, suffering the trauma and after-effects of a brutal interrogation, he would have been feeling not just anxious but desperate. It is not surprising that in that situation he could easily have dropped his usual guard and trusted that fate had brought him a saviour in what could be the last dangerous days of his life.

Whatever the reason, it was a lapse of common sense, most likely brought on by his predicament, the uncertain future of his family and an impending death sentence. Henri was snatching at a last lifeline.

The actual letter to Truus was dictated to Pons by Oelschlägel himself, and Pons presented this letter as a draft for Henri to copy in his own handwriting. He explained this odd procedure by saying that they had to be cautious about what was written down and how it was worded, in case the letter was found. He had an answer for everything. Henri did what Pons suggested and gave Pons the letter so he could take it to Truus once he had been safely released. Pons put it in an inside pocket, and gave it a pat. 'This will be safe with me!'

On the morning of Monday, 28 August 1944, Pons visited Truus at her new apartment in Amsterdam. He presented himself as 'de Bruin' from Rotterdam, making a big show of nervously checking both sides of the street before entering the building. He explained that this was a dangerous mission he had undertaken and he had to be sure he had not been shadowed. Once inside, he handed Truus the letter Henri had written. He went on to assure her that he had the necessary contacts with the prison officers to smuggle items in and out of prison.

He played the role of a sympathetic friend to the hilt, sitting down next to her and taking her hand in a reassuring clasp. Quietly and with sadness in his eyes, he told her that Henri was not in a good situation and needed medical attention. He wanted to help and was in a position to be able to take medicine to him. All this Truus found most upsetting. What had they done to Henri? She then wrote a short letter to Henri, handed it to 'de Bruin' and asked if he could kindly come back the next day, as by that time she would have the medical supplies Henri needed. She was frantic, she told him, and had had hardly any sleep since Henri had been arrested. The children were in a state, and terribly unhappy. Everybody was feeling desperate.

The next day, Pons, playing the knight in shining armour, was back to collect the medication. This he immediately rushed over to Oelschlägel's offices for examination, together with Truus' letter. He was given new instructions and went back to Henri's prison to visit him.

At half past seven in the evening of that same day, Pons again arrived at the Scharrer home with another handwritten letter from Henri to Truus. This time he told Truus that Henri had requested that after reading it, she pass it on to his friend Tom Yardin Millord, as it contained an important request.

In this second letter (also dictated to Pons by Oelschlägel) Henri wrote that 'de Bruin' was now their go-between and could be trusted. The letter requested that Millord assist Truus in raising 10,000 guilders (an enormous sum at that time), which would be paid to a friendly undercover German agent to secure his release. It also requested that Tom use his connections with the NSF (National Support

Funds) to secure the money. That was the crux of the letter to his '*Lieve Truusje*' (dear little Truus) which ended, 'Lots of love and kisses for the children'. Pons then left with more medicine, cigarettes and tobacco that Truus had given him.

Truus was now firmly trapped in Oelschlägel's plot. She found 'de Bruin' to be a pleasant and kind person, and was impressed by the efficiency with which he operated. Pons, too, had urged her to act with all haste, as speed was of the essence. Henri could easily be moved to another location and then be beyond his reach.

This is a step-by-step account of the fateful events that followed.

The first thing Truus did was to alert Henri's Resistance associates, so that a plan could be made to secure his release.

The next morning, she met Pons at the corner of the Kromme Mijdrechtstraat in Amsteldijk, a short way from her home. At this meeting she arranged to introduce Pons to Tom Yardin Millord in order to speed up the raising of the ransom money. Ten thousand guilders for one man's life. All too good to be true!

Meanwhile, in Amsterdam KP circles, hopes were raised about the possibility of rescuing Henri.

Truus sent an urgent message to Betty Millord to meet with her and told Betty that Henri had asked Tom to help her raise the ransom money. Betty rushed home to alert her husband.

On hearing the news about Henri's request, for some reason Tom decided not to raise the money himself. What was Tom's motive here? We know that his story about Henry's suitcase in the train is most unlikely. He later explained that despite his good contacts with the NSF he didn't feel that he would be successful in raising such a large amount in so short a time. After pondering the situation and wondering how to find a solution, Tom decided to approach one of Henri's *strijdmakkers* (comrade-in-arms), Fritz Conijn, the leading member of the KP Alkmaar, known to be a most enterprising and dynamic young man.

We need to take a closer look at young Fritz. He came from a wealthy family and also had good contacts with the NSF. Henri had first met him through Heini Douque, and Fritz played a most important role in assisting Henri and bringing him airmen, including Jim Davies and Ronnie Aitken. Only twenty-one years old, he was a determined Resistance fighter who still lived with his parents and worked for the large family timber firm. At the start of the war the timber business came to a standstill and they switched to yacht building. Fritz's father was Gerhardus (Gerrit) Conijn and his mother Marthe Schroder. He had a sister, Valentine, a brother, Ed, and was close to his brother-in-law, Doeko Bosscher.

Fritz made his way into the Resistance movement by first making official contact with LO (*Landelijke Organizatie voor Hulp aan Onderduikers*), the large organization set up by the SOE-N in London to assist those working in the Dutch underground movement. He then went on to become a leader in the organization of the

KP Alkmaar. Also working with Fritz in the KP Alkmaar were three Limburgers who were essential to the organization – his friends Pierre de Bie, Sjaak Frencken ('Rinus') and Albert Reulen ('Ber'). The KP Alkmaar was successful in staging raids on the distributors of ration cards for food and also on police stations to acquire weapons. On 1 May 1944, they launched a failed but brave attack on the prison on Weteringschans to free Resistance fighters held there.

Henri had given Fritz special travel document paper with blank forms, which would make it easier for him to travel. He was already relatively mobile, as he had authorization to work in the dunes on the bunkers the Germans were constructing.

An instant friendship arose between these two men, despite a twenty-two-year age difference. Van der Wiele and others became concerned at this developing friendship between Henri and Fritz. Who was this a newcomer? Maybe he was a double agent trying to penetrate their group? They were accustomed to working with people they knew and trusted over a period of time, men with proven abilities such as Jan Lowey-Ball and Tom Yardin Millord.

Fritz quickly put an end to this mistrust by supplying Henri and Van der Wiele with information on the building of German fortifications in the area between Den Helder and Wijk aan Zee. Just to make sure the information was not false, Van der Wiele decided to check it out, and he and a friend took a long bike ride to see for themselves what was going on with the dune fortifications. Once it was established that Fritz's information was genuine, London was notified of the construction developments. Soon other Resistance groups, and now the whole of KP Alkmaar, enthusiastically helped collect data to send to England. Alkmaar became the in-between station. Fritz also obtained information on airstrips and the Phillips factories now run by the Germans. This he gave to Henri, who gathered all this intelligence from various sources, organized it and had it transmitted to London through his usual radio sources.

Assisting Allied airmen had not been a speciality of the KP Alkmaar, but the involvement of Henri opened up new opportunities and an extra stream of Resistance activities. Jaap Balder from Broek op Langedijk wanted to meet Henri, and this was arranged. Balder was a linchpin in the North Holland escape networks for airmen. On two or three occasions, Balder's escapees were passed via Conjin and De Bie, then taken through to Henri and Carry and in the usual way helped via Paris and Pau to Spain. There is also in Henri's Stichting files a witness statement made after the war to the effect that the witness personally knew that Henri travelled by train to Alkmaar to pick up airmen from Fritz. How often he did this we do not know.

By May 1944 the Resistance work was more dangerous, as the German security activities had become far more intense. There is a record of a meeting that month involving Fritz Conijn, his friend Pierre de Bie and the Amsterdam KP, concerning a programme that the Amsterdammers had put together which required help from Fritz and Pierre. This needed to be closely examined. The plan concerned the possible liquidation of Henri Eugene de Gruijter, a treacherous political agent living on Amsteldijk. He was described as a most dangerous man who had to be assassinated in the interests of the Resistance. As it happened, although discussed, this assassination did not take place and de Gruijter survived the war; but it gives an idea of the kind of underground work that was planned and activated by the KP in Amsterdam and Alkmaar.

Now it was 28 August, and Tom and Fritz met to discuss the urgent business of raising the ransom money for Henri. Fritz listened to the details of this difficult task, but did not hesitate. He realized its urgency, and immediately sprang into action to save his friend. Henri's fate was close to Fritz's heart, and he optimistically felt that if well prepared, a plan could probably be made to work.

Later the same day, at the Hotel Americain, Truus met Fritz for the first time. Also present was Jan Lowey-Ball, the good friend of both Fritz and Caroline Libourel. Jan explained to Truus that Fritz had the connections that would help Tom raise the money. If Truus felt concerned about the youth and possible inexperience of Fritz, she kept her thoughts to herself.

Later that afternoon, Fritz left for Oudorp to set his plans in motion.

At senior Resistance levels, however, the first reaction was caution and suspicion. Otto Vermeer felt positive, as did Arend Japin. Pierre de Bie, however, a most astute young man, did not feel at all happy about these developments. Unfortunately, Pierre had to travel to Alkmaar that day and so was not closely involved in what followed. Had he been around, it is possible he might have prevented what occurred.

There was one more important meeting that still had to take place. This was between Pons and Tom Yardin Millord, to make arrangements about the handover. It was organized by Truus and would be the first time Millord had met Pons face-to-face. Who was this man who had suddenly sprung to Henri's rescue? He questioned Pons closely and seemed satisfied with his bona fides. He hurried back to Rivierenlaan and advised Truus that the final plan would be that Jan Lowey-Ball would accompany him and Fritz Conijn at the handover. Jan was experienced in intelligence operations, having worked with Field Security, and Fritz believed he would be useful in establishing whether Pons was trustworthy. It would have been reckless in the extreme to go to a meeting with an unknown go-between without an experienced intelligence person present. He went on to explain to her that for her own safety, she was not to be told any details of the plan to raise the money. Once they had the funds they would give her a surprise.

The stage was now set for the disaster that was about to occur.

How Fritz actually obtained the ransom money is not known. There is no record that the NSF guaranteed it. It is possible that he borrowed it from his father, Gerrit Conijn, a wealthy man. If this is true, it was an act of generosity that led indirectly to his son's execution. Had he not provided the money, Fritz might not have attended that fateful meeting. If he had any regrets on this score, in the years that followed, Gerrit said nothing. He died in 1947 and took the truth to his grave. However, the most likely source of the ransom money remains the NSF.

Fritz wasted no time. He was still uncertain about the trustworthiness of 'de Bruin' and contacted underground members in Rotterdam. But Pons' Rotterdam background and his 'de Bruin' bona fides had been well established by the SS. An efficient false trail of friendly contacts and addresses had been set up. Nevertheless, the SS had been concerned that a weak link might be discovered in 'de Bruin's' story and his Rotterdam credentials could be blown. To avoid any mishap of this kind, 'de Bruin' warned Truus that she had to hurry the ransom collection, as Henri's circumstances could change any day.

Before anything could take place, Fritz first wanted to meet 'de Bruin' personally to judge whether he could be trusted. This was urgently arranged. At this meeting, Pons, forever the capable confidence trickster, was able to convince Fritz that all was above board. He would pass the ransom on to a prison go-between and a way would be found for Henri to make his escape.

Everything had been approved from the top by Hugo van der Wiele (Hugo Brandsma) himself. Hugo as the leader of the group had agreed that Scharrer had to be freed and the money raised for his escape. Also agreed by senior Resistance members was that the only three men at the handover would be Fritz Conijn, Tom Yardin Millord and Jan Lowey-Ball. They did not feel it wise for more people to be present. A larger group could arouse suspicions. As an added precautionary measure, the handover area would be kept under surveillance.

The fateful day was 29 August 1944. Fritz had met his mentor, Arend Japin, at ten o'clock that morning and been given a pistol. If the worst happened he might need it. He had no time to waste as he had to rush to the office of Kropman on the Heerengracht, where Jan Lowey-Ball was waiting. Fritz had the ransom money packed in hundreds and laid out neatly in a suitcase. At eleven o'clock he was due to meet Tom Millord. At the Restaurant Victoria the three were given new plans and another location, telephoned through by Truus, who had received further instructions from the Resistance. As Fritz would have a pistol, Tom and Jan did not carry theirs; it had been decided that additional guns would not be needed.

It was a hectic morning. Time was of the essence, with one meeting swiftly following the other.

Truus had originally told 'de Bruin' that the exchange would take place at 1100 hrs at the Victoria, on the corner of Amstellaan and Amsteldijk, on the south side of the famous Berlage bridge across the Amstel River. The arrangement was that Truus would be at the corner of Kromme Mijdrechtstraat to meet 'de Bruin' and walk with him to the Victoria Restaurant. She had been instructed to try and walk slowly, something she found difficult as she wanted the matter over with as fast as possible. By walking slowly, she would allow the Resistance men lurking in the shadows more time to keep the street, Truus and 'de Bruin' under surveillance.

Truus was doing everything in her power to save her husband. That she was taking a grave risk she fully realized. She kept her eye out for any suspicious people in the vicinity, for if she noticed anything untoward she had been instructed to raise the alarm.

All appeared normal, however, with people going about their daily business. At an agreed moment, Truus stopped walking and informed 'de Bruin' there had been a change of plan. They were to turn left in the direction of 12 Verdiepingenhuis, better known as de Wolkenkrabber on Daniel Willinkplein and the corner of Vechtstraat, and to wait at the terrace of the café De Gekroonde Valk (still in existence but under a different name). This new meeting place was a few hundred metres further on, at the corner of Vechtstraat and Amstellaan. Pons did not register any surprise.

Holland had recently been experiencing a heatwave, but on that day the weather was fresh, with temperatures around 18 or 19 degrees. Fritz, carrying the suitcase containing the cash and accompanied by Jan Lowey-Ball and Tom Yardin Millord, made his way to De Gekroonde Valk. The possibility of danger had not been underestimated, and all care and caution was adopted. Had anything amiss been spotted, the plan was that Fritz, carrying the suitcase, would run left in the direction of 12 Verdiepingenhuis and hopefully get away.

Tom, Fritz and Jan sat down at the table outside the café and ordered coffee. Shortly afterwards, Pons and Truus joined them. There were happy greetings all round. Their position at the table gave them a good view of Amstellaan but not down Vechtstraat, which was round the corner. Truus was surprised to notice that Fritz appeared to be the person who had carried the ransom suitcase. She had thought his role was to assist Tom, as Tom was the person Henri had entrusted to raise the ransom.

The tension was agonizing. Truus noticed that her fingers were trembling, and put her hands on her lap to hide her nervousness. Fritz, Jan and Tom wanted to get the handover completed as fast as possible, as although this rendezvous area was under Resistance surveillance, the position could change suddenly, with Germans constantly on the prowl in their motor vehicles.

Jan, who had the most experience with double agents, questioned 'de Bruin' closely regarding his meeting with Henri. How was it possible that he had met up with Henri in prison? Was it a mere coincidence?

Pons' reply was, '*Via een contact in de gevangenis*' (Through a contact in the prison).

He went on to assure them that there was no need to worry, they were pretty safe, as they had a good view of the area from where they were sitting. He was playing his role to the full and enjoying it.

Truus was also carrying the letter she had received from Henri concerning the ransom. She wanted to show this to Jan so that he could make a final judgement on its authenticity, because she also had her concerns about the style of Henri's wording in the letter. Was it really Henri's work?

The coffee was brought to the table by the waiter.

As the cups were being set out, suddenly from around the blind corner, in a matter of seconds, seemingly from nowhere, three German armed vehicles appeared. There were shouts and yells and the screeching of brakes. Everyone sat still in a state of shock. The SS-men rushed up with their guns and rifles pointed, shouting, '*Hände hoch!*'

Cautiously, everybody put up their hands. To have attempted any kind of resistance would have been impossible and foolhardy. A German officer immediately grabbed the suitcase and opened it to check the cash, which would be used as evidence. Pons and Truus were placed under surveillance on the corner of Amsteldijk/ Amstellaan, while the rest were searched; Fritz's pistol was found and seized. The patrons and staff of the café stood silently in shock. In the streets people kept their distance, watching these events unfold.

The direction from which the Germans came was not within the café's line of sight. The men from Euterpestraat came from the back, via Kromme Mijdrechtstraat, Waverstraat and Vechtstraat, which was round the corner from where the party were sitting. The Resistance members lurking in the shadows kept their heads down. They were rendered powerless by the speed and ferocity of the attack.

All the arrestees were bundled into the vehicles and driven off at high speed to SD headquarters in Euterpestraat. Everyone was handcuffed, including Pons. Needless to say, shortly thereafter the handcuffs were taken off Pons and he was later released.

Oelschlägel's plot had worked brilliantly.

Truus remained under arrest, desperately worried about her children being left at home alone. A message was sent to their aunt in the Hague to come and stay in the house and take care of them. Later, a married niece of Truus' came from Amsterdam. The family experienced a few traumatic weeks, before Truus was finally released. Not much is known about her imprisonment, and it would appear that she did not want to talk about it. Richard would comment that from that time his mother was a changed person, suffering bouts of depression and deep grief about the loss of her husband. These events had sapped her usual energy.

A number of high ranking German officials were involved in this 'Scharrer Ransom' plot: Sturmscharführer Wouter Mollis, Kriminalsekretär Friedrich Christian, Hauptsturmführer Hans Blumenthal, second in command at Euterperstraat, SS Ernst Wehner, SS Viermann and SD man Willie Albers. The main officer responsible for this sting operation, as we know from the Pons briefing, was Herbert Oelschlägel.

When the Resistance analyzed these events in the years that followed, it was concluded that even if Pierre's KP Commando had been present, it would not have succeeded in saving Fritz, Jan, Truus and Tom. The presence of the commando would have resulted in a gunfight with disastrous consequences and many casualties, including innocent civilians.

A couple of months later, Raymond and Richard saw 'de Bruin' again, standing on the back platform of a tram. *'Hallo, groeten thuis'* ('greetings to the family'), he shouted to them cheerily. They waved back happily, having no idea at that time that he had betrayed their parents and all those who had tried to help them.

The German security authorities were in a celebratory mood. Drinks were poured and toasts made. Their carefully planned plot had resulted in an important breakthrough. Not only did they have Henri Scharrer, alias 'Sandberg', but also the young KP Alkmaar man Fritz Conijn carrying Arend Japin's pistol – an offence punishable by death. Conijn, Millord and Lowey-Ball were interrogated and charged. Oelschlägel personally interviewed Tom Millord. Brief trials were hurriedly held, and Fritz Conijn was sentenced to death. Millord and Lowey-Ball were charged with assisting the Resistance and sentenced to imprisonment.

Meanwhile, Betty Millord was worried that her husband had not come home, so she went into town to see if she could find him at his usual cafés and pubs. No one had seen him. She then went to his underground address, but Tom was not there either. Next, she visited the Café Americain, a favourite hang-out of Tom, Henri and other Resistance members. She found nothing. Then she went to the Scharrer house, only to discover to her horror that Truus had not come home either and the children were on their own. It had been a frantic, useless search.

The next day, 30 August, after spending a sleepless night, Betty was informed of Tom's last known rendezvous – the Restaurant Victoria and the Café De Gekroonde Valk. She travelled there by tram, and the staff at De Gekroonde Valk told her what they had seen of the arrests. Betty's worst nightmare had come true.

She was not prepared to sit around her house and worry in silence, so decided to take matters into her own hands. Off she went to visit Euterpestraat in an attempt to get an introduction to one of the senior SD men whose name she knew – Willy Albers. With her heart beating and trying to overcome her nervousness, she was told by the receptionist that she would be escorted to his office. Albers received her in a friendly manner. If this show of politeness surprised Betty, it was because there had been developments in the war of which Albers had become aware. The Canadian forces were not far away, and the world of the Third Reich was about to come to an end. He knew that the Allied forces would hunt down all German officials in the occupied territories, that they would be investigated and those suspected of war crimes would be put on trial. It was the right time for a prominent and intelligent German officer to think about his future and provide evidence to show the better side of his nature.

Albers told her that he did have information on this particular case. Henri Scharrer was *'schon erschossen'* (already shot). There was, however, one piece of good news for Betty: unlike two other prisoners, Fritz Conijn and Henri Scharrer, her husband would not be sentenced to death.

Albers then got up from behind his desk and told her he would personally take her to see Tom. He summoned a vehicle and off they went to Weteringschans, where she was ushered into a small room. In a state of anxiety Betty sat there waiting for what appeared to be ages. Finally, Tom walked into the room, looking haggard, limping on bare and swollen feet, unshaven but with no trace of any beard on his neck. The hairs had all been pulled out. With tears in her eyes, she embraced her husband, thankful that he was still alive, and they were able to say a few comforting words to each other.

The following day, Betty returned to Weteringschans with medication for Tom to treat his injuries. Here Betty caught sight of a distressed Truus, eyes red from weeping, but they were not able to talk. After a few weeks, when it was established that Truus was no longer of any interest to her interrogators and could provide no information of value, she was released.

In all innocence, and with bravery and great determination, Truus had tried to raise a huge ransom in a short space of time to secure the release of her husband. In obtaining help to raise the ransom she had been remarkably successful. But she had been deceived by a man who had pretended to be her friend in her hour of need and desperation, and this callous betrayal left her feeling overcome by the extent of evil and deceit to which so-called civilized human beings can resort. What she did not know was that Henri, at the time of his arrest, was on his way to meet the great love of his life, Caroline Libourel. This is one of the ironic aspects of the dramatic events of 28 and 29 August.

The date of 5 September 1944 is referred to in Dutch history as *Dolle Dinsdag* (Crazy Tuesday): crazy because the Dutch started prematurely celebrating, believing they were about to be liberated by the Allied Forces. On that same day, Tom Yardin Millord was transferred to Stalag IV-B in Muhlberg (Brandenburg), a concentration camp on the Elbe.

Somehow in all the confusion and chaos around *Dolle Dinsdag*, the lucky Jan Lowey-Ball, together with a schoolmaster whom he had met while incarcerated, escaped from custody. Jan, as it turns out, was very good at escaping and had successfully done this on a number of occasions. This gave rise to the suspicion that he was not to be trusted, and after the war he was accused of being a traitor, arrested, charged and imprisoned. It took the intervention of Prince Bernhard of the Netherlands, who headed the Council of Resistance, to get him released. This is proof enough that Jan Lowey-Ball, the friend of Henri, Carry and Fritz, was well connected in the Resistance movement at the highest levels and was a brave and enterprising young man, with an untarnished reputation.

The two remaining prisoners, Henri and Fritz, had both been sent to Vught prison camp in the southern Netherlands, part of the Camp Herzogenbusch. This was essentially used for Jewish prisoners before they were moved on to other concentration camps, and for *onderduikers*. The guard staff included SS men and women, as it held both male and female prisoners.

Vught consisted of barracks surrounded by a tall barbed wire fence with a high voltage electric current. Towers stood at the corners manned by guards with machine guns. The camp was also protected by trained dogs, and the ground surrounding the electric fences was heavily mined. On most evenings the sounds of firing squads executing prisoners in the woods nearby could be heard.

The routine for prisoners arriving at Vught commenced with their being herded into a hall, made to undress and then searched standing up and bent over. Next, they were provided with prison clothing. Inside the barracks were rows of metal bunk beds, stacked three high and with little space between. On the other side of the room were a few tables and benches. Across the room was an open bathroom with ten toilets. There was no privacy. Soap was in short supply, as were towels and linen. Most of the time people simply washed themselves in cold water. Food usually consisted of a slice of unbuttered bread in the morning, followed by lunch consisting of a weak, watery soup; dinner would be another slice of bread with a pat of margarine. Once a month, the Red Cross would supply more nourishing food, consisting of thick bean soup, meat and potatoes. Without these Red Cross meals many of the inmates at Vught would have become ill and eventually died of malnourishment.

Early on that chilly autumn morning, 6 September 1944, over 300 prisoners, the largest number in any one group, were taken out to the woods escorted by armed German soldiers. On this walk of death their shoes and boots made loud crunching noises on the fallen autumn leaves and twigs. One can only imagine the horror of this march through the long morning shadows, with so many men knowing that these would be the last minutes of their lives. Their jumbled thoughts would have been of their families, children, all the people they loved and would never see again. Some would have been silently praying to God.

In the group were Henri Scharrer and Fritz Conijn. In an open space among the trees they were lined up. They stood bravely facing the rows of firing squads.

The orders were shouted: '*Zielen! Feuer!*' ('Take aim. Fire.').

All were mowed down. Prisoners not killed immediately were despatched with a bullet to the head. The bodies were immediately and unceremoniously collected and carted away by waiting trucks to the nearby crematoria, including one at Velsen. All the bodies were burnt, so that there would be no evidence of the atrocity.

The families were not informed, and what followed was an anxious and agonizing period of hope that Henri and Fritz might still be alive. Carry Libourel posted notes around Amsterdam asking for information on Henri and giving her telephone number, her address, Oude Delft 233, and Truus' residential address. She described Henri as a Frenchman who spoke good Dutch.

After the liberation, Carry, using Henri's cell number (B2-17), made inquiries about Henri at the prison at Amstelveen, the Canadian Field Security in Apollolaan, the Red Cross in Vught, from people with knowledge of executions at Waalsdorpervlakte and at Overveen, the authorities at camp Sachsenhausen/ Oranienburg, the authorities at Fort Blauwkapel in Utrecht, the Bureau of National Safety, and many other places. She also tried to speak (with little success) to the now detained Germans: Friedich Viebahn, Emil Rühl, Kampcommandant Hans Hüttig van Vught and Joseph Kotälla (The *Beul*, or Torturer, of Amersfoort).

At the head of her list of people who might have assisted her were those with whom Henri had worked, such as Tom Yardin Millord, Jan Lowey-Ball, Jack 'Dick' Bottenheim, Arend Japin, Arnold and Xenia Verster-Molschanowa, Wout Mange (a fellow prisoner of Henri's at Weteringschans) and others. None of them could provide information. Henri had simply vanished without trace.

Betty had passed on to Truus the ominous news of what Albers had told her at the end of August, that Henri was 'already shot'. So the possibility that he was dead was fully understood by Carry and the family. The problem was that they did not know for sure, and without any evidence there was always hope. It was only in November 1945, over a year later, that Carry Libourel discovered the official proof that Henri had been executed.

The question is often asked why so many prisoners were executed, when liberation was so close. It is assumed that this was partly out of revenge, and also because the SS had been given orders from Berlin to destroy as much as possible of the evidence of and the witnesses to their crimes and atrocities.

On the day of the execution, the Canadians were only about 30 miles away from Vught, an easy day's drive in their vehicles. As it happened, however, they would only reach Vught months later, because of a change of military strategy by the Allies.

Today at Vught there is a large and important memorial, the National Memorial Kamp Vught, which attracts thousands of visitors each year. It contains the names of 329 prisoners who were executed there. These are only some, not all, of the hundreds of prisoners who were executed at this site. While the official records at Vught show that Henri Scharrer was executed on 6 September 1944 and then cremated, his name does not appear on the memorial.

Chapter 16

Revenge, Hunger and the Holocaust

The leading Germans known to be involved in these interrogations, trials and executions were themselves being targeted by the Resistance. The spotlight was on Henri's main interrogator, Oelschlägel, and his *V-Mann* inner circle. The KP took the decision that he would be liquidated in such a manner that his body would never be found and that Euterpestraat would have no idea who was responsible; if he simply disappeared, hopefully there might not be any of the usual reprisals against the civilian population. The initiative was taken by Piet Elias and Arend Japin (Fritz Conijn's mentor), who were two leading activists in the Amsterdam KP.

Japin later stated that the plan was to kidnap Oelschlägel, hold him captive and then assassinate him. They had a special place where they could take him, do the deed and hide the body. Others agreed to help. These were Pierre (Otto) Vermeer and 'Tjerk' – the code name of the Amsterdam politician, Jaap Davids.

Less than two months after the execution of Fritz and Henri, on 23 October, on the corner of Apollolaan and Beethovenstraat, Oelschlägel was grabbed by four men who had been trailing him in a vehicle, and tackled to the ground. The chloroform they used did not knock him out, however, and as he struggled with his captors, a gun went off accidentally and a bullet went through his head. The men dived back into their vehicle and fled the scene, leaving behind their victim, dead in the street. There was no doubt in the minds of the Germans as to who was responsible. As a reprisal, 29 *Todeskandidaten* (death candidates) from Weteringschans were shot on Apollolaan and large numbers disappeared. Two houses were set on fire, one of which happened to belong to an NSB member, which was a small solace to the Resistance.

Japin and Pierre accepted responsibility for the plan that had gone terribly wrong, and expressed their deepest regret about the people shot in reprisals. The reality is that it was a poorly executed plan: it was immediately clear to the Germans who was responsible, and many people died or disappeared as a result.

The last year of the German occupation was particularly grim. The winter was harsh and led to 'hunger journeys', starvation, exhaustion, severe cold and disease. These conditions were brought about initially by a general railway strike ordered by the Dutch Government-in-Exile, in the expectation of a general German collapse near the end of 1944. In retaliation, and also because their own supplies were running low, the Germans cut off all food and fuel shipments to the Netherlands' western provinces, in which four and a half million people lived. Severe malnutrition was common, and an estimated 18,000 people starved to death. The period is known as the *Honger Winter* or the Dutch famine.

The people of the Netherlands, including Truus and her two sons, faced appalling hardships. Richard recalled trekking out of town to the farms in search of edible roots and bulbs that had been missed by the Germans. Tulip bulbs were a popular food. Bread was of poor quality, and Truus had to ride her bicycle for about five miles and stand in a long queue to get a daily ration of the miserable stuff.

The two women who loved Henri now supported each other in their grief and in their search for news about him. They wrote each other encouraging letters. Carry brought Truus extra food parcels. They might not have been much, but in that terrible *Honger Winter*, with 500 people dying of starvation in Amsterdam every week, they helped the family survive.

Truus wrote to Carry on 4 March 1945 about the food shortages and conditions in Amsterdam during that terrible winter. She was still hoping that maybe she would see Henri again:

Dear Carry,

Your postcard, of 5th February I received on 1st March and the package on the 24th February, for which I am most grateful.

From the barley meal I was able to cook the youngsters porridge, which they thoroughly enjoyed. With regard to Henri, I haven't heard a word. I trust that there will be an end to all this soon then perhaps the chance exists that I will see him again.

The situation in Amsterdam is horrific. For the first time in 3 months last Saturday we had some meat. Bread [on the black market] price here FL35 but through the Red Cross the price for bread is now FL20. So now and then I buy a loaf of bread as the boys are always hungry. I don't have a stove but manage on a small plate which you fire with small branches called '*sprokel*' locally. This method works fine and quick and then I don't have to go to the public kitchen.

I now receive FL300 per month as there is no man for us who can collect our meals. Richard is so big that I dare not send him to school as there are regularly searches from street to street.

Here in Amsterdam people die regularly. 500 to 600 people per week. There are no more funerals. Corpses lie here sometimes for up to 3 weeks. Daily a delivery bike comes passed with 5 to 7. These coffins go to the funeral storage place. To each coffin they attach a label with your name and when it is your turn they bury you.

The streets are dirty as nobody does garbage removal and in the South the sanitation no longer works with the result that all sorts of illnesses appear. My niece is going to the Hague and will forward this letter and I sincerely hope to hear from you in the near future. Lots of love and a kiss from the boys and me.

Truus.
And once again many thanks.

In 'searching the streets for young boys' Truus was referring to something that was happening daily. Thousands of young Dutch boys and men were deported to Germany for what was known as *Arbeitseinsatz* (forced labour, in German factories). All Dutch men between the ages of eighteen and forty-five who were not in the SS or in German employ were required to do this. Boys who merely looked as if they were eighteen were taken off the streets without question.

The death of his father, and this break in Richard's schooling, had a deleterious effect on him, and it is highly likely that he suffered from post-traumatic stress disorder. After the war he didn't want to go back to school, because if he had to pick up where he had left off he would be a year older than his new classmates. Richard was not alone in this situation, of course, as many Dutch boys had to pick up the pieces of their former lives after the war. In Richard's case, however, he no longer had the firm hand of his father to guide him. So his attendance at school became intermittent. His younger brother Raymond, however, persevered and continued his schooling without interruption.

Relief only came after the liberation of the whole country was finally secured on 5 May 1945. The queen, who had already moved to Breda in the liberated south of the country, spoke over the radio. It is said there was not a dry eye anywhere in the Netherlands. Many people gathered in the town squares and sang the Dutch national anthem, *Wilhelmus*, waving national flags and orange posters and banners – all of which had been banned during the occupation.

The Allied soldiers, too, sang their national anthems, and the pretty blonde Dutch girls kissed everybody. All the Netherlands was celebrating. After the trials and tribulations of the past years it was a particularly joyous occasion and a time remembered happily for many years.

Then came the pictures and reports of the horrors that had been found in the numerous concentration camps. Hardened troops were shocked at what they had stumbled on. In the extermination camps dead and dying people lay everywhere, with piles of naked bodies in hastily dug trenches. Many of those who were sick died after liberation. Some were rushed off to Allied hospitals, but transportation was limited and thousands were not able to receive help.

All Allied forces were involved in the liberating of these camps. The Soviet forces liberated the horrific Auschwitz-Birkenau in Poland. The Americans liberated the forced labour camp at Buchenwald in Germany, to which so many Dutch Resistance fighters were sent. Bergen-Belsen, a holding camp in Germany, was liberated by forces from the United Kingdom, and in the Netherlands the Westerbork transit camp was liberated by the Canadians.

With the war over, Europe was in ruins. Movie clips of the time show women pushing prams with children clinging to their skirts as they walk through the rubble along paths cleared by workers. Would Europe ever recover?

The Red Cross in the Netherlands began compiling lists of names of people, mostly young men, who would not be coming back. Hundreds and thousands of names were published across the country in the newspapers and on lists posted around the towns. For weeks people read these lists in fear they would find the name of a loved one.

Gradually, the extent of the Holocaust and the fact that millions had died began to be understood. How was it possible that nobody had known? The people of the Netherlands were in shock at the barbarity and cruelty of it all. Only a few had known of the existence of the extermination camps, and they were mainly SS officials, pro-German sympathizers involved in the transport of the prisoners, and other civil servants who kept their grim knowledge secret.

According to a German census conducted in early 1941, there were 154,887 Jews in the Netherlands. Most of them lived in Amsterdam, not an easy city in which to hide, although between 25,000 and 30,000 Jewish people were successfully hidden during the occupation.

The unfortunate reality is that the Jewish citizens of the Netherlands had very little chance of escape. Besides its flat landscape, the country has few thick woods and forests in which people could hide. The civil administration of the Netherlands before the war had listed the names, ethnicity, addresses and religions of all its citizens. These vast and efficient records were now under the auspices of the SS, with the unflinching anti-Semite, Reichskommissar Arthur Seyss-Inquart and many Austrian Nazis among its senior officials. They in turn supervised the Dutch civil servants, and this arrangement proved fatal for the Jews of the Netherlands, because the Germans thus had easy access to the identities and addresses of all Jews, and tracking down Jewish families presented no problem at all. It was the same with the Gypsy population. What made it even easier for the Nazis was that they cordoned off the old Jewish quarter in Amsterdam and turned it into a ghetto.

The Dutch people, however, did not take this assault on their fellow citizens lying down. The first show of support for Jews had occurred on 25 February 1941,when the Communist Party of the Netherlands called for a general strike in response to the first Nazi round-up and deportation of Jewish people.

Many citizens of Amsterdam, regardless of political affiliation, joined in this mass protest. The next day, the factories in Zaandam, Haarlem, Ijmuiden, Weesp, Bussum, Hilversum and Utrecht joined in. In retaliation for this strike, 420 Jewish men were taken hostage by the Germans and eventually deported to extermination camps. The records indicate that only two of these men survived.

The strike was put down within a day, with German troops firing on the crowds, killing nine people and wounding twenty-four, as well as taking many prisoners. During the occupation, there were four major strikes against the Germans, including the Jewish deportation strike. The other three were the students' strike, the doctors' strike in 1942 and, in April/May 1943, the railway strike. These demonstrated a strong, overt and unarmed refusal to co-operate with the occupiers, something unmatched in other occupied countries.

These actions had no effect on the Germans' Jewish policy. The Nazis passed a series of regulations which isolated the Jewish population, and many were sent to the transit camps and to the concentration camp at Westerbork. The first deportation of Jews on a train from Westerbork to Auschwitz-Birkenau took place in 1941. From that time trains left Westerbork regularly for both Auschwitz and Sobibor. The prisoners were mostly gassed on arrival at the camps. The last train, staffed by Dutch collaborators, carrying condemned people left Westerbork on 3 September 1944 – three days before the execution of Henri, Fritz and the large Resistance group at Vught.

Speaking of these collaborators, the Nazi war criminal Adolph Eichmann is quoted as having said, 'The transport runs so smoothly that it is a pleasure to see.'

Over a period of three years, transport trains delivered Jews from all corners of German-occupied Europe, to the extermination camps, where they were killed with the pesticide Zyklon B. Over one million Jews perished at Auschwitz alone, and only a few thousand survived to be liberated by Soviet troops in January 1945.

Of the estimated 107,000 Dutch Jews deported to the camps only 5,200 survived. In the 1954 census in the Netherlands, the Jewish population was estimated at only 24,000, less than one sixth of the pre-war number; the majority had survived because they had been in hiding. Five-sixths of the Dutch Jewish population had perished.

By the end of the war, 205,901 Dutch men and women had died of war-related causes. Another 70,000 more Dutch people may have died from indirect consequences, such as poor nutrition or limited medical services. The country had the highest per capita death rate of all occupied territories, with nearly a half of those killed being Holocaust victims.

Now with the war behind them, the Dutch people slowly started to look towards the future. While most turned their backs on the horrors of the past in order to forget, across the country there were many memorials erected in sad and honoured remembrance of the dead.

It was only after Henri's arrest that the extent of Truus' bravery and devotion to her husband was revealed. She took risks that could have resulted in a long term of imprisonment in one of the camps.

Carry's assistance to the Scharrer family continued for several years after the war. She cut through a great deal of red tape to get Truus a pension and life insurance. When she felt additional legal pressure was needed, she requested assistance from the law firm, Van Krimpen, Roelse & Wieringa.

It is interesting to conjecture what Truus knew about Carry and her relationship with Henri. The facts suggest that Truus must have known about it. Carry was friendly with Tom and Betty Millord because she and Tom also worked together at the ANP (the Netherlands Press Bureau). In turn, as we know, Tom and Betty were close friends of Henri and Truus, and it seems unlikely that Betty would not have said something to her closest friend. It would appear that the anxiety caused by Henri's long disappearance, and later the knowledge of his execution, was the shared tragedy that brought the two women together. The war made for strange and unusual bedfellows. Besides, some matters are best left alone and unspoken. Truus was Henri's loyal and devoted wife, and Carry on occasion referred to herself as Henri's fiancée. That was how the matter was and how it rested.

Gradually over the years, as life progressed and people moved on, Carry's ties to the Scharrer family dwindled, although she long remained in contact with Marie Jeanne, Henri's sister, who lived at Cavaillon in the South of France with her husband.

The following is a statement issued by the Area Security Office, South Holland, on 17 July 1945, entitled 'Report on interview with Miss Caroline Libourel':

On being approached by Mr. H. J. Sjollema of P.O.D. for information from SS Hauptsturmführer MUNT, or from any other member of SD Sonderkommando FRANK, concerning the fate of a French Captain SCHARRER, on behalf of SCHARRER'S fiancée Miss CAROLINE LIBOUREL of Oude Delft, I took the opportunity to interview the young lady myself, as it was known to us previously that a SCHARRER had been involved in an organization for the passing through of Allied Dutch youth to the Iberian Peninsula, via Belgium and France, and thence to the UK, whose protégés aroused suspicion on arrival through either being in possession of, or having made use of, allegedly forged SA Ausweises for the purpose of travelling across occupied territory.

This organization included, or had connection with, such characters as CHRIS LINDEMANS alias KING KONG, Domine TEN CARTE, Jan Strangers, the brothers VERLOOP, personnel of the office Nederlandais in Paris, Baron VAN HEEMSTRA, LOUIS DE BRAY,

ANDRE WYSAGOTHA, Baron VAN BOETZELAER, and numerous other individuals, famous or notorious for their activities in resistance and espionage organizations. SCHARRER was known as one of the individuals most intimately connected with the supply of SD documents to would-be 'Engelandvaarders' and as such, was necessarily regarded as somewhat suspect in the absence of proof as to his bona fides.

IDENTIFICATION
On being questioned, Miss Libourel gave me the following information which satisfied me, that her fiancé was without doubt identical with the SCHARRER connected with the escape organizations. His name is HENRI SCHARRER. He was a French National of Alsatian origin, who before the war was employed by the "Algemeene Nederlands Persbureau" in Amsterdam. In 1939 he was called upon to work for the French Legation in The Hague. He was a reserve captain of the French Army. On the invasion of Holland he was interned as a French National at Schoorl but released after the French Armistice in August 1940. He was then compelled to reside in Amstelveen, where he took employment with the Schweizerische Presse Telegraf of Bern.

ACTIVITIES UNDER THE OCCUPATION
Miss Libourel cannot give precise indication as to SCHARRER's introduction into resistance activities, but is aware that for a considerable period before the end of 1943 he had been engaged in assisting shot-down Allied pilots and escaped Allied POWs to travel across occupied territory. He had also similarly assisted a number of Dutch youth to reach England. SCHARRER continued this till June 1944, when things became too dangerous and he gave it up. On the 18th August 1944, he was arrested, while travelling in a train between Amsterdam and Leiden or Haarlem as his identification papers were not in order, and, as he was found to be carrying arms, his case received serious attention. He came under suspicion of having carried out espionage on behalf of the French Deuxième Bureau. During the course of the investigation Miss Libourel was herself apprehended by MUNT and confrontation with SCHARRER took place. Miss LIBOUREL was finally released, but SCHARRER was sentenced to death and the sentence appears to have been carried out. MUNT was questioned concerning his actions in the matter, but claimed that he had been acting on instructions from Einsatz Kommando Amsterdam and that he believed that the whole case was finally turned over to Sonderkommando Frank.

Miss Libourel was aware that SCHARRER had supplied would-be escapers with false SD documents, which he himself had had printed in Amsterdam. She is not aware as to who carried out the actual printing, but gives an account of the origin of the original papers of which copies were made, which corresponds with information already reported in the UK. Her account was to the effect that at the beginning of the latter half of 1943 a Dutch half-caste Indian youth named LOWEY BALL brought genuine SD documents from a SD Dienststelle in France which had issued these papers to him as one of their agents. BALL assisted SCHARRER in his clandestine activities, but as a result of an act of provocation was arrested with two accomplices, FRITZ CONIJN and TOM MILLORD at the end of August 1944 or in the first two or three days of September. Ball was however released in somewhat peculiar circumstances on the so called "Dolle Dinsdag" (5th Sept) allegedly in the confusion of that day. The MILLORD mentioned is TOM YARDIN MILLORD of Amstelveen, Keizer Karelweg 409.

Since the liberation Miss LIBOUREL has met DICK BOTTENHEIM one of the "Engelandvaarders" whom SCHARRER assisted, and LOWEY BALL, both of whom said they were employed by the Dutch FS at Amsterdam but subsequently near Hilversum.

RECOMMENDATION

In view of the above information about BALL and the fact that he was regarded as suspect in the UK as long ago as Feb. or March 1944, it is recommended that his case be investigated before he is allowed to continue in the employment of any Allied Authority. Further information concerning his activities should be available from Dutch Security Records or from UK, whilst references now in Holland include Capt. De Graaf and CELOSSE both former SOE agents.

(SIGNED) A. Braun.

As we see from this report, a few months after the end of the war, in important circles, the brave Jan Lowey-Ball was still considered a suspect requiring further investigation.

Once the occupation was over, *V-Mann* William Pons was speedily tracked down, arrested and charged with treason. His advocate, K. W. P. Klaasen, described him as a church-going man, married and with children, who unfortunately fell under the control of the cunning Oelschlägel. Truus testified at his trial, telling the story of how he had ruthlessly tricked everybody. It was not a pleasant experience for her to face the man who had so deviously and cruelly betrayed Henri and had hoodwinked her and her children with his charm and assurances of friendship and support in her days of desperation. She stared at him with dislike, but he turned his head aside and never met her gaze. At all times his face maintained a disinterested and arrogant expression.

Also present at his trial were Ed and Valentine Conijn, and Toon and Dicky Bosscher, out of respect for Fritz's memory. They sat there in the dark-panelled courtroom, stern yet sad as they faced the man who brought about the death of their beloved son and brother. Their presence at the trial was not because they were hoping to witness Pons' death sentence, but maybe to hear the traitor express regret and remorse for his actions which had led to young Fritz's death. This he never did, remaining a Nazi to the end.

William Pons' defence, that he was a law-abiding family man (his wife had, in fact, long since sent him packing), was of no avail, and he was sentenced to death.

Senior advocate M. H. Gelinck declared, '*Als ere een man is, die de zwaarste straf heeft verdiend, dan is het wel deze man*' ('If ever there is a man who has earned the heaviest punishment, then it is this man'). In May 1948 his sentence was commuted to 24 years imprisonment. After only 16 years spent in various prisons, Willy Pons was released. Shortly thereafter he remarried, but six years later he died in Hoorn aged seventy-one, proving, as we have seen so many times in this tale, the old adage, 'only the good die young'.

After liberation, almost 200,000 Dutch citizens classified as collaborators were interned in camps and prisons and put on trial. Five years after liberation almost 140,000 of these collaborators were pardoned and set free. In spite of the horrors and brutality they had experienced, the Dutch demonstrated that they are a compassionate society, forgiving their invaders and their pro-German fellow citizens.

At Veluwe, a military rifle range, 4,000 Dutchmen who had served in the SS were detained and put on trial. About two hundred people were found guilty of war crimes and given death sentences. On appeal, a large number of these sentences were changed to life.

After the war, numerous Nazi officers were apprehended and charged. The files on the accused, kept in the CABR (*Centraal Archief Bijzondere Rechtspleging*, or Central Archive of Special Justice), were classified and only conditionally opened to the public. Since the year 2000 the majority of these files have been declassified, so we now have more information on how justice was meted out to those Nazis who were captured. Many, however, escaped arrest by fleeing to Germany.

While the majority of German perpetrators of war crimes escaped execution, several of the worst offenders faced the firing squad. The head of the Occupation Government in the Netherlands, the Austrian-born Arthur Seyss-Inquart, was arrested, found guilty of monstrous murders and deportation of Jews, tried, sentenced to death and executed.

The highest SS and Police Officer during the Netherlands occupation, Austrian-born SS-Brigadeführer Johann 'Hanns' Albin Rauter, was arrested by British forces, handed over the Dutch authorities, tried and found guilty of crimes against humanity. Not only was he responsible for the deportation of thousands of Jewish people to concentration camps, he also set up camps in the Netherlands, including Vught, which he proudly showed off to visiting Nazi officials as a 'model' camp. At these camps thousands of people met with maltreatment and often death. Rauter was executed by firing squad in March 1949.

Anton Mussert was arrested on 7 May 1945 at the headquarters of the National Socialist Movement, of which he was the founder and leader. He was tried, and despite making appeals to Queen Wilhelmina, was executed by firing squad exactly one year later, on the Waalsdorpvlakte, where hundreds of Dutch citizens had been executed by the Nazi regime.

Maarten Kuiper, a member of the SS and SD, had taken part in the Silbertanne killings, a series of assassinations carried out between September 1943 and September 1944. More than 50 Dutch people were either murdered or seriously wounded by SS members as retribution for attacks on pro-German Dutch citizens. Kuiper worked with Emil Rühl and Friedich Viebahn, was present at the arrest of Anne Frank and was responsible for the arrest and execution of Ernst Klijzing and many Resistance members, including Henri Scharrer. He presented no mitigating circumstances at his trial, and was executed in August 1948.

SS man Wouter Mollis, a colleague of Maarten Kuiper, who was present at the interrogation of Henri Scharrer, assisted Emil Rühl at the trial of Fritz Conijn and was responsible for the shocking treatment of Klijzing and Balder at Weteringschans, was executed in February 1949.

The German Interior Minister, Wilhelm Frick, was hanged, together with Ernst Kaltenbrunner, Chief of the RSHA.

Willy Lages, Head of the SD, who caused so much death and destruction in Amsterdam, and Ferdinand Aus der Funten, Head of the Centre of Justice *Auswanderung* (emigration) and responsible for the deportation of many Jews, received life sentences. Lages was released on the grounds of ill health and died in Germany in April 1971.

Of the men at Weteringschans and Euterpestraat (SD headquarters), Emil Rühl and Friedrich Verbahn, both involved in Henri's interrogation, were initially sentenced to death but had their sentences later commuted to twenty years' imprisonment. Hans Blumenthal, second in command in Euterpestraat, was sentenced to seven years and went home to Germany in 1951.

Mattis Ridderhof (Georges van Vliet) – a successful Abwehr agent who specialized in penetrating evasion lines – was arrested and convicted. Also arrested was Sergeant Hendrikus Knoppers, who had escaped to England during the war.

After intensive investigation at that time, Knoppers was exonerated by the British Intelligence Service. It was only after the war that it was discovered that he had been a German agent all along. Also working with Ridderhof was Louis de Bray, a Belgian Gestapo agent who was arrested in 1945 and found guilty. He was mentioned in Carry Libourel's report to the Allies.

One of the most interesting men in this saga, Hermann Giskes (Dr German), the man who created the counter-intelligence Operation *Englandspiel* and who recruited Christiaan Lindemans as a double agent, was put on trial together with his associate Josef Schreider. They were both released because of lack of evidence of war crimes. Neither were Nazis. They were simply good at what they did, which was counter-intelligence. After the war, Giskes was considered so proficient at his work that he was employed as a senior official by the US intelligence services in Europe. His memoir *London Calling North Pole*, which tells the story of how he and his team tricked Allied intelligence, was published to critical acclaim and is still available on amazon.com.

Kriminalkommissar Johannes Heinrich Munt, whom Carry visited in an attempt to save Henri, was arrested, briefly imprisoned and then released, as he was found not guilty of any war crimes. While in prison he kept himself busy by writing a novel and poetry.

A number of the Germans in the occupied Netherlands were able to get away with murder. One was the head of the SD's Department of *Gegnerbekämpfung* (combating the opposition) in the Netherlands, Erich Deppner, responsible for the execution at Vught of over 100 prisoners in the first days of September 1944. At one stage he was also stationed at Camp Westerbork. After the war, the Dutch government tried unsuccessfully to get him deported to the Netherlands. He was tried and acquitted of the murder of Russian PoWs in Amersfoort, so he escaped justice and died a free man in December 2005.

One of the main architects of the Holocaust was assassinated three years before the end of the war. SS-Gruppenführer Reinhard Heydrich was attacked in Prague by a British-trained hit squad consisting of Czechs and Slovaks in May 1942, and died of his injuries a week later. Even Hitler referred to him as 'The Man with the Iron Heart'.

And so justice was done.

VICTORY AND SURVIVAL

Chapter 17

New Beginnings

A fter the liberation, Truus appealed to the Allied Military Intelligence Service for assistance with the education of her two sons. It was a long process, and in this task she was assisted by Carry. She worked at it diligently for about two years. In the Washington War Archives there are claim forms and witness statements testifying to how Henri helped Allied airmen. Henri's work with Fritz Conijn is also mentioned in one of the reports dated 1 March 1946, signed with an illegible signature that looks like Paul (Pauki) Schuurbijut and stating that Henri had collected two airmen from Fritz in Alkmaar; the writer of the statement testifies to having been a witness to this meeting.

On 23 June 1947 Truus wrote a letter to Holland Office, 6801 Mis-X Detachment, Military Intelligence Service, United States Army, Bloemcamplaan 36, Wassennaar:

Dear Sirs,
On February 8th of last year Mr. F. Bilgrey, 1st Lt. Air Corps payed [*sic*] me a visit in connection with the help my late husband gave to American pilots who landed in Holland during the war. As you know my husband was shot by the Germans in September 1944. During his visit Mr. Bilgrey told me that in his opinion the U.S. Government would be prepared to undertake payment of the costs of the education of my two sons. In accordance with your letter dated March 2nd 1946, I sent you copies of the birth-certificates of both my boys.
I regret to say that thus far I have not received any news from you. I should be greatly obliged if you would let me know if the help by your Government, which I mentioned above, is still being considered.
Awaiting your much esteemed reply I remain, Yours faithfully w.g. T Scharrer.

Just over two months later, a letter was addressed from Stichting 1940–1945 (an organization to assist victims) to the A.G. Award Decoration, A.P.O.757, U.S. Army, Frankfurt am Main, Germany, dated 7 October 1947:

We, the official "Foundation 1940–1945" that gives social aid to the victims among members of the Dutch Resistance movement during the

occupation provide for – amongst others – the widow and 2 children of
Mr. H. Scharrer, who was shot by the Germans in September 1944 on
account of his prominent work that consisted of bringing back allied airmen via France, Spain or Zwitzerland to their divisions.
From the enclosed copies of a letter dated March 2nd 1946 from lst Lt.
Air Corps Felix Bilgrey, Holland Office, etc. (translation added) and the
reply of 23rd June, you will see that a kind of award was planned for the
education of the 2 children, boys, born 16-10-29 and 19-12-31.
We shall thank you to let us know whether you are still in a position to settle this matter, in which case we shall be glad to give you full particulars
as to the case referred to above, Yours faithfully, Stichting 1940–1945,
District Amsterdam. (signed) Manager.

While there is no further correspondence in the Stichting files, Raymond Scharrer
reports that both he and his mother did actually receive funding.

In 1948, Richard, who was being a difficult teenager and had only been attend-
ing school intermittently, was sent to stay with his Aunt Marie Jeanne in Cavaillon,
France, in the hope that under her influence he would settle down. There is no
doubt that without a father and with no firm hand to guide him, he drifted into an
easy existence of socializing and drinking – popular with a large group of friends,
and always the life of the party.

Raymond, by contrast, was able to concentrate on his studies and attended the
Barlaeus Gymnasium until 1950.

Then, quite unexpectedly, in early March 1950 Truus took ill. She was diagnosed as suffering from a form of acute leukemia that would not give her much
time to live. She faced the sudden onset of terminal illness with her usual bravery,
only taking to her bed the day before she died, on 20 March 1950, less than three
weeks from the time of her diagnosis. Her sudden and unexpected death, just short
of her fifty-first birthday, came as a shock to family and friends.

Raymond remembers talking to Carry Libourel at his mother's funeral, which
was the last time he saw her. An official from the Stichting gave the eulogy. Raymond
does not recall any Resistance people being at the funeral, and Jan Lowey-Ball and
Tom Yardin Millord did not attend. The war was over, and many of its heroes were
dead and buried. Life was moving on.

After his mother's passing, Raymond went to live with Pieter and Elise
Veldhuizen and their daughter Puck at their home at Catherina van Clevepark 59,
Nieuwer Amstel. Pieter was the Technical Director of the British Holland Coal
Company, a business started by his father. They imported anthracite from Wales
and exported it to Germany and had shipyards in Amsterdam and Rotterdam.
Pieter's father also had a stake in Welsh coal mines. As a consequence of the

war and then the nationalization of coal in Wales, the family lost everything and received little compensation. It was while living in their home, which became his safe haven, that Raymond completed his final school exams.

The Stichting also paid Raymond's university fees of 350 guilders a year, and this allowed him to attend the Gemeente Universiteit of Amsterdam, starting a degree in Geology in the autumn of 1950. Puck and Raymond were married on 8 December 1955. Raymond was later offered a position at the Anglo American company in Johannesburg, and the couple moved to South Africa. He was promoted to the position of Manager of the Springs Gold Mine. They lived in a large, rambling Anglo American mining house with a big, beautifully kept garden, and it was here in the mining town of Springs that their children Monique and Denis were born.

Richard returned to the Netherlands after spending a couple of years in France with his aunt and uncle, and started working for KLM at their building on Museumplein, opposite the American consulate. He later worked for Phillips, before joining the Dutch army, where he achieved the rank of sergeant. Sometime around 1958, Richard married Elizabeth (known as Liesje) van Kampen. Liesje, her mother, Ko, her father and two younger sisters (Hennie and Puck) had been interned in a Japanese prison camp in Indonesia during the war. It is not an experience that was ever spoken about, but conditions at the camp were known to have been horrific. At one stage Liesje had to have an operation to remove her appendix. The camp, however, had no anaesthetic for operations and so they operated on her without any painkillers. She simply passed out once they started making the incision. Her father did not survive the prison camp. She was some years older than Richard, tall, slim, quietly spoken and a superb cook of Indonesian dishes.

Richard and Elizabeth followed Raymond and Puck Scharrer to South Africa in 1962, but were divorced in February 1963. They had no children. Richard and Jocelyn were married in East London on 30 March 1963. Elizabeth and Jocelyn remained in touch for a number of years, until Elizabeth married a medical doctor in Switzerland. Jocelyn was requested to organize a second divorce that would be recognized in Switzerland, in order for Elizabeth to remarry, as there was some complication with the papers. This she did, with lawyers handling the necessary court applications.

Richard and Jocelyn's daughter, Nicole, was born in Johannesburg on 6 December 1963, and when she was eighteen months old Richard and Jocelyn returned to Amstelveen, Netherlands, where they lived in a first floor apartment in Pruimenlaan. It was here that Collin and Glenn were born and they were able to meet up with the members of Truus' family. They returned to Johannesburg in 1968, where Richard took up a procurement position with the retail company CNA and Jocelyn started her career in advertising as a copywriter, later becoming Creative Director of the largest agency in South Africa.

Henri Scharrer's younger brother Emmanuel, who was executed in the forests in Arnhem in 1941 as a suspected German agent, and his wife Therese Delaspre, had two daughters. The elder, Claudette, married Jacques Beurnel. They have three children, all boys: Ivan, Serge and Jean Jacques. Nicole (Pouty) Scharrer, the younger daughter of Emmanuel Scharrer, is at the time of writing, seventy-nine years old and lives in the Ardennes. Nicole married Donald Harris in 1958 in Schaerbeek, Brussels. They have a daughter, Myrtille, who married Vivien Benoit and has a daughter by the name of Pimprenelle Benoit.

There has been only limited contact between the sons of Henri Scharrer and their Belgian cousins, although Raymond Scharrer has written to them from time to time.

After the war, Carry Libourel, who had done everything she could to sort out Henri Scharrer's and Truus' financial and legal affairs, packed a haversack, climbed on to her bicycle and pedalled off to France. In keeping with her free-spirited, adventurous nature, she stayed away for months, taking temporary jobs here and there. She waitressed, harvested grapes, planted rice, whatever was going. When she felt capable of picking up the pieces of her life again, she joined AFP (Agence France-Presse) as a journalist, a job at which she excelled.

This news agency, now one of the biggest in the world, suited Carry's experience and background. It has an interesting history, which started in 1940, when German forces occupied France. They took over the original press offices and renamed it 'Office Français d'Information'; only the private advertising company retained the name Havas.

Then on 20 August, 1944, as Allied forces moved on Paris, a group of journalists in the French Resistance seized the offices of the FIO and issued the first news dispatch from the liberated city under the name of Agence France-Presse. And it has been known as the AFP ever since.

Following her time with AFP, Carry had a daughter, Linda, and in keeping with her liberated ideas did not marry the father. Instead, she took up a career in the Netherlands with the General Intelligence and Security Service. It was another position to which she was well suited, given the security and intelligence work she had done with Henri during the war with MI5, the Free French and Belgian security forces. Carry told her Allied Forces interrogator after the war that she continued to keep in touch with both Jan Lowey-Ball and Jack Bottenheim. She worked at a senior level in the Security Service until she retired, then moved to the South of France, where she lived until her death in 1999, when she was in her late nineties.

Linda Libourel now lives in the Hague, working for an investment bank, and is married to Peter Morison. She has children and grandchildren.

After being held at Weteringschans, following the failed ransom attempt, Tom Yardin Millord, who had been tortured while under arrest in order to extract information from him, was transported to Stalag IV-B in Muhlberg (Brandenburg), a concentration camp near the Elbe. From here he was released by Allied forces in May 1945 and went home, traumatized but, unlike so many others, still alive.

Tom survived the war a disillusioned man. A few years later, he wrote a letter to Fritz Conijn's mother offering his condolences. His conscience was plagued by the fact that Henri had specifically requested that he, Tom, help raise the ransom money, but Tom, an experienced man in his forties, had passed the job over to twenty-one-year-old Fritz. He regretted having done so, and he felt partly responsible for Fritz' death. He was deeply affected by his war experiences, and his marriage to Betty soon began to fail. Today he would probably be diagnosed as suffering from post-traumatic stress disorder.

He worked towards raising funds for the building of a national monument on the Dam in Amsterdam, and it was hoped he would assist P. Sanders on a book about the National Support Funds, but to the dismay of the author, Tom's health was not good. Also he wanted his war experiences to be a closed book, as their recollection brought him nothing but bad dreams and tension within his marriage. After he and Betty finally divorced, he finished his days as a motor car salesman. All contact with the Scharrer family came to an end.

Another disillusioned man was Jan Lowey-Ball. There were unpleasant rumours about missing money that had been paid by some of the escapees to secure their documents and pay the guides. Also his involvement in Henri's Resistance business affairs as a go-between was regarded in some quarters as questionable. The Canadians who were investigating collaborators became suspicious. In addition, there was talk in London intelligence circles about anyone who had had a connection with Chris Lindemans, and it was known that Jan had been among his closest contacts. The Allies decided there was something strange about his false Toulouse documents and how he obtained them. Stranger still was his successful escape from imprisonment on *Dolle Dinsdag*, at a time when his colleagues Henri and Fritz were executed and Tom sent to a concentration camp. There is a factor in the poor treatment meted out to Jan that is worthwhile mentioning: one of his parents was Indonesian, so he was regarded as 'half-caste' in those days when racism was predominant. This description of him, which appears on certain documents, did not help matters.

When he returned to the Netherlands from Belgium, where he had been working for the Allies, Jan was arrested and sent to the Interrogation Centre Fort Blauwkapel near Utrecht, where he was locked up with other suspected collaborators for six months.

The Field Security and the BNV (Bureau of National Security), for whom Jan had previously worked, informed the Allied powers that the unfortunate position of one of their colleagues had been brought to their attention, and they requested a proper investigation into any allegations against Jan Lowey-Ball, as they maintained this would clear his name. This had little effect, and he remained locked up without a hearing. Jan had greater success in approaching Prince Bernhard, who knew all about Jan's Resistance work and immediately intervened. Being unaware of his impending release, Jan once again escaped from custody. His freedom, however, did not last long and he was soon recaptured. In February 1946 Prince Bernhard again intervened on his behalf, recommending that as no charges had been levelled against him, he should be released and be appointed an Intelligence Officer, work he had previously conducted most successfully.

Jan was finally released as a result of Prince Bernhard's efforts. He was, however, most disillusioned by his incarceration and decided he had had enough of this unfair and probably racist treatment and would leave the Netherlands. He first worked in Edmonton in Canada and then with Shell in Curaçao. He finally returned to the Netherlands and finished his working career as a director of a Christian organization in Hilversum.

There were many brave men and women who risked everything to help save their countrymen and Allied airmen from harm under the occupation. Their bravery and sacrifice must be regarded as extraordinary. And it was not in vain. The Resistance did not save the Netherlands from German occupation, but it played an enormous role in hiding thousands of people, sending vital intelligence to the Allies and saving the honour of the Dutch nation.

In turn, the Dutch people remembered them. The executed Resistance fighters were honoured after the war, as were those that survived. Letters of condolence poured into their families, and one of those who was high on the honours list was Fritz Conijn – the founder of the KP Noord Holland and the man who raised that enormous ransom for Henri Scharrer in only a couple of days.

There was much soul-searching after the war about the death of the young Fritz Conijn. In looking back at events it is clear that Fritz underestimated the risks and overrated his own chances of success. He felt secure because he had brought along the experienced Millord and Lowey-Ball to the ransom meeting. Did he realize the extent of the risk he was taking in raising the ransom to save Henri? It would appear that he did know. All those who were active in the Resistance and who undertook this dangerous work fully realized that their lives were on the line, just as the brave airmen who climbed on board the bombers and fighter planes knew that the survival odds were stacked against them. The human spirit is such that nobody ever thought that they would be the one to die. So Fritz had faith that his mission would succeed. But luck was not with him that day.

His father Gerrit Conijn found the sacrifice Fritz had made too great for him to bear. He missed his youngest son terribly, and the sadness adversely affected his physical and mental health. He became depressed. Also suffering the effects of the loss of Fritz were his mother Marthe, his brother Ed and his sisters.

While Fritz's achievements became well known and recognized after the war, Ed doubted whether the brave deeds were worth the loss, pain and suffering endured by his parents and the rest of the family. The family could not overcome their grief at this loss and found it difficult to come to terms with it. It is true to say that Fritz Conijn, in all seriousness and dedication, tried to do his duty in those fateful two days, knowing that every day could be his last.

Fritz Conijn was one of the few Resistance men to be posthumously awarded the Resistance Cross, a photograph of which appears on the front cover of Doeko Bosscher's book, *Haast om te Sterven.*

Chapter 18

Extraordinary People We Cannot Forget

Before we leave this story, we need to salute a number of the other people who worked with Henri from time to time; because they too are unsung heroes and deserve acknowledgement.

Their names appear in documents obtained from archives and in the books and memoirs written by survivors. In all these sources there are frequent references to helpers, using real or code names. Sometimes the information on these people is only a few sentences, in other cases it runs to several pages. It is not surprising, however, that when searching the stories around Henri, we find that the same names keep turning up. This was a tight-knit community with controlled contacts with other cell groups. Nobody knew, other than a few trusted people, what was going on. The man or woman next door might be in a Resistance cell, and you would never know.

Many heroes whose names are not mentioned here are recorded by the NIOD (Institute for War, Holocaust and Genocide Studies) in Amsterdam and in other sources available on the internet. We have selected only those few who were actively and directly involved with the Henri Scharrer escapees.

These brave men and women came from all walks of life and included farmers, engineers, students and even members of the aristocracy such as Baron Abraham Van Boetzelaer. He is mentioned as being a person with whom certain Resistance people in the Scharrer Line were associated, including in the Allied report on Carry Libourel's official interrogation by the Allies about the Scharrer Line. The Allied interrogator simply states that a number of people were connected to or associated with the Scharrer organization, including the notorious Christiaan (Chris) Lindemans 'King Kong' already referred to in previous reports, and the Abwehr agent, Louis de Bray, who betrayed Herman Laatsman in Paris. Also included in this list of names are these Resistance fighters and helpers: Jan Lowey-Ball, Baron Van Boetzelaer, Baron Van Heemstra, the brothers Verloop, Domine Ten Carte, Jan Strengers, Andre Wyssogota and the personnel of the offices of Neerlandais in Paris. All have fascinating stories, as we shall see.

Baron Van Boetzelaer was arrested and died in Germany, but his wife Agnes de Beaufort, who was also arrested, survived the war. She later tried to get compensation for the considerable sums her husband had spent helping escapees which, she claimed, consisted of most of his fortune.

Jack Bottenheim, a man whom Henri helped escape and who had travelled to Rotterdam to meet Lindemans, later in London made a long statement to Allied investigators. In this he reported that he knew that when Chris Lindemans first started working in the Resistance he had assistance from two people: Mr (Baron) Van Heemstra and Jonkheer Verspijck. He went on to say that it was Lindemans who gave him the introduction to Baron van Heemstra in Paris. Jack added that the brothers Victor and Albert Swane also joined in with Lindemans and Verspijck. These connections with Lindemans when he was still a loyal Resistance man are corroborated in other reports.

Fritz Conijn's friend, Pierre de Bie, is worth commenting on, as he became a prominent figure after the war. He was the second son of seven children whose father worked in the Maastricht harbour office. A clever young man, Pierre was diligent in all the projects he undertook. During the first year of the war he joined the Nederlandse Middenstandsbank in Maastricht, and in a short time he was promoted to a departmental head, the start of a most successful career.

In May 1944, Ernst Klijzing, a medical student at the University of Amsterdam, also came into the picture. What originally got him into trouble was his refusal to sign the declaration of loyalty to the German occupiers. Through introductions by L. H. Frijda and H. Katan he had come into contact with the small leftist Resistance group CS.6, of which Nicolaas 'Bob' Celosse and Kas de Graaf were members. Ernst was involved in several robberies and attacks organized by CS.6. He also provided assistance to Jews in hiding and distributed illegal publications, including *The Free Lectern*.

In the middle of 1943 the CS.6 group was betrayed and folded as a result of the arrests and executions of many of its members, including its leader Dr Gerrit Kastein, who was betrayed by Anton van der Waals.

Ernst, who until this time had been happily living on the Pieter Lastmankade in Amsterdam, received a warning that the Germans had intelligence on him and that his home was at risk of a Gestapo raid. So he made a dash to Brabant and then Limburg, before trying to get into Switzerland. The Swiss, however, stopped him at the border, and he was forced to return to the Netherlands via France and Belgium.

He was now in serious need of help and protection and made contact with Henri, who decided to help him by introducing him to Fritz and Pierre. The meeting was arranged for Monday, 22 May 1944.

On this particular day, Pierre had gone to the Central Station to meet with Kek, Ber and Rinus to discuss operations. Then he went to the Hotel Americain on the Leidseplein to pick up Fritz Conijn and take him to a café nearby, where the meeting with Henri and Ernst would take place.

Ernst arrived first, took a corner table in a café and as per prior instructions greeted Pierre, Fritz and Henri as long lost friends. Over coffee he quietly explained what his role had been in the CS.6 and that he was on the Gestapo wanted list. From time to time Henri would make a comment. Ernst begged them to help him, and they agreed to do so by finding him a safe house in which to live. After Ernst had left, Fritz and Pierre discussed with Henri their impressions of him and said that Ernst was a worthwhile young man who could be useful in KP Alkmaar. Henri agreed.

For a while the plan was successful, and Ernst worked with the KP Alkmaar. But on 25 June 1944 in Alkmaar he did a silly thing. He rode the motorbike of Fritz Conijn without engine papers and with documents in the name of Van Es, and needless to say he was held at a traffic control. This irresponsible joyride resulted in new SD investigations and had major repercussions, as a link had now been established between the Fritz of the bike and Fritz Conijn. The whole resistance group in Alkmaar had to move to new safe houses. While Ernst Klijzing survived the war as an honoured member of the Resistance, this irresponsible episode left a shadow on his reputation.

Then disaster struck. North Holland Resistance member Jaap Balder, who had been passing Allied airmen through to Henri and Carry, was arrested by the Gestapo. It was a Resistance rule that a person arrested would endeavour not to give away names and addresses of any associates for at least twenty-four to forty-eight hours. This allowed colleagues time to make their escape, or if possible to make arrangements for the release of the arrested person. It was usually after about two days of extreme interrogation that a prisoner would finally give away information, and more arrests would then follow. The officer responsible for the interrogation and torture of Balder was the brutal SD man, Sachbearbeiter Emil Rühl, who bragged to his men about how he had wasted no time in getting Balder to talk. This left everybody with little time to take evasive action.

The result was that within two days of the arrest of Balder, Ernst Klijzing was arrested at what until now had been considered a safe house. When word got out that Ernst had been arrested, everybody in the KP Alkmaar knew they would be in immediate danger. All members, including Fritz and Pierre, hurriedly took evasive action and disappeared before the Gestapo could catch up with them.

Karst Smit was another highly decorated Resistance man, awarded the Medal of Freedom with Silver Palm on 16 November 1946. After serving with the Dutch army during the invasion, he then joined the Marechaussees, the Dutch mounted police, which was responsible for patrolling the country's borders. He was based at Baarle-Nassau, where *Englandvaarder* Jack Bottenheim made his first crossing from Belgium to the Netherlands. This has a sister town in Belgium by the name of Baarle-Hertog and the two became joined as the result of medieval boundary changes. When American escape line researcher, Bruce Bolinger, visited Karst after the war, he was shown a house in the town with a white boundary line running up the owner's front door. During the war the owner kept pigs, and his pigsty was on the Dutch side of the house. Owning pigs was forbidden in the Netherlands but permitted in Belgium. So he moved the pigsty from the Dutch side of the house to the Belgian side. Strange but true!

Smit's resistance work started as the result of an unexpected meeting. While on patrol in April 1942, Smit and another policeman encountered two escaped French prisoners-of-war. They had crossed into the Netherlands from Germany at a point on the German–Dutch border near Twente, and were trying to reach France via Belgium. Smit volunteered to guide them across the border and thus set up the beginnings of his network, which he developed together with Eugene van der Heijden. When they first worked for the Resistance they transported men from Tilburg to Brussels across the Dutch–Belgian border, and provided them with money and identity papers.

In November 1944 his escape line was smashed and he transferred his services to another, organizing the southern part of a line through France and over the Pyrenees. Then he was betrayed by Christiaan Lindemans, arrested and spent March 1944 to April 1945 in a concentration camp. In the last days of the war he was able to escape, joined the advancing American forces and survived the war.

In an email to Megan Koreman, Rudy Zeeman also mentions the names of other people who were in separate cell groups in Paris. This was the city where so many escapees landed up, either as a result of their own efforts or through the escape lines of the Netherlands and Belgium. The lucky ones made it to the Resistance safety net, were looked after and helped on their way.

What is interesting is that so many of these Resistance fighters and helpers worked together at different times. Sometimes they would be in a group that would link up with another group, work together for a few weeks, then split away again. So a Resistance fighter from the Dutch–Paris Line would link up with the Belgian Comete Line, Christiaan Lindeman's Line, or be helped by Christiaan's wife, Gilberte 'Gilou' Letoupe, Henri Scharrer, Albert Starink, Piet Felix or Victor and Albert Swane. Or they might even send escapees to England by boat with Anton Schrader.

These were only a few of the brave individuals linked in various ways to Henri. They and many others formed the backbone of the Dutch Resistance and it was their efforts and dedication that made it such an effective organization in extremely dangerous times.

They are all unsung heroes.

Chapter 19

Richard Scharrer Writes about his Father

*I*n 1996, three years before he died of a heart attack in his sleep, Richard Scharrer wrote down these memories of his father. The idea was that they would form a framework on which Jos Scharrer could write the story of Henri Scharrer.

27-10-96

<u>Attention: Jocelyn Scharrer</u>
HENRI JEAN SCHARRER
BORN – 21-04-1900 in Ostend, Belgium.
NATIONALITY: FRENCH
Father: Henri Scharrer – Born in Metz – France
Mother: Mlle Decoo. Birth place unknown
Brother: Manuel Scharrer. Birth place unknown
Sister: Marie Jeanne Scharrer. Birth place unknown
But both born presumably in Belgium or France.

Brother was in the Resistance in the Ardennes and got killed when warning a group in the Ardennes that SS forces were on to them. Date of death unknown.

Sister married Henri de Vittecoque – French military attaché in the Netherlands – rank Major. Died at young age of cancer. Had large military funeral in the Hague. From the hospital to the cemetery streets were lined with army personnel, and I remember that his coffin was on a gun carriage and an army band played over and over the Death March. Marie Jeanne remarried Henri Viallat, then a commandant in the French Forces. Both died five and a half years ago. A month before their deaths I had the pleasure of seeing them.

Father worked for A.F.P. [*sic*] as a foreign correspondent. He was away a lot and in the years prior to 1939, the outbreak of the war, he was involved in military intelligence. In +/– 1940 he worked for S.P.A. (Swiss Presse Agentur), a Lausanne based agency – which was in reality a semi-intelligence operation. We did see from time to time articles by him – but we hardly ever saw him.

After 53 or 54 years one does not remember all that had happened.

The first time I met his partner was in 1941 (January) – Tom Yardin Millard [*sic*] who was, it was said, involved in British Military Intelligence. It was also rumoured that Dad had been to England and the both of them set up networks in France, Belgium and Holland:

a. To get the resistance on a military basis
b. To get Allied Airforce men to Spain via Holland – Belgium & France as most of the daylight bombing by the USAAF (US Army Airforce) was targeted to Bremen–Kiel–Ruhr area–Berlin.

The French connection came in when raids were in the Dresden–Frankfurt & Scheinfurt areas (Scheinfurt Ball Bearing) – vital to the Luftwaffe, tanks and all rolling stock of the Wehrmacht.

After many years I have tried to put my father's picture together and from references I concluded that they had 'Dad & Tom' embarked on a marathon task, fraught with danger (S.S. – Gestapo) deceit, informers, paid so-called agents, trips to Spain over the mountains near Andorra (Les Pyrenées Mountains), etc. Only a little help from the Allied Commando.

Once you are there you are on your own which even today can be regarded as a non-commitment.

My father, from what I recall, was dedicated – and my mother stood by that 'I think'. When you are young your parents do not confide in important matters with their children.

War went on and Dad came home after curfew. I remember the day that he walked down the street and a German patrol stopped him, sub-machine guns, pistols, rifles pointed at him. I do not know what he said, but after taking out his papers, they all jumped to attention. He walked down to our house with a big grin, and I asked him what happened. All he said was, 'I'm an Obergruppenführer' (+/– Colonel). 'Never say that to anyone, but I'm really a Lieutenant Colonel in our army.'

Dad never spoke anything but French to me, and he was fluent in German having lived with my grandmother and grandfather part of his life in Alsace-Loraine, where the prevalent language is French 20% – German 80%. How it is now I do not know.

I remember vividly asking my Dad that I wanted to see my Aunt Jo, because I loved her like Tante Jeanne.

The answer was 'Get to the station tomorrow at +/– 09.00 hrs, platform (I do not remember). I arrived there, no father. Suddenly I got tapped on the shoulder and there was that imposing, SS whatever, and it was my father.

He said to me, 'Speak only German.' And he gave me a magazine called 'Der Adler' – a German Airforce publication.

We went to a compartment which said 'Für Wehrmacht Offiziere'. There was one man in the compartment. A flight commander (German) with the rank of major. I never forget that. He said to Dad. 'I'm posted away. I will sleep.' In other words, 'FU S.S'.

Dad organized escapes with Tom. They raided the 'Coupon' offices (without food coupons you could not exist). We had 3 Allied Airmen at home – one a gunner, one a navigator of the USAAF and a Flight Officer of the R.A.F.

The young USAAF gunner gave me a little silk American flag, which I put on the wall of my bedroom. Removed by the Gestapo after Dad was arrested.

Family During the War

Totally disrupted. Since 1940 we did not have a father, though he was there sometimes.

Personal Memories of my Dad

I loved him. But in retrospect he was what I would call a modern day buccaneer. He had a great sense of values, but not always to the benefit of his family. I think I can understand his ways somehow, because the whole Scharrer family were military men – adventurous but not to the detriment of your family. The main concern has been, which I found out at an early age, of his relationship with Miss Carry Libourel – an attorney and cell-leader. But maybe living a day to day life like that, we should forgive him. If possible.

His Last Days

Dad was on a certain mission with Tom from Amsterdam to Paris [sic]. At Leiden the usual Gestapo check was made, but now also in all the compartments of the Wehrmacht. Dad & Tom never travelled in the same compartment.

Dad's travel papers were in order, but they also asked for his S.S. identity. He pulled out the wrong identity, not corresponding with the name of the S.D. card. He was arrested, had a silenced 'US gun' in his possession. Tom, a trained paratrooper, jumped out of the train – phoned my mother and told her the story [sic].

Date of arrest +/– 10th September and executed on 14.09.1944 [sic]. The day that the Allied forces were +/– 35 kms away from the execution site.

Beryl & I had the opportunity to go there last year and we could feel how these men have felt. We have photos of the camp & the names of the dead! His final titular rank was Colonel. His awards have been from Gen. Eisenhower. Air Marshal Tedder. Crox [sic] de Guerre (posthumous). Also French & Belgian medals. 2 or 3.

To my recollection from a young age I think my father cared for us all.

The nature of his work, his involvement in military intelligence, the turbulent years 1935–1939, and the subsequent invasion of Europe in 1940 by the German forces, destabilised countries, societies and most of all families.

In Western Europe, Great Britain and later the U.S.A. family life was totally disrupted, not by choice, but by necessity in order to overcome the Nazi menace.

Men were affected. They had to fight, but mainly the families they left behind, were the victims. Who do we blame? The soldiers or the often irresponsible governments who cause all this.

1. You win. We did it for a cause. Destruction of what.
2. You lose. We did it for a cause. Destruction of what.

Until now the world has not seen the light. Live in co-existence? Where? Europe is nearing it. U.S. is meddling in the Mid-East. A time bomb. Africa a total disaster.

In my opinion 'now' my Dad was a Family man. The war got in the way. [Illegible].

Epilogue

One cannot help wondering what the purpose was of all this sacrifice and death. These personal tragedies and millions like them became the foundation of a new world built on the ashes of the old. The history of the world following the Second World War is one in which the great successes outweigh the failures. Countries across the globe obtained full independence from the colonial empires. The United Nations was created. The world economy boomed and living standards improved across the planet. New technologies have changed the way people live. International travel has become a way of life. We have placed men on the moon, have an international space station and have sent rockets to Mars.

Then we have the individuals who survived the war due to the help of others: Rudy Zeeman, Frank Hart, Jack Bottenheim, Jim Davies, Ronnie Aitken, Eugene Halmos and countless others. They were able to go home, live full, active lives with hope and optimism, and tell their stories.

In 1996, the navigator on Frank Hart's Liberator, Eugene Halmos, wrote a best-selling war memoir, entitled *The Wrong Side of the Fence* and still available through Amazon. The jacket states that Halmos takes the reader back to a time of mass warfare, when survival and liberation were the dominant obsessions of American prisoners-of-war. After he returned home he became managing editor of *Engineering News Record* and continued his career there and at other well-known publications. He also became mayor of Poolesville, Maryland.

Rudy Zeeman remained in contact with many Dutch survivors. He wrote in his memoir that the Escapees to England Association had come into being through the initiative of a number of *Engelandvaarders* who had started meeting on a regular basis in the 1960s. During a business and holiday visit to Europe in 1977 he learned about its existence and, together with Robert van Exter, attended the annual reunion of 1977. He continued to attend these reunions whenever he visited the Netherlands, up until 1994.

Most *Engelandvaarders*, like many members of the Dutch Resistance, were eligible for the Dutch Resistance Cross, and their patron HRH Prince Bernhard pinned the award on the chests of a few recipients at the reunion at the Air Base Soesterberg on 19 September 1982. At this event, Rudy was given the opportunity to present His Royal Highness with his painting depicting his crossing of the Pyrenees in the bitter weather of January 1944. The painting is now at the Resistance and War Museum at Overloon in Brabant, in the south of the Netherlands.

The Scharrer family survived, and the families of Richard and Raymond have grown and flourished.

Jocelyn and Richard divorced in 1978. Richard Scharrer died in 1999 of a heart attack while in his sleep at the age of seventy. At that time he was married to his fifth wife, Beryl. Most of his adult life he was haunted by memories of the war and the death of both his parents. The disappearance of Henri for nearly a year, when they did not know what had happened to him, was highly traumatic for the whole family. It happened at a time when Richard was at a young and impressionable age.

He was well read and enjoyed reading French. He also read extensively on the Second World War and the rise of Nazi Germany – a subject on which he became an expert. His other interests included jazz and classical music, especially German music, with Wagner being one of his favourites. He was also an excellent cook and would spend Sunday mornings in the kitchen preparing a classic French dish or paella.

Raymond Scharrer and his wife have lived a full and successful life in South Africa, Italy and Belgium. They now live in Brussels and spend a lot of time travelling.

Henri Scharrer has five grandchildren. In South Africa are Richard's three children. Nicole is married to Michael Bruce, who runs his own motor business. She is a leading figure in South African advertising and heads up Geometry – an international Ogilvy company. Collin Scharrer married Kathy Bowyer, a TV producer. He runs his own TV and film production company under the name of Film Machine. Glenn Scharrer runs his own mobile catering company branded as Longtom Foods.

The children of Raymond and Puck Scharrer are Denis, an international marketing consultant, and Monique Scharrer Twynholm, a microbiologist with Smith Kline Glaxo. Both live in the United Kingdom.

Henri has eight great-grandchildren. Collin and Kathy Scharrer's children are Georgina, studying for her Honours in English Literature at Stellenbosch University with a view to becoming a journalist; Alexandra (Lexi), a student at Cape Town University, hoping to make a career in international affairs; Olivia, at the time of writing a first year student at the University of Pretoria. Robert, Ashley and Shelby Bruce, the triplets, children of Nicole and Michael Bruce, are all students at the University of Pretoria. Shelby is interested in Sports Science and excels at rowing, Ashley plans to become a journalist and Robert is hoping to become a lawyer.

In the United Kingdom there are: Peter, the son of Denis and Lyn Scharrer, currently a student at Cambridge University majoring in Chemical Engineering, and Denis' daughter, Christine, a graduate of the London School of Economics and qualified in the United States as a commercial pilot. She is currently a pilot with the airline EasyJet. Monique Scharrer Twynholm's son, Ross, is studying Sports Science at the University of Manchester.

Henri never received any acknowledgement of his espionage and intelligence work from the British, French and Belgian authorities, although this was the charge made against him by the Nazis on his arrest and for which he was found guilty and sentenced to death.

In all likelihood, this was due to the fact that most of the information available on wartime espionage and intelligence was classified, and even remains classified to this day. Henri's honours and the published information about him, Truus and Carry, only relate to the work he did in the Resistance movement, the false travel documents he organized and the help he gave to Allied airmen and young Dutch people who wanted to escape. There is no reference to his intelligence work.

Henri's descendants do not know his story. This book was especially written for them.

Concise Bibliography

Books

Bosscher, Professor Doeko, *Haast om te Sterven*, Prometheus Bert Bakker, 2015

Clutton-Brock, Oliver, *RAF Evaders. The Comprehensive Story of Escapers and Their Escape Lines, Western Europe, 1940–1945*, London Grub Street Publishing, 2009

Eman, Diet with James Schaap, *Things We Couldn't Say*, William B. Eerdmans Publishing Company, 1994

Evans, Richard, *The Coming of the Third Reich*, The Penguin Press, New York, 2004

Giskes, Hermann, *London Calling North Pole*, Marks Publishing, 1949

Halmos, Eugene, *The Wrong Side of the Fence*, White Mane Publishing, 1996

Marks, Leo, *Between Silk and Cyanide – A Codemaker's War 1941–1945*, The History Press

McDonough, Frank, *The Gestapo – The Myth and Reality of Hitler's Secret Police*, Coronet, 2015

Meyerowitz, Seth, *The Lost Airman. A True Story of Escape from Nazi-occupied France*, Penguin Random Books, 2015

Rees, Laurence, *The Dark Charisma of Adolf Hitler*, Ebury Press, 2012

Whittock, Martyn, *The Third Reich. The Rise and Fall of the Nazis*, Robertson Running Press, 2011

Zeeman, Rudy, *Luck Through Adversity*, P. R. Zeeman, self-published

Articles, notes and other sources

Air Forces Historical Research Agency (AFHRA)

Report from Linda Libourel Morison. Scan of Caroline Libourel's interview report with A. Braun of the Allied Forces, 1945.

ArmyAirForces.com of World War II

Article by Matt on his great uncle Sergeant John Currie, who was a crewman on the flight of Frank Hart's Liberator 41-28832 'Heaven can Wait'.

Article on another Liberator that came down on September 18, 1944. Its pilot, Captain Claude Lovelace, and others were killed and were buried in a Catholic Church in the town of Hommersum, Germany.

Baxter, Bob

Bomber Command article on the internet.

Bolinger, Bruce. United States

Supplied numerous website details and scans from the National Archives II, including:
http://wwii-netherlands-escape-lines.com/links-to-other-escape-and-evasion-websites/
    united-states-army-air-forces-usaaf/world-war-ii-u-s-airfields-on-the-u-k/
http://wwii-netherlands-escape-lines.com/links-to-other-escape-and-evasion-websites/
    united-states-army-air-forces-usaaf/http://wwii-netherlands-escape-lines.com/
    links-to-other-escape-and-evasion-websites/united-states-army-air-forces-usaaf/
http://wwii-netherlands-escape-lines.com/links-to-other-escape-and-evasion-websites/
    united-states-army-air-forces-usaaf/http://wwii-netherlands-escape-lines.com/
    links-to-other-escape-and-evasion-websites/united-states-army-air-forces-usaaf/
    world-war-ii-bomb-groups
http://wwii-netherlands-escape-lines.com/links-to-other-escape-and-eva-
    sion-websites/united-states-army-air-forces-usaaf/http://wwii-neth-
    erlands-escape-lines.com/links-to-other-escape-and-evasion-websites/
    united-states-army-air-forces-usaaf/9th-air-force
http:llwwii-netherlands-escape-lines.com/research/aircraft-crash-sites/
hhtp://www.nmkampvugt.nl/biografieen/scharrer-Henri/
http://airwar.texlaweb.nl/
http://wwii-netherlands-escape-lines.com/library/netherlands/netherlands-king-kong
http://wwii-netherlands-escape-lines.com/evasion-of-tom-applewhite/
    air-force-service/missiobn-report-385th-bombardment-group-11-nov-1943

Bosscher, Professor Doeko, University of Groningen

Various scans of personal information on Henri Scharrer, including:
Letter written by Truus Scharrer to Carry Libourel dated 4 March 1945.
Various photographs of Henri, Truus and Caroline Libourel.
Afschrift. Area Security Office, South Holland dated 17ᵗ July 1945. Report Copy of Henri
    Scharrer Business Card, copies of sketches made by Henri at Schoorl prison. Official
    residential information. Photograph of William Pons. Forged Identity and Travel
    documents produced by Henri Scharrer. Afwikkelingsbureau Concentratiekampen
    Taalstraat 60, Vught. Dated 3ʳ October 1945. Confirmation of the execution of Henri
    Scharrer signed by A. Timmenga. Textielkaart in the name of Hendrik J. Scharrer.
    Headquarters European Theatre of Operations. Military Intelligence Service, Claim
    for family Scharrer, Raymond Scharrer, together with witness statements.

British National Archives, Kew, United Kingdom

http://discovery.nationalarchives.gov.uk/details/r/C10852534 to C10852540
Also their files on Giskes, Schreider, Lindemans and others.

Christos, T.

Christos military and intelligence corner

Courtois, Robert, Brussels

Articles, press cuttings on Emmanuel Scharrer and genealogy of the Scharrer family. Scharrer family information obtained during his research.

HistoryNet

'Tiny Mulder: Teenage World War II Resistance Heroine'

Hobday, H. S.

Dam Buster. Article written by him on his escape to Spain. Reports by him to Allied authorities after his arrival in London.

Koreman, Megan, Paris

http://dutchparisblog.com/
Copies of articles on 'How to Flee the Gestapo', posted on the internet.
Also emails.

LeBlanc, Michael Moores, Canada

Diagram of SOE Contacts in Holland. Photographs of Anna Maria Verhulst Oomes. Report on Christiaan Lindemans formerly labelled secret by Mr E. R Stamp (slightly illegible) to Colonel R. Stephanus Camp 020. Information of the SOE. Scans of other reports by escapees and shot-down Allied pilots. Scans on reports by 'Dam Busters' Fred Sutherland and Harry Hobday, whom Christiaan Lindemans claimed he had helped save. Reports on Mrs R. Laatsman and Captain J. Weidner, of the Paris connection to Major White. Report by Gabrie Nahas. Report on Francois-Georges, Toulouse Service Logement. Report on Suzy Kraay – declassified, by Head Netherlands Security Service, Paris. NARA reports Authority NND 735001 1973 on shot-down Liberator bearing the names of Frank Hart and Eugene Halmos. Letter from Frank Hart to Mrs Xenia Verster. Report by Frank Hart dated 11 December 1945. Letter by Mrs Frank Hart (mother) to Mrs Verster.

Morison, Linda Libourel

Photograph of her mother Caroline Libourel.
Various emails containing information on Caroline and Henri Scharrer.

Scharrer, Richard

Essay on his father Henri Scharrer, 27 October 1996.

StrolZand

Internet Articles on Piet Felix and Frank Hart.

US Military Archives, College Park, Washington Registry & Archives

'Subject: Jack Charles Bottenheim'. By G.J. Baker, Lieutenant.

US National Archives (NARA)

http://www.8thafhs.com/get_one_acgroup.php?acgroup_id=21
Report on Aircraft Groups. 489th Bombardment Group (Heavy)

Wikipedia

Christiaan Lindemans

Index

ANP (Algemeen Nederlands Persbureau), 5, 65, 145
Aachen, 24–5, 119
Abbeville, 104
Abor, 47
Aerdenhout, 8
Africa, 166
Agence France-Presse (AFP), 155, 163
Aitkens, Ronnie, 87, 89–91, 120, 129, 167
Albers, Willie, 135–6
Alkmaar KP, 126, 129–30, 135, 161
Alkmaar, 52, 86, 89, 130–1, 152, 161
Alsace-Lorraine, 63
Amersfoort, 138
Amstel River, 6, 61, 78, 133
Amsteldijk, 129, 131–2, 134
Amstellaan, 132–4
Amstelveen, 61, 117, 137, 146–7, 154
Amstelveenseweg, 9
Amsterdam District, 153
Amsterdam Golf Club, 28
Amsterdam KP, 130, 140
Amsterdam University, 160
Amsterdam, 2, 5–7, 9–11, 20, 25, 28–31, 39, 43, 53, 55, 57, 61–2, 134, 137, 140–1, 143, 146–7, 149, 156, 159–60, 165
monument on the Dam, 156
Andorra, 164
Antwerp, 24, 73–4, 85, 89–90, 104, 111, 119–21
Antwerpen, 25
Apollolaan, 138, 140
Arbas, 37
Ardennes Forest, 64, 155
Arnhem, 7, 60, 104, 111–12, 115, 155
Atlantic, 84
Aus Der Funten, Ferdinand, 149
Auschwitz-Birkenau camp, 143–4
Avenue Foch, 32

Baarle-Hertog, 161
Baarle-Nassau, 75, 94, 161
Bach, 61

Badhoevedorp, 127
Baker Street, 46
Balder, Jaap, 53, 130, 149, 161
Baltimore, 22
Barcelona, 39
Barlaeus Gymnasium, 153
Barnes, Wallis, 86
Barrere-Charbonnier, 57–8
Baserques-Charbonnier, 57–8
Bavaria, 63
Baxter, Bob, 87
Beethovenstraat, 28–9, 140
Beishuizen, Henk, 69
Belgium, 2, 6, 21–3, 25–6, 28, 43, 59, 63–4, 73–4, 89, 94, 104, 108–109, 119–20, 145, 156, 160, 162–4, 168
Belgium-France border, 78
Belize, 87
Benoit, Pimprenelle, 155
Benoit, Vivien, 155
Ber, 160
Berlage Bridge, 133
Berlin, 111, 119, 138, 164
Bern, 68, 146
Bernhard, Prince, 2, 111, 114, 137, 157, 167
Beurnel, Ivan, 155
Beurnel, Jean Jaques, 155
Beurnel, Serge, 155
Biarritz prison, 44, 80
Bidot, Pauki Schuur, 89
Bijzitter, 89
Bilbao, 59
Bilgrey, Mr F., 152–3
Bille, Joe, 120
Bingham, Major, 47, 50–1
Birmingham, 19
Bletchley Park, 47, 110
Blizard, Major Charles, 47
Bloemcamplaan, No. 36, 152
Blumenthal, Hans, 135, 149
Blunt, 51
Boetzelaer, Baron Abraham, 81, 85, 105, 146, 159

Boissevain, 'Janka', 53
Bolinger, Bruce, 161
Bolt, William, 87–8
Bong, Richard I, 87
Boon, Elsie 'van Loon', 59, 80, 95
Bordeaux, 80, 93, 118
Bos, Carel, 69
Bosscher, Prof. Doeko, 7, 62, 65–6, 68, 148, 158
Bosscher Senior, Doeko, 129
Bosscher, Toon, 148
Bottenheim, Jack, 40, 42, 45, 57, 59, 71–85, 94, 103, 120, 138, 147, 155
Boussens, 36, 70, 81
Bowyer, Kathy, 168
Brabant, 160, 168
Brand, 103
Brandenburg camp, 136, 156
Braun, A., 147
Breda Prison, 114
Breda, 29, 142
Bremen, 164
Breslau Station, 43
Brighton, 23
Bristol, 19, 43
Britain, 3, 47, 65, 92
British Empire, 19
British MI5, 69
British National Archives, 53
Broek op Langedijk, 130
Bruce, Ashley, 168
Bruce, Michael, 168
Bruce, Nicole Scharrer, 168
Bruce, Robert, 168
Bruce, Shelby, 168
Brussels, 25, 29, 31, 43, 45, 57, 64, 74–5, 85, 95, 105, 114–15, 121–2, 162
Bryne, Gerard, 58
Buchenwald camp, 64–5, 106, 120, 143
Bureau of National Security, 157
Burgers, J.M., 71
Burto, Leslie 'Crash', 87

CS.6 resistance cell, 53
Cabbane du Gauch, 38
Café Americain, 135
Cambrelin, Simone, 85
Camp Herzogenbusch, 137
Campo Miranda del Ebro, 41
Canal du Midi, 34
Canejan, 38, 70

Cape Town, 87
Carcassonne, 71
Carnaris, Admiral, 48
Cassady, Leonard, 34–5
Catherina van Clevepark, No. 59, 153
Cavaillon, 145, 153
Cazères, 36
Celosse, Lieutenant Nicholas 'Bob', 57, 71, 92–3, 117–18, 147, 160
Central Station, 11, 31, 160
Chait, Edmond, 56
Chamberlain, Neville, 65
Channel, 84, 87
Charise, Lieutenant A. B., 45
Chateau de la Fougeraie, 114
Chester Square, No. 77, 28
Chez Emile restaurant, 34–5
Chiat, Salamon, 57, 85
Chicago, 22–3, 25
Chivenor, 93
Christian, Friedrich, 135
Christmann, Richard, 108–109, 113
Churchill, Winston, 3, 46, 91
Coedy, William, 23
Cok, Leo, 45
Col de Port d'Aspet, 37
Cole, Bob, 13, 15, 17
Cole, Harold, 109, 113
Coleman, Derrick, 23
Comete Line, 59, 74, 119, 162
Compter, Kees, 64
Concertgebouw, 61
Conijn, Ed, 129, 148, 158
Conijn, Fritz, 11, 86, 89, 102, 129–33, 135–8, 140, 143, 147–9, 152, 156–8, 160–1
Conijn, Gerhardus 'Gerrit', 129, 132, 158
Conijn, Marthe, 158
Conijn, Valentine, 129, 168
Connewitz, 91
Convoy to England, 84
Corellistraat, No. 6, 53
Courtois, Robert, 64
Croix de Guerre, 45
Cuit, Lieutenant, 57,
Curaçao, 157
Currie, John, 13

Daelemans, Marcel 'Victor', 119
Dam Square, 5, 78, 156
Daniel Willinkplein, 133

Dansey, Colonel Claude, 103
Davids, Jaap 'Tjerk', 140
Davies, Jim, 72, 86, 88–91, 120, 129, 167
D–Day landings, 110, 121
De Beaufort, Agnes, 159
De Bie, Pierre, 130–1, 135, 160–1
De Bliqui, 59
De Braan, Lieutenant, 57
De Bray, Louis, 85, 120, 145, 159
De Gekroonde Valk 133, 135
De Geuzen, 64, 105
De Graaf, Jonklaar, 117
De Graaf, Kas, 50, 52–4, 57–8, 60, 71, 92–4, 117–18, 147, 160
De Gruijter, Henri Eugene, 131
De Jong, 59
De Jong, Andree 'Dedee', 59
De Jong, Dr L., 53–4
De Jong, Hanje, 88
De Jong, Roelfke, 88
De Kooy airfield, 43
De Lairessestraat, No. 96, 39
De Vittecoque, Henri, 163
De Vries, Rudolf, 70
De Waals, Anton, 160
De Wilp, 88
De Wit, 117
De Wolkenkrabber, 133
De Zitter, Prosper, 119
Decoo, Mlle., 163
Decoo, Jean Baptiste, 63
Decoo, Johanna, 63
Delft, 8, 67, 70–1, 94, 104, 116
DeMay, Marie-Louise, 120
Den Helder, 4, 130
Deppe, Arnold, 59
Deppner, 150
Deram, Madelaine, 113
Der Funten, Ferdinand Aus, 149
Desmet, Freddie, 103
Deventer, 92
Dijckmeester, Frans, 40
Dijkstra, Piet, 89
Donker, Dr, 49
Donny, Baron, 59
Donostia, 70
Dordrecht, 22, 126
Douque, Heini, 129
Downe, Charles 'Chuck', 35–6, 39
Downing Street, 46

Dresden, 43, 164
Driebergen, 113
Dubois, Henri, 69
Dumont, Georges, 64–5
Dupon, Henri, 69, 116
Dutch Chamber of Commerce, 117–18
Dutch-Belgian border, 162
Dutch-Paris escape line, x, 29, 34–5, 44, 56–9, 80–1, 85, 105, 120, 122, 162

Eastern Front, 10
Easyjet, 169
Ebenezer, 47
Edmonton, 157
Eichmann, Adolph, 144
Eindhoven, 111, 113
Eisenhower, President Dwight D., 2, 23, 110, 165
El Greco, 40
Elbe, 136, 156
Elias, Piet, 140
Emmakade, No. 21, 20, 76,
Enfield, 23
England, 19, 28, 42, 46–7, 53, 58, 71, 73–5, 84, 86, 92–3, 112, 149, 162, 164
Englandspiel, 48–51, 60, 90, 107–109, 120
English Channel, 16, 58
Entvald, Aart, 105
Escape lines, 44, 56–9, 74, 81, 93, 109, 117, 119, 123, 162
Essen, 64
Europe, 19, 46, 48, 50, 62, 91, 98–9, 110, 143–4, 150, 165–7
Euterpestraat, 6, 100, 134–5, 140, 149
Evers, 79–81, 84

Far East, 28
Felix, Piet, 22–3, 26–7, 59, 90, 162
Fleuri, Panier, 123
Fort Blauwkapel, 138, 156
Foundation 1940–1945, 152
France, 2–3, 6, 15, 22, 24–6, 28–9, 33–4, 43–6, 63–4, 67, 69–71, 78, 90, 108, 110, 116, 145, 147, 153–6, 160, 162–4
Franco, General, 41
Frank, Anne, 9, 149
Frank, German officer, 145–6,
Frankfurt am Main, 152
Frankfurt, 24–5, 164
Frederiksplein, 55

French-Spanish border, 36
Frencken, Sjaak 'Rinus', 130
Fresnes Prison, 107
Frick, Wilhelm, 98, 149
Frijda, 160

Gallo, Russell, 34
Gans, Sergeant Alexander, 42, 57, 71
Gare d'Austerlitz, 34, 80
Gare du Nord, 31
Garip village, 89
Gelinck, Advocate M.H., 148
Gemeente Universiteit of Amsterdam, 154
General Intelligence & Security Service, 155
German, Dr, see Giskes, Major Hermann
German-Dutch border, 162
Germany, 2–3, 14–19, 26, 36, 41, 44, 59, 63–5,
    67, 74, 99–100, 102, 107, 110, 112, 114,
    142–3, 148, 149, 152–3, 162
Gestapo, 98, 100, 106, 109, 117, 150, 160
Ghent, 94
Gibraltar, 21, 41–3, 84, 93
Giskes, Major Herman, 7, 48–51, 53–4, 59–60,
    90, 93, 107–12, 114–15, 120–1, 150
Glasgow, 19
Glysynski, Eugene, 23
Godfrey, Sir John, 51
Gold Beach, 110
Göring, Hermann, 99
Goya, 40
Grand Hôtel du Palais Royal, 44
Grave Bridge, 111
Great Britain, 166
Grebbe Line, 3
Greidaniges, Lieutenant, 57
Greter, Captain, 75–7, 84–5
Grobzschoche, 91
Groningen Province, 91
Groningen, 88
Grubb, Ernest, 35–6, 38–9

Haarlem, 8, 144, 146
Hague, 4, 6, 8, 22, 50, 58, 64–5, 69, 89, 102,
    106, 134, 146, 163
Halesworth, 14
Halmos, Eugene, 13–15, 17–18, 26, 167
Handel, 61
Hank, 119
Happe, 73
Harris, Donald, 155

Harris, Myrtille Benoit, 155
Hart, Frank, 6, 13–14, 16–18, 20–4, 26–7, 72,
    87, 90, 120, 167
Hart, Genevieve, 26
Hartman, Erich, 87
Hartzog, 73
Harwich, 2
Havas, 155
Hayden, Alan, 23
Heerengracht, 132
Heineburen hamlet, 88
Heiterblick, 91
Helmer, Karl 'Stahl', 120
Hertzberger, Captain Edmond, 40
Heuilly, 118
Heydrich, Reinhard, 98, 150
Hilterman, Suzanne, 45, 56–7, 122
Hilversum, 144, 147, 157
Himmler, Reichsminister, 48, 98
Hitler, Adolf, 3, 19, 98, 100, 150
Hoetink, Hans, 92
Holland, 3, 5, 8, 19, 30, 39, 45, 49–50, 63, 73,
    77, 80, 88, 93, 107, 115–20, 133, 147, 164
Holland Office Stichting 1940–1945, 152
Holland Offices of the US Army, 152
Holland Waterline, 3
Holocaust, 143
Hoorn, 19, 148
Hôtel Americain, 29, 78, 131, 160
Hôtel de Medicis, 33, 42
Hôtel de Noailles, 31
Hôtel des Deux Hémisphères, 70–1, 79, 93, 117
Hotel International, 93
Hôtel Monsieur le Prince, 31, 70
Hotel St Maria, 117
Hôtel Venezia, 80–1
Hussong, James 35–6

Iberian Peninsula, 145
Idsings Zee, 88
Ijmuiden, 144
Indo-China, 34
Indonesia, 58, 154
Ireland, 84
Isbrücker, 94
Italy, 168

Japin, Arend, 131–2, 135, 138, 140
Java, 92
Johannesburg, 154

Jonkerbos War Cemetery, 119
Juliana, Princess, 2
Juno Beach, 110

Kaatsheuvel Zundet-Chaam, 22, 27
Kager Plas, 61
Kaltenbrunner, Ernst, 149
Kamp Amersfoort, 102
Kastein, Dr Gerrit, 53, 100–102, 160
Katel, Gideon, 53
Katel, Jan, 53
Keizer Karelweg, No. 409, 147
Kek, 160
Kennedy, President, 10
Kennedylaan, 10
Ketting, Dirkie, 126
Kibble, William 'Billy', 87
Kiel, 164
Kiesewetter, Major, 113
Klaasen, K.W.P., 147
KLM line, 90, 116, 119–20
Klijzing, Captain Ernst, 54, 149, 160–1
Knoppers, Hendrikus, 149–50
Koekemoer, Sergeant, 44, 57
Koersen, Theo, 32, 62
Koetter, 116
Kole, Eric, 34
Koreman, Megan, 45, 162
Kottälla, Joseph, 138
Kraay, Suzy, 45, 58, 122–3
Kremer, Willem, 93
Kromme Mijdrechtstraat, 129, 133–4
Kroone, 117
Kuiper, Maarten, 9–10, 149
Kupp, Willy, 108–109, 115

La Cabane des Evades, 37
La Couple restaurant, 33
Laatsman, Hermann, 45, 56–7, 80, 118, 120, 159
Lages, Willy, 149
Lahnemann, Mr, 31
Lancaster bombers, 86, 88
Laurens, John, 87–8
Lausanne, 163,
Lauwers, Hubert, 47–8
LeBlanc, Joseph Thomas Lloyd, 119
Le Bourget Airport, 116
Le Dôme, 33
Le Havre, 25
Leiden City Council, 95

Leiden University, 42, 80, 94
Leiden, 146
Leidseplein, 29, 160
Leipzig, 86–7, 91
Lems, Ernst, 23
Leonard, Walter, 13
Leone, Clement, 23
Lerida, 39
Les, 38
Libourel, Caroline 'Carry', 6–8, 10–11, 21–2, 24, 26–7, 65, 67–71, 85, 94–5, 103–104, 114, 130–1, 136–8, 141, 145–7, 150, 152–3, 155, 159, 165, 169
Libourel, Dr P.H.B., 65
Libourel, Hans, 10
Libourel, Linda Morison, 8, 67–8, 155–6
   see also Morison
Liège, 122
Lille, 104
Limburg, 160
Lindemans, Christiaan, 7, 44, 71, 74–7, 79, 85, 94, 103–108, 110–19, 145–6, 150, 159–60, 162
Lindemans, Christianne, 107
Lindemans, Gilbert 'Gilou', 74, 106–109
Lindemans, Henk, 106
Lindemans, Jan, 104, 109
Liverpool, 19, 42, 71, 84
Lleida, 43, 82
London School of Economics, 169
London Underground, 19
London, 5–6, 9, 11, 19, 28, 43, 46, 48–9, 52–4, 69, 71, 90, 92–4, 104, 108, 121, 129–30, 156
Low Countries, 2–3, 104
Lowey-Ball, Jan, 7–8, 10–11, 33, 70–1, 79, 103–105, 114, 116–17, 130–3, 135, 137–8, 147, 155–7, 159
Ludford Magna airfield, 86
Luret, Henrietta, 118
Luxembourg, 2
Lyon, 56

Maas River, 112
Maastricht, 79, 117, 160
Madrid, 39–40, 82–4, 93
Madurodam, 95
Manchester University, 73
Mane, 36–7
Marks, Leo, 47–9
Marret, Henri 'Mireille', 35–6, 57

Mars, 167
Martin, Marguerite, 63
Marum, 88
Maryland, 167
Maudan, 38
Mauthausen camp, 49
Medal of Freedom, 161
Memphis, 23
Mermignaux, Pierre, 57
Mersey River, 84
Metz, 63
Meyer, Mr, 122
MI6, 103
Mid East, 166
Midlands, 73
Millord, Betty, 8–10, 129, 135–6, 145, 156
Millord, Tom Yardin, 8–10, 100, 102, 128–33,
    136–6, 138, 145, 147, 153, 156–7, 163–5
Model, Field Marshal Walter, 111
Mohr, M.J., 45
Mohr, Oscar, 68–9
Mollis, Wouter, 9–10, 135, 149
Monnier, Wilhelmus, 23
Montaigu-de-Quercy, 34
Montgomery, General Bernard, 110
Montparnasse, 33
Moores-LeBlanc, Michael, 116, 119
Moorish Castle, 42
Moos, James, 13
Mora, Cyril, 58
Morison, Linda Libourel, 8, 67–8, 155–6
Morison, Peter, 156
Muller, 54
Müller, Heinrich, 99
Munt, Johannes Heinrich, 11–12, 145–6, 150
Museo del Prado, 40
Museumplein, 154
Mussert, Anton, 5, 53, 100–101, 149

Napoleon, 65
National Support Fund, 156
Natsweiler Camp, 34
Nazi Germany, 98
Nederlandsche Bank, 55
Nederlandsche Press Bureau, also Algemeen
    Nederlands Persbureau (ANP), 5, 145–6
Neerlandais, Paris, 159
Netherlands South, 168
Netherlands Western Provinces, 141
Netherlands, 2–4, 11, 13, 16, 18, 21–2, 25,

27, 43–4, 46–51, 53, 61, 66–7, 69, 71, 73–5,
    84–5, 88–9, 93–5, 100, 104, 106, 108–109
Neyessel, Anika 'Neis', 44, 80, 122
Niebert, 88
Nieuwe Kerk, 78
Nieuwendijk, Th. H.A., 127
Nieuwer Amstel, 153
Nijmegen Bridge, 111
NIOD (Institute of War, Holocaust & Genocide
    Studies), 159
Noesgen, Rudolf, 68
Noord Holland KP, 157
Noordsingel, No. 176, 75
Normandy, 14, 41, 50, 110–11, 113
North Africa, 84, 87
North Brabant, 22
North Holland, 130
North Sea, 17, 58
North Wales, 91
Northern France, 34
Nothomb, Jean Francois 'Franco', 59
Nuremberg trials, 98, 107

Oberursel, 19, 24–5
Ockhuizen, Catherine 'Okky', 57, 80
Oelschlägel, Herbert, 6, 9–10, 126–9, 135, 140
Oldenzaal, 74
Omaha Beach, 110
Oosterhaut, 23
Operation Bodyguard, 110
Operation Fortitude, 122
Operation Market Garden, 111–13
Operation Neptune, 110
Operation Silbertanne, 102
Oranienburg, 33, 138
Ostend, 63, 163
Oude Delft, No. 233, 145
Overloon, 168
Overveen, 138
Owens, William, 23

Packham, George, 23
Pahut, 85
Pamplona, 93
Paris Metro, 31
Paris, 21, 28–33, 42–5, 56–7, 59, 70–1, 76–7,
    79–81, 104–105, 107, 109, 115–18, 120, 122,
    130, 159–60, 162, 165
Park Hotel, 75, 78
Pas de Calais, 43, 50, 109, 122

Pattle, Marmaduke 'Pat', 87
Patton, General, 24
Pau, 29–30, 44, 80–1, 130
Peeters, Martin 'Arno', 120
Pétain, 68
Phillips company, 154
Pic de l'Aube, 37
Picasso, 34
Ping Pong, 92
Pinto, Oreste, 112
Place St Georges, 34
Plaza Mayor, 40
Plymouth, 19
Poland, 3, 65, 143
Pons, William, 123, 126–9, 131–4, 147–8
    'De Bruin', 127–8, 132–3, 135
Poolesville, 167
Portugal, 93, 104
Post, Bob, 13
Prague, 150
Puerta del Sol, 40
Putten, 101–102
Pyrenean foothills, 81
Pyrenees, 21, 28, 31–2, 35–6, 43, 70, 81–2, 117,
    162, 164, 168

RAF (Royal Air Force), 165
Rauter, General Hanns Albin, 53, 101–102, 149
Ravensbrück camp, 74
Raviol, Miss, 122
Reile, Colonel Oscar, 106
Rens, Jacques, 24, 34–5, 56
Resistance & War Museum, Overloon, 168
Restaurant Victoria, 132, 135
Reulen, Albert 'Ber', 130
Reydon, 53, 102
Rhine River, 112
Ridderhof, Mattis, 119–20, 149
Rijksmuseum, 78
Rinus, 160
Rivierenlaan, No. 16, 10, 131
Roelof Hartplein, 9
Rommel, Field Marshal Erwin, 110
Roquefort-sur-Garonne, 70
Rosseeuw, André, 120
Rostock, 24–5
Rotterdam, 2, 4, 75–7, 102, 104–106, 108–109,
    117–18, 126–8, 132, 153, 160
Royal nightclub, 108
Royal Palace, 78

Royston, Albert, 87–8
Rue Alex Fourtannier, No. 3, 80–1
Rue de Grenelle, 109
Rue de la Michodière, 31
Rue des Matiers, 70
Rue Franklin, 122
Rue le Goff, 34
Rue Lord Byron, No. 3, 79
Rue Monsieur-le-Prince, 33, 56–7, 70
Rühl, Sachbearbeiter Emil, 9–10, 138, 149, 161
Ruhr, 86, 164
Ruys, John, 33–4
Ruys, Commander R.E., 34

SOE-N, 11, 46, 48, 51–2, 54, 93, 129
Saarbrücken, 24–5
Sachsenhausen camp, 138
Sagan, 19
Saigon, 34
Sainsbury, Alfred, 114
Saint-Denis, 107
Saint-Omer, 43
Salerno, 42
San Antonio, 24
San Sebastian, 70
Sandberg, 6, 29, 44, 127, 135
Sanders, P., 156
Santora, Joseph, 13
Sarrat De Bouch, 37
Schaar, Joseph, 84
Schaerbeek, Brussels, 155
Scharrer, Alexandra 'Lexi', 168
Scharrer, Beryl, 165, 168
Scharrer, Christine, 169
Scharrer, Claudette Beurnel, 155
Scharrer, Collin Earl Peter, 154, 168
Scharrer, Denis, 168–9
Scharrer, Emmanuel, 64–5, 155, 163
Scharrer, Georgina, 168
Scharrer, Glenn Walther David, 154, 168
Scharrer, Henri, 2, 5–13, 20–4, 28–33, 42–6,
    50, 52–3, 56–7, 59–60, 65–71, 73, 76–80, 85,
    89, 92–4, 99–100, 102–105, 113, 116–17, 120,
    123, 126–41, 143, 145–7, 149, 152, 155–7,
    160–1, 163–6, 168–9
Scharrer, Henri Senior, 63
Scharrer, Jean, 63
Scharrer, Jocelyn, 154
Scharrer, Johanna, 63
Scharrer, Kathy Bowyer, 168

Scharrer, Lyn, 168
Scharrer, Marie Jeanne, 64
Scharrer, Monique Twynholm, 169
Scharrer, Nicole Harris, 155
Scharrer, Nicole 'Pouty', 155
Scharrer, Nicole Simone, 154, 168
Scharrer, Olivia, 168
Scharrer, Peter, 168
Scharrer, Puck, 154, 168
Scharrer, Raymond, 10, 20, 27, 61–3, 65, 135,
  153–5, 168
Scharrer, Richard, 10–11, 16, 20, 22, 27, 43, 62,
  65, 67, 76, 86, 89–90, 134–5, 141–2, 153–4,
  163–6, 168
Scharrer, Thérèse Delaspre, 155
Scharrer, Geertruida 'Truus', 2, 5, 10–11, 20,
  61–2, 65, 67–8, 128–9, 131–6, 141–2, 145,
  152–3, 155, 169
Scheinfurt Ball Bearing, 164
Scheinfurt, 164
Scheveningen, 9, 101–102, 114
Schiphol, 62
Schleubig, 91
Schnaufer, Heinz-Wolfgang, 87
Schoorl, 5, 67–8, 146
Schrader, Anton 'Tonny', 21, 54, 58–9, 162
Schreieder, Josef, 48, 50, 150
Schroder, Marthe, 129
Schuurbijut, Paul, 152
Scotland, 43
Seyffardt, General, 53, 92, 100–102, 110
Seyss-Inquart, Arthur, 12, 100, 143, 148
Shawcross, Sir Hartley, 51
Sheffield, 23
Shell, 157
's-Hertogenbosch, 44
Siegers Woude, 88
Silver Palm, 161
Sjollema, H.J., 145
Slotboom, Frans, 101
Smart, Dave, 13, 17–18
Smit, 59
Smit, Karst, 114, 161–2
SOE (Special Operations Executive), 46
Sobibor camp, 144
Soesterberg air base, 167
Sommer, Otto, 101
Sorensen, Jack, 13
South Africa, 154, 168
South of France, 156

South Friesland, 74
South Holland, 145
Soviet Union, 126
Spain, 6, 21–2, 28, 39–41, 43, 57, 59, 70–1, 76,
  93, 104, 116, 130, 153, 164
Speer, Albert, 76
Sprang-Capelle, 23
Springs Gold Mine, 154
Springs, 154
St Augustin Metro station, 33
St Gaudens, 35
St Gilles prison, 64, 90, 95
Stalag IV-B Muhlberg camp, 136
Stalag Luft III, 43
Stalag Luft IV Gross Tychow, 19, 24
Stalag VII Brandkau Kreulberg, 90–1, 156
Stamp, E.B., 71
Starink, Albert, 29, 31, 33–4, 43–5, 47, 59, 71,
  80–1, 105, 117, 162
Staryn, E.B., 116–18
Stevens, Col., 114
Stichting 1940–1945, 152–4
Stock, Ernest, 34
Strangers, Jan 'Strengers', 44, 59, 85, 105,
  145, 159
Strassburger, Adolf, 74
Stubbe, 117
Suffolk, 14
Swan, Victor, 44, 59, 74, 105–106, 117–18, 120,
  160, 162
Swane, Albert, 44, 59, 160, 162
Swiss Press Telegraf (SPT), 68–9, 146, 163
Switzerland, 68, 153–4, 160
Sword Beach, 110

Taconis, Thijs, 47
Tank, Frank, 34
Tasmania, 28
Technical University, 70
Tedder, Air Chief Marshal Sir Arthur, 2,
  23, 165
Ten Carte, Domine, 85, 145, 159
Texas, 24
Thames, 3
Todt, Fritz, 76
Tolbert Protestant Church, 88
Tolbert, 88, 91
Toulouse, 34–5, 43–4, 70–1, 78, 80–1, 117
Traitors, 120
Treillet, Etienne 'Palo', 35–8, 57

Trocadero Station, 31
Tromme, Camille, 105
Turnhout, 23, 25
Tusenias, 57
Tuts, Lieutenant Phillipus Christiaan, 57, 71, 116–17
Twente, 162
Twynholm, Monique Scharrer, 169
Twynholm, Ross, 169

United Kingdom, 11, 46–7, 60, 92–3, 143, 145, 147, 168
United Nations, 167
United States Army, 152
United States, 11, 14, 20, 24, 26, 28, 43, 166, 169
University of Amsterdam, 28
University of Cambridge, 168
University of Cape Town, 168
University of Delft, 31
University of Groningen, 62
University of Manchester, 169
University of Pretoria, 168
University of Stellenbosch, 168
Ursem, 18
USAAF (United States Army Airforce), 164–5
Utah Beach, 110
Utrecht Police station, 53, 92
Utrecht Station, 31
Utrecht, 138, 144, 56
Utrecht-Tuindorp, 58

Vaes, Andre, 84–5
Van Asbeck, Ima, 9
Van Boetzelaer, Baron Abraham, 146, 159
Van de Pol, H. H. J., 66–7
Van Den Berg, 122
Van der Heijden, 59, 162
Van der Hoof, A., 23
Van der Stok, Bram 'Bob', 42–5
Van der Stok, Petie, 43
Van der Waals, Anton, 49, 53, 160
Van der Wiele, Ben 70
Van der Wiele, Hugo, 70, 130, 132
Van Exter, 45, 57
Van Exter, Mr, 31
Van Exter, Mrs, 31
Van Exter, Robert, 22, 28–35, 39–40, 42, 44–5, 62, 167

Van Eycklei St, No. 17, 90, 120
Van Hall, Walraven, 55
Van Hattem, 69
Van Heemstra, Baron, 145
Van Heemstra, Baron John, 76, 79, 81, 85
Van Heukelsfeld-Jansen, Marinus, 93
Van Kampen, Elizabeth 'Liesje', 154
Van Kampen, Hennie, 154
Van Kampen, Po, 154
Van Kampen, Puck, 154
Van Krimpen, Roelse & Wieringa, 145
Van Muylem, René, 26, 42–3, 49, 60, 90, 116, 119–21
Van Nagel, 75, 77
Van Nerom-Duickers, Cecile, 59
Van Roggen, Mathijs, 44
Van Tienhoven, 54
Van Vught, Hans Hüttig, 138
Vassias, Eve, 44
Vechtstraat, 133–4
Veen, Jan, 88
Velasquez, 40
Veldhuizen, Elise, 153
Veldhuizen, Pieter, 153
Veldhuizen, Puck, 154
Velsen Crematoria, 137
Veluwe, 148
Venlo, 19
Verdiepingenhuis, No. 12, 133
Verhulst-Oomes, Anna Maria, 23, 26, 49, 89–90, 190
Verleun, Jan, 92, 101
Verloop, Brothers, 85, 145, 159
Verloop, Cornelius, 108–9, 111, 113–14
Verloop, David, 57
Vermeer, Pierre 'Otto', 131, 140
Verspijck, Jonkheer, 76, 79, 160
Verspyck, Matilda, 74, 84, 105
Verster, Arnold, 6, 138
Verster, Xenia, 6, 22, 24–7, 138
Verzetsmuseum, 30, 62
Viallat, Henri, 163
Viallat, Marie Jeanne, 163
Vichy, 78
Viebahn, Friedich, 9, 138, 149
Vielle, 82
Viermann, SS Officer, 135
Villa Real de San Antonio, 41
Vimy, 34
Vlaming, Pauline 'Pam', 120

Von Küchler, General Georg, 4
Voorburgwaal, 5
Voortman, Martin, 115
Vught Red Cross, 137
Vught, 93, 95, 137, 139, 144, 149–50

Waal River, 112
Waalsdorpvlakte, 137, 149
Waalwijk, 22, 24
Waffen-SS, 98
Wagemakers, Toon, 22
Wagner, 61
Waight, Cassian, 87–8
Wales, 153–4
Washington War Archives, 152
Wassenaar, 85, 152
Waverstraat, 134
Weesp, 144
Wehner, Ernst, 135
Weidner, John, 44–5, 56, 58, 81, 85, 105, 122
Weidner, Miss, 122
West Virginia, 23
Westerbork camp, 5, 143–4, 150
Western Europe, 3, 166
Weteringschans, 9, 11, 100, 130, 136, 138, 140,
    149, 156

Whitchurch, 43
White, Horace, 23
Wijk aan Zee, 130
Wijkstra, Sietse, 88
Wijlen, André, 23
Wijnhaven, No. 8, 104, 116–17
Wilhelmina, Queen, 28, 58, 85, 94, 149
Winkelman, General, 4–5
Woerden, 58
Wurr, Walter, 108
Wyssogota-Zokozenski, André, 44, 57–9, 81,
    85, 103, 146, 159

Xolberg, 24–5

Ypenburg, 4

Zaandam, 144
Zaragoza, 40
Zeeland, 4
Zeeman, Rudy, 21–2, 28–35, 38–42, 44–5, 58–9,
    62, 70, 72, 78, 81–4, 162, 167
Zhukov, Marshal, 24–5, 129
Zuiderzee, 17, 19